NEW ACCENTS

General Editor: TERENCE HAWKES

Psychoanalytic Criticism:
Theory in Practice

IN THE SAME SERIES

* Not available from Routledge in the USA

Psychoanalytic Criticism:
Theory in Practice

ELIZABETH WRIGHT

ROUTLEDGE
London and New York

For my daughter and son

First published in 1984 by
Methuen & Co. Ltd
Reprinted 1985
Reprinted with a new appendix 1987
Reprinted in 1989 by
Routledge
11 New Fetter Lane, London EC4P 4EE
29 West 35th Street, New York, NY 10001
© 1984 Elizabeth Wright

Photoset by Rowland Phototypesetting Ltd
Bury St Edmunds, Suffolk
Printed in Great Britain by
Richard Clay Ltd, Bungay, Suffolk

British Library Cataloguing in Publication Data

Wright, Elizabeth, 19—
Psychoanalytic criticism.—(New accents)
1. Criticism   2. Psychoanalysis and literature
I. Title   II. Series
801'.95   P.N98.P75

ISBN 0-416-32650-1
ISBN 0-415-04583-5

Library of Congress Cataloging in Publication Data

Wright, Elizabeth, E.
Psychoanalytic criticism.
(New accents)
Bibliography: p.
Includes index.
1. Psychoanalysis and literature.   2. Psychoanalysis
and art.   I. Title   II. Series: New accents
P.N56.P92W75 1984   801'.95   84-14752

ISBN 0-416-32650-1
ISBN 0-415-04583-5

Contents

General editor's preface

It is easy to see that we are living in a time of rapid and radical social change. It is much less easy to grasp the fact that such change will inevitably affect the nature of those disciplines that both reflect our society and help to shape it.

Yet this is nowhere more apparent than in the central field of what may, in general terms, be called literary studies. Here, among large numbers of students at all levels of education, the erosion of the assumptions and presuppositions that support the literary disciplines in their conventional form has proved fundamental. Modes and categories inherited from the past no longer seem to fit the reality experienced by a new generation.

New Accents is intended as a positive response to the initiative offered by such a situation. Each volume in the series will seek to encourage rather than resist the process of change, to stretch rather than reinforce the boundaries that currently define literature and its academic study.

Some important areas of interest immediately present themselves. In various parts of the world, new methods of analysis have been developed whose conclusions reveal the limitations of the Anglo-American outlook we inherit. New concepts of literary forms and modes have been proposed; new notions of the nature of literature itself, and of how it communicates, are current; new views of literature's role in relation to society flourish. *New Accents* will aim to expound and comment upon the most notable of these.

In the broad field of the study of human communication, more and more emphasis has been placed upon the nature and function of the new electronic media. *New Accents* will try to identify and discuss the challenge these offer to our traditional modes of critical response.

The same interest in communication suggests that the series should also concern itself with those wider anthropological and sociological areas of investigation which have begun to involve scrutiny of the nature of art itself and of its relation to our whole way of life. And this will ultimately require attention to be focused on some of those activities which in our society have hitherto been excluded from the prestigious realms of Culture. The disturbing realignment of values involved and the disconcerting nature of the pressures that work to bring it about both constitute areas that *New Accents* will seek to explore.

Finally, as its title suggests, one aspect of *New Accents* will be firmly located in contemporary approaches to language, and a continuing concern of the series will be to examine the extent to which relevant branches of linguistic studies can illuminate specific literary areas. The volumes with this particular interest will nevertheless presume no prior technical knowledge on the part of their readers, and will aim to rehearse the linguistics appropriate to the matter in hand, rather than to embark on general theoretical matters.

Each volume in the series will attempt an objective exposition of significant developments in its field up to the present as well as an account of its author's own views of the matter. Each will culminate in an informative bibliography as a guide to further study. And while each will be primarily concerned with matters relevant to its own specific interests, we can hope that a kind of conversation will be heard to develop between them: one whose accents may perhaps suggest the distinctive discourse of the future.

TERENCE HAWKES

Acknowledgements

My thanks are due to the following for their help: Marilyn Butler and Ann Jefferson for patiently reading the whole manuscript and offering invaluable criticism and suggestions on its general coherence and intelligibility; Geoff Bennington, John Forrester, Peter Henninger and Richard Klein (Oxford) for giving specialist advice on selected portions; Samuel Weber for reading an earlier draft and encouraging the project; Terence Hawkes for his meticulous reading of the finished product, for suggesting many minor improvements and demanding (and I hope getting) more clarification on certain sections; Janice Price of Methuen for helpful and encouraging letters throughout. Most of all, I would like to thank Edmond Wright for his unstinting availability whenever (that is constantly) there was a critical issue to be untangled, and for his philosophical expertise in helping me to keep to a consistent viewpoint.

My work has been greatly stimulated by participation at annual conferences organized by Georg Christoph Tholen at the Research Centre for Psychoanalysis and Literature of the University of Kassel.

The staff of the following libraries have aided me considerably during the time this book was conceived and written: the Taylor Institution, the Bodleian Library, and the library of the Tavistock Centre.

I would like to thank the editor of *Poetics Today* for permission to use material based on a review of a book by Christian Metz.

I am grateful to Girton College and to Trinity College, Cambridge, for granting me leave at exactly the time when I needed it.

E.E.W.

Girton College
Cambridge

There was once a red-haired man who had no eyes and no ears. He also had no hair, so he was called red-haired only in a manner of speaking.

He wasn't able to talk, because he didn't have a mouth. He had no nose, either.

He didn't have any arms or legs. He also didn't have a stomach, and he didn't have a back, and he didn't have a spine, and he also didn't have any other insides. He didn't have anything. So it's hard to understand whom we are talking about.

So we'd better not talk about him any more.

(Daniil Kharms 1974)

Introduction

The purpose of this book is to give a critical overview of what has become a very wide field: the relationship of psychoanalytic theory to the theories of literature and the arts, and the way that developments in both domains have brought about changes in critical practice. Psychoanalysis addresses itself to the problems of language, starting from Freud's original insight concerning the determining force within utterance: he draws attention to the effects of desire in language and, indeed, in all forms of symbolic interaction. The language of desire is veiled and does not show itself openly. To read its indirections, to account for its effects, is no simple matter. What is at issue?

Psychoanalysis explores what happens when primordial desire gets directed into social goals, when bodily needs become subject to the mould of culture. Through language, desire becomes subject to rules, and yet this language cannot define the body's experience accurately. What is of peculiar interest to psychoanalysis – some would say peculiar in the sense of both special and bizarre – is that aspect of experience which has been ignored or prohibited by the rules of language. Words fail to match it but it is actual none the less. The energies of this desire become directed outside conscious awareness, attaching themselves to particular ideas and images which represent unconscious wishes. *Wunsch* in Freud's terminology has this special sense, as desire associated specifically with particular images, whereas 'desire' is better retained for those underlying energies which are not yet bound to specific aims.

Only through its effects do we come to know the unconscious: through the logic of symptoms and dreams, through jokes and 'Freudian slips', through the pattern of children's play, and most crucially in the mutually affective relationship which human beings develop as a consequence of their past total helplessness and dependence on another person. These emotions, regenerated in the analytic situation, may be taken as evidence that no experience the body has is ever totally erased from the mind. In the unconscious the body does not take the social mould, and yet the conscious mind thinks it has. On the basis of clinical evidence psychoanalysis has built up a theory of how this difference comes about. It hypothesizes that there are certain stages of socialization each of which have their own problems of invasions from the unconscious. The joint re-creation on the part of patient and analyst of the earliest stages in the patient's development is to be taken as evidence that no phase of development is ever totally outlived, no early satisfaction wholly surrendered. The neurotic and psychotic disorders which bring human beings to the consulting-room symptomatically speak of the mismatch between bodily desire and sexual-cum-social role.

None of this as yet can be scientifically proved, despite the efforts of the founder. If science is given a positivist definition, psychoanalysis cannot count as one of the physical sciences. What psychoanalysis has to offer therefore cannot be assessed without raising the problem of what a science is or can do. It is through its implicit questioning of traditional philosophic theories of how knowledge is acquired that psychoanalysis makes its most interesting contribution. Accounts of 'the standing of psychoanalysis' (Farrell 1981) continue to take for granted that psychoanalysis must situate itself in relation to other modes of knowledge and to 'common sense', and that therapy is the yardstick by which theory is to be measured. On the contrary, psychoanalysis is a theory of interpretation which calls into question the 'commonsense' facts of consciousness, facts which it maintains can only be reconstructed after the event. The assumption of a plain objectivity susceptible to a rigid true/false analysis is itself open to question. Science may continue to be reliable without necessarily accepting that label-ling and measuring can do justice to that to which they are applied. The progress of science has been marked by revolution-ary changes in the understanding of concepts, leading to defi-nitions that are incompatible with those they replace, not merely falsifications of them (Kuhn 1970). At the most basic level of science, quantum physics, the question of interpreta-tion emerges irrepressibly. Science is itself a highly interpretative activity, and it is as a science of interpretation – that is, in part, as a science of science – that psychoanalysis must be viewed (Foucault 1974, p. 373; see pp. 160–1 below). This is not to say that the theory must be accepted uncritically. The emphasis must be on the interpretative force of the theory instead of on a simplistic true/false analysis of what are highly subjective phenomena. There is a positivist error in thinking that subjec-tive phenomena cannot be objectively studied. The effects produced in a body by its perilous entry via language into culture take the form of repetitions and patterned interactions from which laws can be derived, thereby making the uncon-scious a legitimate object of a special science (Althusser 1977).

This book tries to show in what way Freudian theory has been and still is part of an ongoing debate. As a body of knowledge acquired in the clinical situation it is itself open to more interpretation. One might consider whether it should focus on liberating the self in its efforts to achieve pleasure and avoid unpleasure (instinct- or id-psychology); whether it should strengthen that part of the self capable of social adaptation (ego-psychology and its offshoot, object–relations theory); whether it should centre on the division of the subject in language (structural psychoanalysis); or whether it should openly serve a revolutionary purpose by opposing and accusing social institutions (anti-psychiatry). All these positions are paralleled by the changing relations in literary theory and critical practice.

If there is a single key issue it is probably the question of the role of sexuality in the constitution of the self, and crucially, how this sexuality is to be defined. This raises the question why we should still be bothering with psychoanalytic theories of sexual-ity in the context of literature and the arts. Critics from Kenneth Burke and Lionel Trilling onwards have warned against it while at the same time hallowing the process by which psychoanalysis can be made literary. This now familiar theme has been taken up again in a recent collection of critical essays on Freud:

> Freud's principal literary speculation is not to be found in the familiar psychosexual reductions that tend to characterize his own overt attempts at the psychoanalysis of art. [It lies] instead in his notion that the very mechanisms of the mental agencies are themselves the mechanisms of language.
>
> (Meisel 1981, p. 2)

This kind of declaration is usually intended to protect literature and art from the unwary psychoanalytic critic who would ineptly perpetrate psychobiography and all manner of vulgar Freudianisms on the innocent art-object. Freud has anticipated this objection. 'It may be', he writes in his analysis of Jensen's story *Gradiva:*

> that we have produced a complete caricature of an interpretation by introducing into an innocent work of art purposes of which its creator had no notion, and by so doing have shown once more how easy it is to find what one is looking for and what is occupying one's own mind.

But, he argues, even if the author was unaware of the work's 'rules and purposes', 'nevertheless we have not discovered anything in his work that is not already in it. We probably draw from the same source and work upon the same object, each of us by another method' (Freud 1953, IX, pp. 91 and 92).

Author and reader are both subject to the laws of the unconscious. To concentrate on 'mechanisms' without taking account of the energies with which they are charged is to ignore Freud's most radical discoveries: it is precisely the shifts of energies brought about by unconscious desire that allow a new meaning to emerge. A desexualized application of psychoanalytic criticism, a confining of it solely to the mechanisms of language – whether as an example of the plenitude of ambiguity (New Criticism and its offshoots: the 'work' of an author) or as a set of perpetually shifting ambivalences (deconstruction: the 'workings' of language in a 'text') – does not engage the full explanatory force of psychoanalytic theory. An essential point is missed. Psychoanalytic theory brings out the unconscious aspect of utterance through its concentration on the relationship between sexuality and social role. Clinical practice has borne out to what extent sexuality, in its wider Freudian sense, is the component of intention, how all utterance is concerned with the satisfaction of the needs of bodies which have become socialized. The literary text, the work of art, is a form of persuasion whereby bodies are speaking to bodies, not merely minds speaking to minds. The plays of Samuel Beckett graphically present us with images of bodies, or parts of bodies, sometimes comically, sometimes desperately, struggling to channel their desire through speech. Conversely, the theatre of Antonin Artaud assaults us with images of the body's violent refusal to become entrapped in language. Creative activity can here be seen as a material process, with both author/actor and reader/viewer implicated as desiring bodies.

This emphasis upon the bodily aspect of art poses a problem for psychoanalytic criticism because it neglects the public and the social. It is a problem with which psychoanalytic aesthetics battles intermittently on two fronts: first, there is the worry as to how the work of artistic merit is to be distinguished from the 'work' involved in the construction of dreams or fantasy; second, there is the question of regarding the work as 'text', no longer the property of a single author, but produced in a network of social relations. Each of these questions is concerned with the part that consciousness (whether true or false) plays in the creative process, and the way ideology affects the reading and writing of texts: the language of desire has both a private and a public aspect and that is why the literary and artistic work is a 'text', the proper reading of which is no simple matter.

Though psychoanalytic criticism is irresistibly drawn to those texts that are classified as literature (and art), it has not been able to provide a satisfactory theory of aesthetic value, but then neither has any other approach. It contributes rather to an understanding of the creative process, both before and in language, and this has implications for aesthetics. Beginning with Freud, this account deals with those psychoanalytic theorists who have been the main contributors to the criticism of literature and the arts, either directly or indirectly (through their work being taken up by others). Included also are theorists

(Derrida, Foucault) who have had an effect on psychoanalytic criticism.

The outline follows a historical course, though like Freud's famous sequence of sexual maturation, no stage ever totally supersedes another. On the contrary, recent French contributors have tried to merge an id-centred approach, focusing on the emotions attached to the sexual drives, with the abstract linguistic one of structural psychoanalysis. Tracing out a sequence of development in chronological order does not therefore imply that there is a necessary logical order. Such a method merely enables me to give as clear as possible an exposition of the field while still leaving room for critical appraisal. The aim will be to show how psychoanalytic theory and practice, not always working in concert with each other, have contributed to the theory and practice of criticism. There are four variables here, which makes for a complex set of interactions. At the same time I shall attempt to trace out the ideological assumptions that underlie successive developments in both theory and practice. Though the overall aim is exegesis, which must include showing what is of worth even where there are deficiencies, there will be an underlying and unconcealed attempt to point to what has now emerged as the most valuable aspect of psychoanalytic criticism.

My criteria derive from a three-fold scheme: first, I see psychoanalytic criticism as investigating the text for the workings of a rhetoric seen as analogous to the mechanisms of the psyche; second, I argue that any such criticism must be grounded in a theory which takes into account the relationships between author and text, and between reader and text; and third, I argue that these relationships be seen as part of a more general problem to do with the constitution of the self in social systems at given moments in history.

PART I

2

Classical psychoanalysis: Freud

Theoretical principles and basic concepts

Though the summary of Freudian theory given here cannot but be selective, it aims to indicate what sort of knowledge psychoanalysis has to contribute to the understanding of literature and the arts. The same mechanisms which Freud shows as determining in normal and abnormal behaviour come significantly into play when we are engaged in aesthetic activities of any kind. The theories which follow offer various explanations of how the unconscious functions in the production and consumption of the arts. This section will introduce the main concepts of psychoanalytic theory: the models of the psyche, the concept of repression, the role of the sexual instincts – their nature and place in Freud's theory of the unconscious, and the phenomena of transference.

Sigmund Freud (1856-1939) gives a genetic explanation of the evolutionary development of the human mind as a 'psychical apparatus'. He regarded such an explanation as providing a scientific basis for a theory of the unconscious, by which he relates it directly to the needs of the body. He looks at the mind from three points of view: the 'dynamic', the 'economic' and the 'topographical' (see Freud 1953, XX, pp. 265–6 for a brief summary). These are not mutually exclusive interpretations but emphasize different aspects of the whole. All three are evidence of Freud's attempt to derive the mind from the body.

The 'dynamic' point of view stresses the interplay of forces within the mind, arising from the tensions that develop when instinctual drives meet the necessities of external reality. (The German word for these drives is *Triebe*, translated as 'instincts' in the Standard Edition, but because, as will be seen, they are to be distinguished from instinct in animals, it is now more usual to translate *Triebe* as 'drives', particularly when the notion of pressure is at stake.) The mind comes into being out of the body. What is necessarily given at the start are the needs of the body itself: these are inseparably connected to feelings of pleasure and pain.

From the 'economic' point of view pleasure results from a decrease in the degree to which the body is disturbed by any stimulus. Unpleasure results from an increase in disturbance. In the interaction of the body with the external environment a part of the mind Freud calls the 'ego' evolves to mediate the actions of the body so as to achieve the optimal satisfaction of its needs. In particular the ego is concerned with self-preservation. This of its nature implies that there has to be control of these basic instincts if there is to be an adjustment to reality. Under the economic model this is viewed as a struggle between the 'reality principle' and the 'pleasure principle', in which the body has to learn to postpone pleasure and accept a degree of unpleasure in order to comply with social demands.

The third point of view is the 'topographical' of which there are two versions. The psychical apparatus is here conceived of in a spatial metaphor as divided into separate sub-systems, which together mediate the conflict of energies. In the first of the two versions Freud sees the mind as having a three-fold division, conscious, preconscious and unconscious. Consciousness he equates with the perception system, the sensing and ordering of the external world; the preconscious covers those elements of experience which can be called into consciousness at will; the unconscious is made up of all that has been kept out of the preconscious–conscious system. The unconscious is dynamic, consisting of instinctual representatives, ideas and images originally fixated in a moment of repression. But these do not remain in a fixed state; they undergo a dynamic interplay in which associations between them facilitate the shift of feeling from one image or idea to another. In Freud's terminology they are regulated by the 'primary process', a type of mental functioning where energy flows freely by means of certain mechanisms. These mechanisms, of crucial interest for psychoanalytic criticism, will be explained later in this chapter in the sections on dreams and art, where their function as strategies of desire will be discussed. The second version of the topographical scheme was introduced by Freud in 1923, when he came to view the mind as having three distinct agencies: the 'id', a term applied retrospectively to the instinctual drives that spring from the constitutional needs of the body; the ego as having developed out of the id to be an agency which regulates and opposes the drives; and the 'superego', as representative of parental and social influences upon the drives, a transformation of them rather than an external agency. This model of the psyche is often called the 'structural' model and is the one drawn on by ego-psychologists.

With the appearance of these agencies, the picture of dynamic conflict becomes clearer. The id wants its wishes satisfied, whether or not they are compatible with external demands. The ego finds itself threatened by the pressure of the unacceptable wishes. Memories of these experiences, that is images and ideas associated with them, become charged with unpleasurable feeling, and are thus barred from consciousness. This is the operation known as repression: 'the essence of repression lies simply in turning something away, and keeping it at a distance from the conscious' (XIV, p. 147).

Unfortunately this theory, what there is of it, is far from simple. If the notion of there being unconscious mental processes is to be seen as the key concept of psychoanalysis, it has of necessity to be linked with the theory of repression, 'the cornerstone on which the whole structure of psychoanalysis rests' (p. 16). Freud makes a distinction between two senses of the term. 'Primal repression' initiates the formation of the unconscious and is ineradicable and permanent. Although the forces of instincts are experienced before socialization, such experience is neither conscious nor unconscious. Freud cannot account for how such forces find representation in the mind. He has to hypothesize that these instincts have become bound to thoughts and images in the course of early (pleasure/pain) experience. Primal repression consists of denying a 'psychical representative' (that is an idea attached to an instinct) entry to the conscious: a fixation is thereby established, splitting conscious from unconscious. Without these initial imprintings the later entrance into language that establishes personhood could not be achieved. For Freud primal repression marks a pre-linguistic entry into a symbolic world. Lacan, on the other hand, reserves the term for the second stage of symbolization, the entry into language (for further discussion of this problem see Weber 1982 on Freud, pp. 39–48; see also Laplanche and Leclaire 1972, on Freud versus Lacan, pp. 155–63).

The term 'repression' in its second and more generally known sense is used by Freud to designate repression proper or 'after-pressure' (XIV, p. 148): it serves to keep guilt-laden wishes out of conscious experience. The symptoms, dreams and parapraxes ('Freudian slips') that turn up in the course of this process represent the 'return of the repressed', a mechanism that marks both the emergence of the forbidden wish and the resistance to it. Within the unconscious, the flow of energy becomes bound up with certain memory-traces, developing the character of unconscious wishes that strive continually to break through against the counterforce exerted by the ego. Where the primary process allows the psychical energy to flow freely, the 'secondary process' transforms it into 'bound energy', in that its movement is checked and controlled by the rational operations of the ego. The censorship of the ego can be subverted, however, precisely because of the free shifting of energy in the primary process. The drives or wishes can get through in disguise, as the so-called 'compromise formations' of the return of the repressed. It is the nature of these disguises that has occupied classical psychoanalytic criticism. Where the earlier 'instinct-psychology' emphasizes that which gets through the disguise, that is the content of the wish, the later 'ego-psychology' concentrates on that which 'controls' the wish, the work's formal devices.

Freud's theory of the instinctual drives was dualistic throughout his work; he always opposes one drive with another. It is with the earlier theory that we are concerned for the moment; the opposition of the sexual instincts to the instincts of self-preservation. The sexual instinct plays a major role in psychical conflict precisely because it is always opposed by another instinct. This is invariably forgotten when Freud is accused of 'pan-sexualism', tracing all action to the sexual instinct; his radical notion of sexuality is confused with the popular understanding of the term. He calls the total available energy of the sexual instinct 'libido', and it is essential to realize that it is not solely directed towards sexual aims *per se*. Sexuality is to be understood as not specifically limited to the process of reproduction: 'Sexual life includes the function of obtaining pleasure from zones of the body – a function which is subsequently brought into the service of reproduction. The two functions often fail to coincide completely' (XXIII, p. 152). The prime example is the infant, who gets the pleasurable stimulation of the region or 'zone' around the mouth, hence called an 'erotogenic' (eros 'love'; -gen- 'create') zone. The infant later, in sucking its thumb, is fantasizing the repetition of that sensual pleasure in the absence of nutritional need:

> The baby's obstinate persistence in sucking gives evidence at an early stage of a need for satisfaction which, though it originates from and is instigated by the taking of nourishment, nevertheless strives to obtain pleasure independently of nourishment and for that reason may and should be termed *sexual*.   (p. 154)

The concept of what is sexual is thus greatly extended and complicated. Freud is showing that sexuality is not a mere matter of a biological urge but involves the production of fantasies under pressure of external circumstances. There is then a disjunction between mere physical need and mental satisfaction. In Freud's view human sexuality is to be understood as what in 1910 he came to call 'psycho-sexuality' (XI, p. 222).

The libido is checked when it comes up against the environment and can only achieve partial satisfaction. In the course of an infant's development those instinctual drives which Freud came to designate sexual or 'libidinous' in nature are channelled into zones. At each stage the infant has to give up a part of its bodily satisfaction: the breast, the faeces – its first product – and the unconditional possession of a penis. Its selfhood will depend on its assumption of a sexual identity, not merely anatomically determined, but psychically constructed. Until this is achieved the infant's sexuality is 'polymorphous': it is at the mercy of the 'component instincts', functioning independently and varying in their aim, their object and their source (*Three Essays on the Theory of Sexuality*, in VII, pp. 191 and 167ff). Only gradually and with difficulty do they become organized into what our culture considers to be adult sexuality. The match of biological sex with the sexual role determined by society is thus achieved, not given.

For Freud this matching is accomplished via the combined workings of the Oedipus complex and the castration complex. It is impossible in this short introduction to give an account of how Freud's theory of gender evolved from the *Three Essays* (1905) through to his lecture 'Femininity' (1933) (XXII, pp. 112–35). The development of his theory has been of particular import to women (see Chasseguet-Smirgel 1981; Mitchell and Rose 1982), since it started out with the notion that until puberty the little girl sees herself as a little man. The account that follows can be no more than a summary of Freud's later position, given on the most general lines.

Freud sees the child's relationship with its parents as critical for the achievement of its proper sexual identity. The difficulties begin with the child's dependence on the nurturing mother. Not only are there problems specific to the very formation of a self-concept in the initial separation from the mother's body, but the love of the mother remains dominant in the early formative years. Inevitably, according to Freud, a perception of the father as rival in this love becomes insistent for the boy-child to the point where he is drawn into fantasies of the killing of this rival and of possessing the mother. This is the Oedipus complex. The way out of it is provided by the fears of the castration complex. The father is experienced as the source of all authority, all direction of desire, and thus as capable of castrating the boy-child, who unconsciously believes this to be the reason for the absence of the penis in the girl. The boy thus abandons his love for the mother and moves towards identification with the father, with the understanding that he too can in time occupy such a position of power.

The trajectory for the girl-child is not so straightforward. In her case the complexes work in reverse, and the castration complex ushers in the Oedipus complex. She interprets the absence of a penis as a failure in provision on the part of the mother. Under the influence of this disappointment she turns away in hostility from her mother, but in the unconscious the wish for a penis is not abandoned: it is replaced by the wish to bear the father a child. Hence the girl becomes the rival of the mother for the father's love. Freud saw the fading of the Oedipus complex in the girl-child as a more uncertain process, because the identification with the father's law, facilitated for the boy-child by the anticipation of power, is not so secure. Nor has he an adequate explanation of how the girl overcomes her jealousy of the mother and attains identification with her.

The Oedipus complex is for Freud the nucleus of desire, repression and sexual identity. Its residue is a life-long ambivalence towards the keeping and breaking of taboos and laws. As the complex declines, the superego is formed and becomes part of the topography of the psyche. The struggle to overcome the complex is never quite resolved. It is the cause of neurotic illness and *raison d'être* of the psychoanalytic process, where the patient is offered a chance to emancipate himself anew, by dint of a better compromise with authority. The psychoanalytic encounter restages the old drama through 'transference'.

Transference and countertransference might be regarded as the 'reader theory' of psychoanalysis. In the non-clinical sense these phenomena are present to some degree in all our relationships: transference is a mode of investing persons and objects with positive and negative qualities, according to our early memories of significant experience of familial figures and the expectations founded thereon. 'Countertransference' defined in this mundane sense manifests itself in the 'knots' which result from the unending chain of mutual misreadings:

> Since Jack is afraid
> that Jill will think that
> Jack is afraid
> Jack pretends that Jack is not afraid of Jill
> so that Jill will be more afraid of Jack.

(Laing 1974)

This process is unconscious: at its worst it leads to a futile reaction and counterreaction, but at its best it may lead to the shifting of old agreements and the making of new ones that better satisfy desire.

The managing of these phenomena in the clinical situation is directed towards helping this process where it has got stuck. The 'free association' of the patient, her saying whatever comes to mind (see the beginnings of this technique in Freud 1953, II, p. 63), gradually reveals that which determines her. Freud distinguishes between two kinds of transference (for a detailed account see Laplanche and Pontalis 1973, on whom this discussion in part relies; see also Wollheim 1971, pp. 152–4). In the first instance transference was for Freud the displacement of feelings from one idea to another (see the section on dreams below). In the analytic situation intense feeling, or 'affect', is transferred to the analyst (the dreams the patient brings may have been dreamt 'for' him), and becomes organized around a group of hostile and loving wishes. The patient's wishes and demands are devices of resistance, the attempt to win the analyst by undermining his authority, so that the repressed wish may at last be granted. The interpretation of the resistance – the words and actions which block off access to the unconscious – is thus the key technique of psychoanalysis. The mechanism of transferring past experience onto the figure of the analyst is set in motion just when the repressed wish is in danger of emerging. Psychoanalytic reader-theory, as will be seen, looks for such points of resistance in both readers and texts, as manifestations of the compulsion to repeat.

The second kind of transference develops in the course of the treatment. Freud calls it the 'transference neurosis'. The nearer the analyst gets to the repressed complex which induced the illness the more the patient's behaviour becomes pure repetition and divorced from present reality. He is in the grip of the 'repetition compulsion', the uncontrolled return of the repressed. Freud's fascination with art is partly due to his admiration of the artist for the ability to control the return of the repressed, as his discussions of art show (see particularly his essay on 'The uncanny' in Part III).

Freud's view of countertransference was cautious: he saw it as the analyst's uncontrolled response to the patient's transference, an inappropriate reaction to be taken care of in the training-analysis. Laplanche and Pontalis define it as 'the whole of the analyst's unconscious reactions to the individual analysand – especially to the analyst's own transference' (1973, p. 92). For some analysts the psychoanalytic encounter becomes the mutual playing out of the subjectivities of analyst and analysand: there is transference and countertransference on both sides (see André Green in Part II, who works out a parallel relationship for writer and reader). For others, such as Jacques Lacan, transference and countertransference can only be negotiated via the spoken word: resistance that is played out between two bodies will only close up the unconscious. Speech, on the other hand, will open it up, for here resistance is directed against the father's law, the order of language, which implicates both analyst and analysand in something beyond a dual relation (Lacan 1977b, pp. 123–34). It is the narration of the analysand, rather than his behaviour, which will therefore enact the reality of the unconscious, which for Lacan is in the very structure of language (for a literary demonstration of narration as transference, see Shoshana Felman in Part III).

The most general implication of all this for a theory of reading is as follows: if the patient's 'text', his presentation of experience, can cause a disturbance in the analyst which allows for a new interpretation, this turns upside down the notion that the reader is the analyst and the text the patient, which has so infuriated opponents of psychoanalytic criticism. Readers do not only work on texts, but texts work on readers, and this involves a complex double dialectic of two bodies inscribed in language.

The value of Freud's opening up of the 'royal road' to the unconscious is that it led to the realization of the universality of this endless conflict and adjustment that bodies must perforce engage in if they are to effect any kind of social compromise, if they are to speak at all.

The dream and the strategies of desire

Dreams have a privileged place in Freud's metapsychology: 'the interpretation of dreams is the royal road to a knowledge of unconscious activities of the mind' (V, p. 608). As a result of investigating them, in himself and his patients, he found himself more and more engaged with conflict and the overlapping of interpretations. Dreams, *par excellence*, reveal themselves to be boundary phenomena, in that they occur where intentions are in opposition, where bodily desires have to come to terms with society.

Whichever of the three models of the psyche is drawn upon, what takes place at the frontiers of the divisions is of prime importance. For the 'dynamic' model one can ask how the primary process affects the secondary process; for the 'economic', how the reality and pleasure principles are evidenced in psychic conflict; for the two 'topographical' models, how the unconscious interacts with the preconscious and conscious, or how id and superego each invade the realm of the ego. Undecidability at the boundaries is likely whenever the restraining power is at its weakest, not only under times of unusual stress, but at the most normal ones, such as that of sleep.

In the condition of sleep the force of repression, according to Freud, is relaxed, because there is no immediate likelihood of unconscious impulse being carried through into dangerous action. Constraint is still operative in that the incursions of what is repressed are deflected from action, that is, from awakening the sleeper. This is why Freud calls dreams 'the GUARDIANS of sleep and not its disturbers' (IV, p. 233). This view has now been challenged as an empirical hypothesis by the fact that dreams have been shown to be regularly occurring events during a distinct state of sleep, with the implication that dreaming is something given which may be capitalized upon by unconscious impulses, not something which is *causally dependent* on being a dual creation of impulse and repressing force (for a thorough review see Jones 1978). However, the duality, and moreover the ambiguity, of dreams remains. It is Freud's vigorous exploration of the workings of these ambiguities that is of special relevance for the language of the arts, and for the activities of reading, writing and criticism. All the arts deal in illusion and Freud's exploration of the ruses and stratagems of the psyche is of immediate relevance to aesthetic experience, at the level of both the medium (the sounds and colours of the dream) and its interpretation.

A summary of Freud's account of the genesis and nature of dreams must precede a description of these workings, because they cannot be adequately assessed without acknowledging their causes in desire. According to Freud, the energizing force of dreams springs from an unconscious impulse seeking fulfilment, a desire not fulfilled in waking life. Unable to find expression in action, the impulse gathers to itself material both from recent experience, such as the effects of present bodily need plus the recollections of the previous day (the 'day's residues'), and from distant memories involving infantile sexual wishes. An unconscious wish meets up with a preconscious thought and strives for an illusory satisfaction. But the 'censorship', the force of repression, at the frontier between unconscious and preconscious will not allow these powerfully charged memories to reach representation in their original form. Instead, under the influence of this censorship, the material is transformed into a series of images, that is the dream. Hence Freud's dictum: 'A dream is a (disguised) fulfilment of a (suppressed or repressed) wish' (IV, p. 160). The disguise may be total as regards the judgement of the dreamer, or it may be insufficient. In either case, the repressed material has both reacted to and evaded censorship by this encoding into a not immediately recognizable form. Hence Freud calls the dream a 'compromise' between the demands of impulse and the intensity of the repressing force. The more intense the force of repression, the more obscure the encodings: the distortions of the material present in the dream are thus traceable to the power of the censorship.

The apparent irrationality of the dream is not only traceable to the resistance to censorship of the unconscious material. That material is already in a form to which the word 'rational' cannot be applied. It is subject to the flow of the primary process, that activity of unconscious desire, whereby an impulse seeks the repetition of achieved satisfaction by finding again the perception that accompanied it: more is included in the perception than the conscious mind can recognize. Hence this perceptual sorting is not some pre-given recognition but a perceptual 'identifying' of sensory patterns, complexes of colour, shape and sound across time, that do not necessarily correspond to what the repressing force, involved in the secondary process, takes as identical. Linkages made in the (unconscious) primary process are already absurd from the point of view of the conscious mind, and these have a profound effect upon the dream. It is therefore difficult to understand precisely the distinction, if it is indeed viable, between the irrational connections pre-existing in the primary process and the 'distortions' insisted on by the censorship. The mechanisms involved seem to serve at one and the same time a subversive purpose (primary process functioning) and a defensive purpose (the censorship of the dreamwork). As Freud said, 'in any case the censorship profits from it' (XV, p. 173; quoted by Laplanche and Pontalis 1973, p. 83). When a patient reports a dream later, the rationality of daytime experiences gives the censoring force another opportunity, in that it can impose on the apparent absurdity of the dream-sequence a narrative sense and coherence, what Freud calls 'secondary revision'. This further distortion-towards-coherence represents another clue from the mode of the actual censoring as to what is being repressed. It would be a mistake, however, to view the question as being an exclusive distinction between the subversions of the primary process (its determination to have its wishes fulfilled) and the distortions of the secondary process (its determination to prevent those wishes from being realized). It is much more a matter of the two forces in some way interacting simultaneously, though Freud himself did not reach this theoretical position, in that he kept primary process and secondary process separate. It is precisely this lacuna in Freud which led to the polarization between id-psychology and ego-psychology and the consequent opposing literary-critical positions.

Nevertheless, Freud's discussion of the individual mechanisms of the dream-work show him to be operating with a concept of ambiguity. It is significant, and has been remarked upon before (see for instance, Lacan 1980, p. 268, and Jones 1978, pp. 11–13, who make this point for and against Freud respectively), that in *The Interpretation of Dreams* Freud is nowhere engaged in tracking down the repressed infantile wish. What Freud is interested in is not the same old primal wish, but the forms taken by the language of desire, that which he calls the 'dream-work'.

The dream-work transforms the 'latent' content of the dream, the 'forbidden' dream-thoughts, into the 'manifest' dream-stories – what the dreamer remembers. Latent content goes piece by piece into the dream-stories via a string of associations.

It is the reverse process from that traversed by the analyst, who therefore requires the patient to retrace the chain of associations in order to decode the dream. The operations of the dream-work, its subversions and distortions, take four forms: condensation (*Verdichtung*), displacement (*Verschiebung*), considerations of representability (*Rücksicht auf Darstellbarkeit*), and secondary revision (*sekundäre Bearbeitung*). These mechanisms are of crucial interest to literary critics of all persuasions, though, as has been indicated already and as will become increasingly apparent throughout this book, the ideological perspective brought to bear upon these workings will vary considerably; a detailed description is therefore called for.

According to Freud, 'the first achievement of the dream-work is *condensation*. By that we understand the fact that the manifest dream has a smaller content than the latent one, and is thus an abbreviated translation of it' (XV, p. 18). But this is far from being a simple process of the mere omission of elements. Composite figures and structures are formed so that as little as possible is left out. Hence the concept of 'overdetermination', whereby several latent wishes converge on one manifest item, or the reverse, where one wish is represented a number of times in the same dream-sequence. The result in each case is a superimposition of elements. This ambiguity is most clearly demonstrable in the way condensation treats words or names. A thing with one name may be associated in a dream with an event with a similar name, even though neither *word* occurred in the dream. Freud relates a case, where someone dreamt that '*his uncle gave him a kiss in an automobile*. He went on at once to give me the interpretation, which I myself would never have guessed: namely that it meant 'auto-erotism' (V, pp. 408–9). The co-presence of the car and the kiss matches the linking of the two parts of the term 'auto-erotism' (inducing sexual pleasure in one's own body). Condensation is also one of the essential features of the joke since, as the above example shows, it produces an ambiguous word in which two thoughts come together. In his book on jokes Freud quotes a saying that old people tend to fall into their 'anecdotage' (VIII, pp. 21–2). Here condensation creates a neologism: the phonetic sequence /dout/ is the element where two meanings coincide – anec*dote* and *dot*age. Instead of saying that old people bore us with their endless stories in their old age, the two ideas are condensed into one sound-unit.

Rational associations with words can be disrupted even more markedly. It is in the nature of the primary process that the distinction between word-as-symbol and word-as-actual-sound can sometimes be wholly ignored. Words, which as sounds have an auditory form, are things in their own right, and associations can be made between the word-as-thing and the thing for which it stands. This is what happens in the case of the schizophrenic, where something in his experience has attracted a chain of associations onto a noise, and the actual word/thing distinction disappears altogether; the world gets sorted out according to private symbols instead of public ones. It is because absurdities of this kind occur in the dreams of normal persons that Freud was able to demonstrate that the unconscious has its own mode of operation.

The second activity of the dream-work is *displacement*, which, according to Freud, 'might equally be described [in Nietzsche's phrase] as "a transvaluation of psychical values"' (V, p. 655). This transvaluation is achieved by the elements in the manifest dream replacing elements in the latent dream-thoughts via a chain of associations for the purpose of disguise; this results in the intensity of an idea becoming detached from it and passing to other ideas, which in themselves are of little value. There is also the consequence that the manifest dream has a different centre from the dream-thoughts and does not reflect their relative importance: indeed they need not appear in the dream at all. Freud regards displacement as 'the most powerful instrument of the dream-censorship' (XV, p. 233). Displacement too has an affinity with the mechanisms of the joke in that a switch of context affords a play on words whereby the dream-work achieves its forced and often far-fetched linkages. One such example is cited by Freud and concerns a patient caught up in a series of dreams, in which her father, whom she recently lost, reappears. In this particular dream the father said: 'It's a quarter past eleven, it's half past eleven, it's quarter to twelve.' To this she made associations that her father set great store on punctuality, but this did not explain the source of the dream. Another chain of associations, apparently unconnected with the dream, led to a remark which occurred in a conversation she had heard the previous day: 'The *Urmensch* [primal man] survives in all of us.' This had provided her with the pretext to bring her dead father back to life, for she had turned him into an *Uhrmensch* [clockman] by making him proclaim the regular passing of the quarter hours (XV, pp. 234–5). The displacement here consists of a shift of association between the authoritarian father who insisted on punctuality and the clock to which he repeatedly made reference. What was associated with the father is shifted onto the telling of the quarters, in itself a trivial event. This example also illustrates the occurrence of condensation and displacement together, for not only is there a displacement from father to the recurrence of the quarters, but there is a pun between *Ur-* (primal) and *Uhr-* (clock). A number of displacements onto one element of itself produces condensation and facilitates overdetermination. Displacement and condensation are thus not exclusive and there is no limit to the modes of their occurrence.

Freud's examples in his explanations of condensation and displacement make no distinction between the associative links that depend on likeness (similarity) and those that depend on proximity (contiguity). When a professor's name, 'Gärtner' (gardener) reminds Freud of a botanical monograph, word-likeness is involved; when a laboratory reminds him of a colleague who works there, the association is of A being found with B, one of contiguity. Both these associations come into his discussion of condensation. Under displacement similar linkages operate: climbing stairs is metaphorically linked with 'going up in the world' socially; a girl born in May and married in May associates herself with may-beetles, a plague which once appeared in that month. It is only after Freud that similarity and contiguity have been singled out as the two fundamental poles of language (Jakobson 1956, pp. 76–82) and subsequently equated to the rhetorical figures of metaphor and metonymy, by confining condensation to metaphoric shifts of association (based on similarity) and displacement to metonymic ones (based on contiguity). All these tropes are based on one thing being a reminder of another, on one's memories. No limits can be laid down beforehand to dictate to the memory whether it should provide similarities or contiguities or both: that two entities are found together is no bar to their being in some way significantly alike and that two are alike is no bar to their being significant in their proximity. Freud realized the inextricability in practice of similarity and contiguity; Jakobson's theoretical distinction helps to clarify what happens when memories produce tropes. It implies no contradiction of Freud, being merely an analysis of the varieties of troping.

Both condensation and displacement can produce visual and auditory images for abstract thoughts, thus contributing to the actual process of representation in dreams. *Considerations of representability*, the way the dream-thoughts achieve representation in the dream via images, is the third activity of the dream-work. Freud stresses the affinity of this process to what already obtains in language. Just as words are created by appeal to sensory items, so latent material becomes imaged by them. The German for 'adultery' is *Ehebruch*, literally 'breach of marriage': 'you will forgive the dream-work for replacing an element so hard to put into pictures . . . by another breach – a broken leg [*Beinbruch*]' (XV, p. 176). The representation is a strange language, however, in that it is divested of logical and syntactical relations. It is nearer to a rebus, a series of ideograms or pictographs, in which the syntactical connections are left to be made by the dreamer (IV, pp. 227–8). The dream has its own order of relations, which can be deduced from the visual elements that actually appear. Contradictions can coexist in an image, for one image can stand for the opposite poles of conflict. Freud cites the phenomenon found by philologists that there are a number of words which are used equally for opposite meanings (Latin *sacer* meaning both 'sacred' and 'profane'). One thing that is the cause of another might appear in a close temporal sequence but without the causal relation being demonstrated. A chronological succession of events might be turned into an image containing them all in spatial proximity. All these transformations of rational linkages are accompanied by regression to infantile modes of thought and feeling.

Representations also make use of symbols that are independent of the individual dreamer, deriving from a variety of cultural sources: they either already have a fixed conventional meaning or else they are 'typical symbols' that recur in the reports of a large number of patients. In the first case, some feature of a familiar legend may make its appearance; in the second, there is a common identification of the male sexual organ with upright objects, and of the mother's body with horizontal ones or with enclosures of all kinds. The interpretation of such 'typical symbols' has led to what has become known as 'vulgar Freudian symbolism': a given and rigid code in which all images have a specific bodily association. Freud, while under the influence of Wilhelm Stekel, did accord a greater place to the conventional symbol, but in the course of his clinical practice he rejected such a mechanical approach, asserting that the interpretation of any symbol, however public, has to be mediated by the context in which it is found: 'as with Chinese script, the correct interpretation should be arrived at on each occasion from the context' (V, p. 353). Freud was thus no vulgar Freudian, even though as analyst he could not ignore the stock-in-trade of familiar symbols that are present in the culture.

The analyst is not the first interpreter of the dream: in narrating a dream the dreamer already acts as his own biased interpreter. *Secondary revision* is logically the last distorting activity of the dream-work. It can occur in the course of the dream, in that the censorship may already be singling out and emphasizing certain elements of the dream, operating 'simultaneously in a conducive and selective sense upon the mass of material present in the dream-thoughts' (V, p. 499). But secondary revision or 'elaboration' (*Bearbeitung*), as Freud also called it, is most obviously at work when the dream is presented in the form of a verbal account. The conscious mind prefers to put the irrational dream-sequence into recognizable and familiar logical order, involving a further distortion of the 'distortion' already achieved by the three mechanisms discussed above. This final revision is in the form of a gestalt-switch in that the dream-sequence is not altered, but the sorting of it is. The 'intelligible pattern' which the conscious mind wants to impose on the visual material can ignore or falsify what is patently there, in the manner of a reader who is so engaged in the text that he ignores the misprints (ibid.). What was visible to the mind's eye in the dream remains unchanged, but the conscious perspective produces a re-vision of it. The material is ignored in the determination to arrive at an acceptable rational narrative: the ready-made formulations of the dream are abandoned, and new ones are made of the very same material. One might illustrate this with an example from Afferbeck Lauder's *Let Stalk Strine*, the comic guide to Australian pronunciation, taking the phrase 'Baked Necks'. The first clue, the actual letters as spelled out, suggest that a curious Australian cooked meat is being offered – perhaps an exotic 'prepared neck-end of lamb'. This clue is subverted in the context by the rival second clues that follow: 'A popular breakfast dish. Others include emma necks; scremblex; and fright shops' (Lauder 1965, p. 14). This is a fair analogy for the process of secondary revision: a first interpretation of a visual experience (the letters) was 'revised' by its being placed in a new context. In the patient/dreamer's account the censorship in its conflict with the primary process overlooks in its secondary revision obvious contextual clues. Secondary revision shows that it is a danger for all systematic thinking to ignore elements that do not fit into a desired pattern. Reading shares this danger with the reporting of a dream. Boundaries shift with contextual placings of the visual material of the dream or of any symbolic medium, including what we call art: the rivalry of interpretations both within subjects (conscious versus unconscious) and between subjects (teller versus hearer) remains a common characteristic of dream and art, in whatever other respects they may differ.

Art and the strategies of desire

Although Freud's essays on art and literature are admired for their elegant exposition, they have not, until fairly recently, received much serious critical attention. This is because in the past these writings have been invoked reductively, quoted selectively against his aesthetic argument as a whole. He relates art to the dream, along a path that leads 'from the investigation of dreams to the analysis of works of imagination and ultimately to the analysis of their creators – writers and artists themselves' (XIV, p. 36). He relates the artist to the neurotic, this being his most notorious statement:

> An artist is once more in rudiments an introvert, not far removed from neurosis. He is oppressed by excessively powerful instinctual needs. He desires to win honour, power,

> love, wealth, fame and the love of women; but he lacks the
> means of achieving these satisfactions.   (XVI, p. 376)

Finally, the object of the whole enterprise is the fulfilment of an
infantile wish: 'In the exercising of an art it [psychoanalysis]
sees once again an activity intended to allay ungratified wishes –
in the first place in the creative artist himself and subsequently
in his audience or spectators' (XIII, p. 187). Id-psychological
criticism is founded on these reductions: the content of the wish
is paramount and as a consequence a direct relation between
the artist and the work is presupposed and usually made the
centre of the inquiry.

The key question around which these issues circle, 'from
what sources that strange being, the creative writer, draws his
material, and how he manages to make such an impression on
us and arouse in us emotions of which, perhaps, we had not even
thought ourselves capable' (IX, p. 143) has not stirred many
minds outside psychoanalytic circles. The question is confined
to motivation: it asks about the nature of the subject and not
about the value of the object. It would therefore seem to testify
to the inferiority of the psychological approach to aesthetics as
compared to the philosophical. In the past this kind of argument has been influential (see Langer 1942, pp. 207–8), but
more recently Paul Ricoeur (1970) and Richard Wollheim
(1973) have argued for the relevance and modesty of Freud's
investigations into aesthetics. Freud does not profess to deal
with the question of aesthetic criteria: 'Before the problem of
the creative artist analysis must, alas, lay down its arms' (XXI,
p. 177). Throughout his work he never departs from this
view.

In 'Creative writers and day-dreaming' (1908) Freud
frankly admits that psychoanalysis cannot say how the artist
achieves his 'innermost secret'. Ricoeur takes this essay as a
prototype to argue that these writings on art are fragmentary
in a highly systematic way. First, Freud proceeds by a series of
analogies. Far from being reductive, these analogies make up
the organizing principle of Freud's essays on art. By a series of
displacements he works from the child at play, to the writer's
fantasy-world, to the novelist's hero, bringing together dream
and fiction in their joint function of fulfilling a wish (Ricoeur

1970, pp. 165–6). But Freud, as Ricoeur points out, also distinguishes daydream from artistic creation, by including the role of play, which goes beyond hallucinatory wish-fulfilment, and by stressing that the daydream makes use of the relation of fantasy to time, by taking 'an occasion in the present to construct, on the pattern of the past, a picture of the future' (IX, p. 148). Second, Freud has something to say about how the pleasure the artist gives us (from 'what we are inclined to take to be his personal daydreams' (p. 153)) is connected with the dynamics of the work of art, and this Ricoeur sees as the systematic aim of the Freudian aesthetic. Variously interpreted, there is no doubt that this theory has been an all-pervasive influence within psychoanalytic applied criticism. Dreams and art are not merely linked because they fulfil wishes, but because both have to make use of strategies in order to overcome the resistance of consciousness: 'work' is done by the dreamer and the artist to transform their primitive desires into culturally acceptable meanings. In order to undermine our resistance, the artist masks his egoistic daydream and at the same time lures us with the

> purely formal – that is, aesthetic – yield of pleasure which he
> offers us in the presentation of his phantasies. We give the
> name of *incentive bonus*, or *fore-pleasure*, to a yield of pleasure
> such as this, which is offered to us so as to make possible the
> release of still greater pleasure arising from deeper psychical
> sources.   (p. 155)

For this Freud has continued to come under fire, not only from aestheticians and literary critics, but also from the proponents of ego-psychology, who wish to argue that aesthetic form has to do with the ego's attempt to maintain and extend its boundaries over the id. Freud is damned out of his own mouth: 'In "Creative Writers and Day-Dreaming", Freud reduced form and beauty to resistance and defence . . . Form sugar-coats an offensive content, bribing critical powers with aesthetic pleasure (analogous to sexual forepleasure)' (Rose 1980, p. 7). While this school must be given credit for its attempts to relate form and content, it makes art, as will be seen, into an altogether fervent and solemn affair. It ignores the connection between the technique of the work of art and the effect of pleasure it produces, which Freud here adumbrates, albeit in a reductive fashion. For a full elaboration of his theory one needs to look at Freud's work on the technique of jokes, where the connection between the fore-pleasure generated (by the word-play) and the deeper instinctual pleasure released is brought out (Ricoeur 1970, pp. 167–8). The saving of the repression, the needless expenditure which gives rise to laughter, can only occur by means of the linguistic devices the 'joke-work' employs in order to divert the attention of those involved in the joke (Wollheim 1973, pp. 216–17).

Freud does not stop at asking where the artist gets his material and how he achieves his effects; he is also interested in the devices whereby the wish gets through. In an essay entitled 'Freud and the understanding of art', Richard Wollheim (1973) examines what part these devices play in Freud's view of art. He argues that Freud was fully aware of the difference between treating art as biographical evidence and treating it as an aesthetic object. The essay entitled 'Leonardo da Vinci and a memory of his childhood' is first and foremost an attempt at psychobiography, whereby Freud wishes to trace the continuing effects of sexuality as experienced in childhood on the adult life of a great man. In the course of tracing his subject's complex history Freud purports to explain why Leonardo turned from art to science and why even his homosexuality was present merely in an idealized form. Freud's study is rooted somewhat tenuously in a supposed 'childhood memory' of Leonardo's, a 'vulture' that opens the infant's mouth with its tail (and which turns out to be a mistranslation of the word *nibio*, meaning kite). He relates these biographical findings (which do not depend on the species of bird in any significant way) to certain of Leonardo's paintings, the *Mona Lisa* and the *Madonna and Child with St Anne*. As Wollheim stresses (1973, p. 207), Freud does not derive his biographical evidence from the paintings: he finds contextual information embedded within them which he decodes with the help of the findings already established. As regards the *Mona Lisa*, Freud argues that the smile condenses two images of Leonardo's first mother, one signifying tenderness and reserve, the other sensuality and seduction. As regards the other picture, both natural mother and equally loved stepmother are present and linked in a pyramidal structure; here the enigmatic smile can be read on both faces, doubly condensed in dreamlike fusion. The focus is thus on processes whereby a conflict of meanings can be discerned within the work itself: in psychoanalytic terms a wish, to yield to the tenderness of the mother, is confronted by a defence, the danger of yielding to this wish. In artistic terms there is an ambiguous element the viewer cannot account for, what has been called 'the daemonic magic of this smile' (XI, p. 108).

Dreams and fantasies require a frame of reference, the associations the dreamer/patient is expected to bring to them, that make salient their ambiguity for the analyst. The work of art has already itself provided that ambiguity. In his study of Jensen's story *Gradiva* Freud feels justified in investigating 'the class of dreams that have never been dreamt at all – dreams created by imaginative writers and ascribed to invented characters in the course of a story' (IX, p. 7). He finds all the associative elements in the story itself; his interpretation in no way depends on the intention of the author, conscious or otherwise. This is not to deny that Freud was primarily interested in the several ways in which the story corroborated his theories: indeed he treats it as an allegory of psychoanalysis, with patient as hero, analyst as heroine, and analytic setting as archaeological building-site. The clinical object of Freud's study may be summarized as four-fold; the fourth point brings together psychoanalytic and aesthetic ambiguity.

First, Freud plays on the obvious analogy between archaeology and psychoanalytical investigation, a favoured image to which he returns again and again. In *Gradiva*, the hero, Norbert Hanold, is an archaeologist who is investigating the buried remains of a city, Pompeii, and also, unknowingly, his '"buried" childhood'.

Second, the story illustrates for Freud what he regards as one of the cornerstones of his theory, the return of the repressed: 'There is, in fact, no better analogy for repression, by which something in the mind is at once made inaccessible and preserved, than burial of the sort to which Pompeii fell a victim and from which it could emerge once more through the work of the spade' (p. 40). In the story the hero is wholly absorbed in his studies and has turned away from life and its pleasures. As

Freud puts it, the emotions he is unable to give to women of flesh and blood he gives to women of marble and bronze. His fantasies come to centre upon a Roman relief and grow into a full-scale delusion. The sculpture is of a girl stepping out in an idiosyncratic way, whom he therefore names Gradiva, 'the walking one'. After searching for her in vain in his native city, Vienna, he has an anxiety-dream in which he sees her in Pompeii, where he had assigned her in his fantasy, as she lies down and is buried by a fall of rubble. Like the hero of Thomas Mann's *Death in Venice*, Hanold is now driven by 'an inner restlessness and dissatisfaction' to seek an uncertain destination until he finally 'finds himself' in Pompeii (p. 13). There he is disgusted by the presence of couples all about him and soon his thoughts and feelings drift from the moderate carnality of mating couples to the gross animality of copulating houseflies. When he sees his Gradiva in flesh and blood he knows at last what drove him to Pompeii. Subsequently it becomes clear that Hanold's fantasy is not a hallucination, but derives from the repressed memories of his childhood, 'a kind of forgetting which is distinguished by the difficulty with which the memory is awakened even by a powerful external summons, as though some internal resistance were struggling against its revival' (p. 34). What Freud is interested in is not the mere fact of the return of the repressed, but in 'the highly remarkable manner of that return' (p. 35). The instrument used to repress the unconscious, the name Gradiva, becomes the very means by which the repression is subverted. The unconscious fulfils the wish by means of a trick: 'Gradiva' turns out to be the translation into Latin of the repressed surname of Hanold's childhood love, Zoe Bertgang, meaning 'one who steps along brightly'.

Third, Freud wishes to show (and this is what first draws him to this story) that dreams have a meaning and can be interpreted. Though they cannot foretell the future, as antiquity would have it, they do have intentional significance; when the dream-text is finally revealed it represents the wishes of the dreamer as fulfilled. The creative writer, Freud says with one of his favourite gestures, knows better than the scientist. Dreams are not mere somatic stimuli, but have sense and purpose: they are 'the physiological delusions of normal people', giving access to the unconscious (pp. 62–3). But can literary dreams be analysed, when there is no dreamer to supply the associations for each piece of the manifest dream? Freud says this can be done by dint of 'borrowing' from his *Interpretation of Dreams*.

One of the principles he laid down is that some element in the dream is a piece of reality. Taking Hanold's first dream, in which Hanold is in Pompeii at the same time as Gradiva, Freud transcribes this circumstance as signifying 'the girl he was looking for was living in a town and contemporaneously with him' (p. 58). This is true inasmuch as it applies to Zoe Bertgang, the real elements being 'in a town contemporaneously with him'. But it is a displacement by way of a double reversal, because in the dream Hanold is living at the same time and in the same place as the historical Gradiva, whereas in 'reality' (the story's empirical world), she is living in *his* time and place, the Vienna of his day. It is this displacement which enabled the repressed wish to get through. According to Freud's dream theory there is a current wish which attaches itself to a wish to do with the past. In this case, the admissible wish of the archaeologist, 'to have been present as an eye-witness at the catastrophe in the year 79 A.D.,' attached itself to the inadmissible wish of the would-be lover, 'to be there when the girl he loved lay down to sleep' (p. 93).

Fourth, Freud notes the overlap of psychoanalytic and artistic ambiguity in the course of the story's unfolding. The author of the story leaves the reader in suspense as regards the level of its reality, whether the Gradiva Hanold finds in Pompeii is a revenant or a hallucination. Freud points out that the reader's knowledge of the situation is in advance of the hero's and that this is part of the author's conscious strategy: 'Anyone who reads *Gradiva* must be struck by the frequency with which the author puts ambiguous remarks into the mouths of his two principal characters' (p. 84). The Gradiva in the streets of Pompeii is Hanold's old childhood friend Zoe and she understands what is going on. Both Zoe and Hanold share the symbolism which structures the story, the analogies between childhood and Pompeii, repression and burial. Zoe can therefore maintain her Gradiva role and yet at the same time try slowly to free Hanold from his delusion. Like a good analyst she works towards her goal indirectly, cultivating the ambiguities of the situation. What happens is that Gradiva/Zoe sees two meanings where Hanold sees only one. Freud gives a number of examples, one when she says to her patient: 'I feel as though we had shared a meal like this once before, two thousand years ago; can't you remember?' (p. 85). Freud calls this handling of a double language 'a triumph of ingenuity and wit', but carried away by the psychoanalytic parallel of heroine-cum-analyst he seems to wish to assign the credit to the character rather than the author. This is because in the first instance he wishes to press home the analogy to psychoanalytic procedures: 'This striking preference for ambiguous speeches . . . is nothing other than a counterpart to the twofold determination of symptoms, in so far as speeches are themselves symptoms and, like them, arise from the compromises between the conscious and the unconscious' (ibid.). Freud sees a relationship between the symptomatic character of speech (all words as compromise-formations even when not obvious Freudian slips) and the writer's skill in the strategic use of language. The author achieves his effects by means of ambiguity: he speaks to the reader through Zoe, thus sharing his superior knowledge. Two meanings go to the reader, where only one goes to the hero. In his analysis of the story Freud shows that the strategies of desire are partly performed by the text. Here the author is not the one who is being analysed (although Freud did write to Jensen, and despite getting no lead, indulged in some lively speculation). However, he discusses the workings of the text only from the analyst's point of view, whether as himself, the author, or Zoe in her role as analyst; he does not here pursue any analogy between 'patient' and reader.

In the essay 'Psychopathic characters on the stage' (orig. publ. 1905/6) the spotlight is more on the audience. One question which occupies Freud in this highly condensed essay is how the audience's understanding of the repressed material will affect their response. If too much gets through, resistance will come into force and the spectator will not allow himself to be drawn in. The dramatist will fail to purge the spectator of his emotions and thus, according to Freud, not open up a possible source of pleasure. It is once again a question of strategy. In 'Creative writers and day-dreaming', the reader was to be 'lured' away from the writer's personal unconscious by the work's formal properties. In the present essay the spectator is to be drawn into the character's psychopathology by means of having his attention 'diverted'. The focus has thereby shifted from the author's need to that of the reader.

Freud's argument takes a somewhat roundabout route. The spectator wishes to identify with the hero, to have an illusion of greatness, but he does not want to undergo any real suffering. 'Accordingly', says Freud, 'his enjoyment is based on an illusion.' There speaks Freud the positivist, the same Freud who assumes that the child at play is like the creative writer in separating his world 'sharply' from reality (IX, p. 144; on this point see also Trilling 1964b, p. 44). This seems only to stress the negative aspect of illusion, not the positive one developed by Freud's later followers (see Part II). Freud does come round to the pertinent question as to how this illusion, that is 'only a game' (VII, p. 306), is to be maintained, but he never answers it straightforwardly. He approaches the problem of audience response by making a distinction between the theatre of the Ancients and the Moderns.

Greek tragedy essentially involves conflict with an authority, be it a struggle against divinity (religious drama), against the state (social drama), or against another individual (psychological drama); in all these examples two conscious impulses are in opposition. But, Freud argues, when instead of psychological drama we have psychopathological drama, 'the source of the suffering in which we take part and from which we are meant to derive pleasure is no longer a conflict between two almost equally conscious impulses but between a conscious impulse and a repressed one' (VII, p. 308). The neurotic spectator will react to the lifting of repression with a mixture of enjoyment (on account of the energy saved in not having to hold down the repression) and resistance (on account of any anxiety that may be caused). The dramatist, says Freud, must proceed with care to attune the *non*-neurotic spectator, whose gain is not so obvious; he must draw him in 'with his attention averted', lower his resistance, so that he does not know exactly where his emotions are leading him: 'After all, the conflict in *Hamlet* is so effectively concealed that it was left to me to unearth it' (pp. 309–10).

At the beginning of the essay Freud argues that in drama in general the spectator can identify with the hero without suffering: he can have the glory without paying the price. He knows his enjoyment is based on illusion and hence he does not mind plunging in. With 'psychopathological drama' there is the problem of coming up against resistance. Rebellion against an inner authority is a painful process. Even so, there might be a yield of 'masochistic satisfaction' in identifying with the hero's defeat (p. 306; Freud is here touching on his later economy of the drives as it appears in *Beyond the Pleasure Principle*). Hence a different strategy is required to draw in the spectator who does not consciously wish to be the person on the stage, one which takes account of an unconscious satisfaction. The first case, illusion, and the second case, 'diversion of attention', together are a joint strategy, applicable to all drama. The opening of Freud's essay is in keeping with the wish-fulfilment theory of 'Creative writers and day-dreaming', in that it stresses the play aspect, now in the light of the spectator's willingness to enter the illusion created by the playwright and the actor, who 'enable' him to play. At the end of the essay, however, the 'dramatist's skill' is presented as creating a surrogate neurosis. There is aesthetic pleasure in both, in providing the unconscious with a release, but in the former, play partakes of a collusion that is publicly validated, while in the latter the collusion is private. A new kind of space is thus created, a neurotic space. In his essay 'Theatricum analyticum', Philippe Lacoue-Labarthe points out that this has wide implications for a theory of the theatre, in that it marks a break with Aristotle's poetics of the drama. What takes place can no longer be taken as a representation of reality, the mere imitation of an action, but is to be seen as the production of reality 'outside representation' (Lacoue-Labarthe 1977, p. 25). Theatre, in Jean-François Lyotard's words, is 'de-realized space' (see 'Beyond representation', preface to the French translation of Anton Ehrenzweig's *The Hidden Order of Art* (Paris: 1974), cited by Lacoue-Labarthe; Ehrenzweig's theory of the creative unconscious is discussed in Part II).

'Psychopathic characters' has something of the richness of Freud's essay 'The uncanny,' where he also stresses the power of the writer to control the return of the repressed and demonstrates, albeit unconsciously, how it is done: in foregrounding the uncanny effects in E. T. A. Hoffmann's 'The Sandman' via an argument for the Oedipus complex, he succeeds in 'diverting attention' from the uncanny effects of the repetition-compulsion as figured in the essay as a whole. In these writings Freud discusses theory and practice together: he is interested in the work's devices and the pleasurable effect thereby achieved. Unfortunately id-psychology dropped this two-fold concern and took for granted that the ultimate task of the psychoanalytic critic was the recovery of a latent and true meaning, and that this meaning would inevitably be directly connected with the way the author was caught up in his private fantasy. Since, however, the scrupulous critics were interested in the way this fantasy was *figured* in the text, their readings, however predictable in terms of themes, already, before Trilling, linked psychoanalytic processes with rhetoric.

It must be said, however, that Freud's notion of collusion between writer and reader assumes that there is always a challenge from a neurotic infantile wish, never a wish that could be corrective of the repressive system, against that system. The ambiguities always work one way only, allowing spurious satisfaction, returning the repressed whence it came. This is indeed, as will be seen, the burden of D. H. Lawrence's objection, and, from an anything but radical position, that of the ego-psychologists and archetypal critics. Freud's theory, though it recognizes the subversive force of the unconscious, here neglects the possibility that on some occasions it may overcome the censor and produce an aggressive correction. As will be seen in Part III, his theory of the joke does something to make up for this omission.

3

Classical Freudian criticism: id-psychology

Instinct-psychology (or id-psychology, as it came to be called) centres on the role of the sexual instincts as the determining force of an individual's life. In Freud's early topography of the mind, the dualistic one, the conscious and preconscious are engaged in conflict with the unconscious – or, to put the contrast in terms of instinct – the ego-instincts, concerned with self-preservation and the need to relate to others, are in conflict with the sexual instincts as the dynamic core of the energies in the unconscious (the term 'id' had not yet been adopted by Freud). The unconscious is thought of as close to the bodily sources of the pressure of need, from which libido derives, with its power to invade and transform experience, particularly in dream and fantasy. Its ability to mask itself thus enables it to appear in disguised form in activities wherein the sexual origin is apparently unrecognizable and only to be decoded with difficulty, even though the feeling they give rise to loses none of its intensity by such disguise.

The aesthetics of id-psychology are grounded in the notion that the work of art is the secret embodiment of its creator's unconscious desire. Classical applied psychoanalytic criticism related the work back to the author's psyche, which it explored via the analysis of his earliest childhood experiences gleaned from what is known of his life, the analysis of his fictional characters, and the analysis of his 'typical symbols' (vulgar

Freudianism). Despite its obvious shortcomings, in that it neglects the art-aspect of the work, such an approach can be very illuminating for the way it works with figures of repetition. Its less scrupulous exponents, those who translate without due regard for context (a cigar, as Freud said, is sometimes just a cigar), have given it a bad name, but often it is dismissed out of hand from hearsay on account of the polemics of other critics. What follows below are three examples of classical applied psychoanalytic criticism where the practitioners each pay close attention to context. If one is disposed to give them credit for this close examination of the text one must acknowledge the inadequacies of the mode in which it comes. All treat the work as symptomatic in that its effect is dependent on an uncontrolled return of the repressed, thus privileging the unconscious of the author over his conscious mastery.

Psychoanalysis of the author: Bonaparte on Poe

The study of an artist's life to explain his works, or the study of his works to explain his mind, was already an established mode in the latter half of the nineteenth century, when pre-Freudian psychology made various attempts to relate genius to madness. Cesare Lombroso, an Italian professor of legal medicine, argued that creative genius was a by-product of psychosis, in that the advance of this condition can turn someone with an average mind into a genius (Lombroso 1891). This provoked a controversy as to who was sick, the creative genius (whose state of health does not in any case reflect on his work) or the society who chose to assign this status to decadents such as Wagner, Nietzsche and Baudelaire. The artistic products of the accused were investigated and brought in as proof of their decadence and as evidence of their lack of genius: 'Degenerates are not always criminals, prostitutes, anarchists, and pronounced lunatics; they are often authors and artists' (Nordau 1895, p. vii). What was at stake was thus not just the status of the artist, but what the criteria for morality were to be: 'Books and works of art exercise a powerful suggestion on the masses' (ibid.).

This is the background to what came to be called 'pathography': a study of the artist not for the sake of the work or even the man, but for the purpose of classifying a particular pathology. Studies of this type appeared in a periodical called *Imago* (published in Vienna, Leipzig and Zürich), from 1912 to 1937 the chief organ for the publication of writings dealing with the relation of psychoanalysis and the arts to all aspects of culture (see Fischer 1980 for examples). Freud was ambivalent in his attitude to pathographical studies, even though he designated his Leonardo essay as such (Freud 1953, XI, p. 130). He claimed he was working within the definition of the term, but then criticized others of his circle who were unable to match his commitment to the cause. Rather than being bent on validating a particular pathology he wished to throw light on the psychoanalytic process as such. This shift of concern seems to be reflected in the now more commonly used term 'psycho-biography'.

Marie Bonaparte's full-length study of Edgar Allan Poe (Bonaparte 1949; orig. publ. 1933) is the classic example of what has become known as 'psychobiography', although she called it *étude psychanalytique*. Freud's preface to it shows not only his approval but also his awareness of the delicate ground 'investigations of this kind' were treading on:

> In this volume my friend and pupil, Marie Bonaparte, has directed the light of psycho-analysis upon the life and work of a great writer of a pathological type. Thanks to her inter-pretative efforts, we can now understand how much of the characteristics of his work were determined by their author's special nature; but we also learn that this was itself the precipitate of powerful emotional ties and painful experiences in his early youth. Investigations of this kind are not intended to explain an author's genius, but they show what motive forces aroused it and what material was offered to him by destiny. There is a particular fascination in studying the laws of the human mind as exemplified in outstanding individuals.
>
> (XXII, p. 254)

Bonaparte begins her study with Poe's life-story, which she gives in considerable detail, drawing her material from the best available scholarly sources of the time. A brief synopsis can do no more than outline the parallels she wants to make between the man and his work. Poe was born in 1809. His father disappeared when he was 18 months old; his pretty and childlike mother died of consumption about a year later. He was brought up by foster-parents, and he was neither legally adopted nor later left any money by his foster-father. He married his cousin Virginia when he was 26 and she was 13 and already sickening; she died of consumption some ten years after their marriage. Poe died at the age of 40, after a life of poverty, debts, drink, drugs and depression, having completed a considerable mass of essays, poems and stories. Bonaparte goes to work on the stories, subjecting them to a minute scrutiny, and relating the events and figures (persons) in Poe's life to the events and 'figures' (in its rhetorical sense) of the text. Her basic contention is that Poe was a necrophilist, someone for whom corpses have an erotic attraction (necrophilia being a pathological extension of the part played by normal mourning, when the mourner for a time refuses to accept the event). Bonaparte argues that Poe, through a fixation on his mother, was condemned to an eternal fidelity. He remains physically faithful to her, his first love, by marrying an ailing cousin and thus sparing himself the need to consummate the marriage. So now at last comes the point: as a psychoanalytic critic what does she do with this material? She declares the principle of her enterprise at the outset:

> Works of art or literature profoundly reveal their creator's psychology and, as Freud has shown, their construction resembles that of our dreams. The same mechanisms which, in dreams and nightmares, govern the manner in which our strongest, though most carefully concealed desires are elaborated, desires which often are the most repugnant to consciousness, also govern the elaborations of a work of art.
>
> (Bonaparte 1949, p. 209)

Marie Bonaparte takes the characters in Poe's stories as imagos, that is as internalized images which are the result of past experience. She takes them as father-, mother- and sister-figures which have made their way from Poe's unconscious into his tales. The women particularly, consumptive and ethereal figures, she sees as prototypes, and hence she labels the second section of her book 'Tales of the mother'. In her analyses of these tales she wishes to show how the repressed feeling is transferred, via a displacement (dream-theory) onto fictional figures and objects. Thus a building too can do duty, the famous house of Usher, for instance, or the sea, the earth's depths and the stars. This is what is implied by Freud's notion of symbolism. The whole world can be absorbed narcissistically, the sexual drives can attach themselves to anything the senses perceive. In each tale, according to Bonaparte, Poe is reliving Elizabeth Poe's last agony and death. The third section of her book is entitled 'Tales of the father', in which male figures become the return of the repressed, the father who comes back to avenge Poe's imaginary parricide and incest.

For psychoanalysis Poe's work is thus an example *par excellence* of the compulsion to repeat – in Bonaparte's reading the repetition of a content in accordance with her interpretation of Freud's early instinct theory; in Lacan's reading (see Part III) the repetition of a structure in accordance with his interpretation of Freud's later instinct theory. Since the central tenet of Freud's theory of dream-formation was that dreams are wish-fulfilments, the compulsion to repeat raised a problem for him when it came to anxiety dreams, such as he found with those suffering from war neuroses, where the dreamer returned over and over again to the memory of his traumatic experience. Freud came to think of anxiety dreams in general as attempts to fulfil wishes accompanied by the performance again of the ego's initial repression of the dangerously challenging upsurge from the id, as if to renew and strengthen the resistance to that wish (XXII, pp. 27–30). Poe's fiction, according to Bonaparte, embodies the wish to become reunited with his dead mother; since this must needs be a censored wish we should not be surprised that Poe's tales hardly read like wish-fulfilments.

In carrying out her task Bonaparte avails herself of Freud's theory of dream-interpretation. She takes Poe's tales as the manifest part of the dream and believes that, by finding associations from persons and incidents in Poe's life, she is recovering the latent part. The problem is not so much in what she does (which is very interesting), but in what she claims: that this is where the true meaning is to be found. '[It] is as though Poe himself were to declare "*Because* I am still fixated on my mother, I cannot love another woman"' (Bonaparte 1949, p. 655). Freud warned against such a view:

Now that analysts at least have become reconciled to replacing the manifest dream by the meaning revealed by its interpretation, many of them have become guilty of falling into another confusion which they cling to with equal obstinacy. They seek to find the essence of dreams in their latent content and in so doing they overlook the distinction between the latent dream-thoughts and the dream-work. At bottom, dreams are nothing other than a particular *form* of thinking.

(V, p. 506n.; see also p. 580)

In her operations on the text Bonaparte goes beyond her reductive statements. The fourth section of her book is devoted to an explanation of the mechanisms of the dream-work, of which she has made use throughout. The nearest she gets to literary criticism is in her analyses of the configurations within the text. A brief example can be extracted from her reading of 'The Black Cat'. She places this tale in the second section of her book, 'Tales of the mother', under the sub-title of 'Tales of the murdered mother'. The psychoanalytic theme here is the part the woman plays in the arousing of castration-anxiety. There are two cats in the story. The first one is an all-black cat, which the narrator loved greatly. One night he returns home drunk, and fancying that the cat is avoiding him, he seizes it roughly, only to get bitten. In a fit of rage he gouges out one of its eyes, whereupon the mutilated creature fills him with such horror that he finally hangs it. Not as finally as he thinks, for there appears a second cat, which according to Poe has 'a large, although indefinite splotch of white, covering nearly the whole region of the breast'. Since it already has a missing eye it too inspires horror in the narrator, becoming a victim of his hatred, and the cause of his downfall.

In the course of her interpretation Bonaparte makes use of the activities of the dream-work, particularly the mechanisms of condensation and displacement. She sees the ambivalent emotions which Poe (according to her biographical findings) feels for his mother displaced onto the cats. The first cat represents the mother seen as all bad (figured as all-black in contrast to the second cat), avoiding him and thus arousing memories of unfulfilled needs. The second cat, on the other hand, momentarily arouses memories of fulfilled needs, for its white splotch, she argues, represents milk both by its colour and its position. Moreover, she points out, the second cat is found in a tavern, where one drinks, and it is sitting on top of a barrel of gin. Here one might see an example of condensation since two images to do with drinking are condensed into one scene. What provokes the fate of both cats, however, is the missing eye, because it is through this mutilation that each cat inspires such horror: this is another displacement in that fear of castration is displaced onto the disappearance of the eye (Bonaparte 1949, pp. 472–3).

In her analysis Bonaparte seeks to understand the psychology of the author by unravelling the meaning which a vast number of objects in Poe's own life have acquired in a chain of addition and substitution. To this extent her reading corresponds to the sign-system of the dream. She shows how a manifest meaning is subverted by a latent meaning or meanings via an associative link. The link is in the form of a trope, metaphorical (white is *like* milk) or metonymic (milk is *found with* breast). The meaning was changed as a result of the irruption of a wish; there is thus a link here between the role of desire in dreams and the figuration and structuring of the text.

There are two levels of objection to this. The first is one of complete sceptical negation of such decodings. This, of course, implies a wholesale rejection of the findings of psychoanalysis, and thus a rejection of such configurations outside this text, both in other texts and in life, which invite this kind of reading, and a rejection of the possibility that, if Poe's tales were an anonymous *oeuvre*, such readings could be adduced. The second level of objection concedes that a neurosis appears in the text, but maintains that dramatically it belongs to the narrator. This is the argument of the orthodox critic:

> Poe's narrators should not be construed as his mouthpieces; instead they should be regarded as expressing, in 'charged' language indicative of their internal disturbances, their own peculiarly nightmarish visions. Poe, I contend, is conscious of the abnormalities of his narrators and does not condone their intellectual ruses through which they strive, only too earnestly, to justify themselves.
>
> (Gargano 1967, p. 171)

This is merely the converse of Bonaparte's position. The one is trying to assign the figures of desire exclusively to the unconscious of the author, the other is trying to assign them to a neurotic narrator under the detached control of an authorial consciousness. One is making the dream encapsulate art, the other is making art encapsulate the dream. Bonaparte disregards the public aspect of Poe's utterance and classifies it as belonging to 'that conscious, logical and aesthetic *façade* which we call creative writing' (Bonaparte 1949, p. 663, my italics), behind which the true unconscious is at work. The orthodox critic disregards the private aspect of Poe's utterance in believing the unconscious can be safely confined within the boundaries of a character.

Can one separate Bonaparte's reductive principle from the results of her application of it, the effects she displays in the text? Although her argument from biography is gratuitous because one cannot estimate how true or false it is, this need not mean that her criticism is worthless, given that there is an undeniable typicality in the symbolism she reveals. Her aim was the vindication of psychoanalysis, yet her reading of Poe does not depend on the truth of the psychobiographical method. She took for her frame of reference the author's life, but it is the stories which get her going. She calls them 'transference stories', since, in accordance with her reading of Freud and Poe, they are subject to 'repetition compulsion which dominates our instinctual life, and impels us always to seek the same emotions in the same forms, whatever the object' (pp. 221–2). Like many others she has herself succumbed to the 'Poe-etic effect' (see Felman 1980, pp. 119–25, for an analysis of critical reaction to Poe in terms of transference phenomena) but the rigour of her approach, its very reductiveness, makes her analysis of the tales into a compelling fantasy, rather like a strange poem in its own right, as much her own as Edgar Allan Poe's. She ignores what is commonly regarded as literary in refusing to remain at the level of public symbolization, yet her reading partakes of literary criticism because she is a gifted reader with an eye for picture-puzzles, a gift she shares with Poe. Paradoxically, she has shown him to be a master of ambivalence, and, above all, a provoker of fantasy, but she gives all the credit to his unconscious, whereas her unconscious too is actively involved.

Though she believed herself to be the analyst of the text, she was as much an analysand as her patient. It is not only the author who is in transference to his medium, who has unconsciously invested it with his fantasies; her reading is equally subjective. This throws new light on the supposed reductiveness of psychoanalytic interpretation: the very reductiveness, instead of achieving the objectivity of which it was in search, reveals, in the intensity of its concentration, a subjective response given public articulation. The analysis she pursues of Poe contributes to an interpretation of the stories.

Psychoanalysis of the character: Crews on Hawthorne

The psychoanalysis of literary characters has not fallen into as deep a disrepute as the psychoanalysis of the author. It is still a flourishing industry, even if under the sophisticated guise of post-Freudian developments in psychoanalytic theory. That is to say, although the id-psychological model, with its emphasis on the sexual instincts trying to find representation in images and symbols, has been abandoned, other models, based on Freud's second topography and focusing on pre-oedipal conflict, have taken its place. This means that the terms of the equation have changed but the assumptions and attendant problems have not. I quote as an example from a recent psychoanalytic interpretation, entitled 'Melville's lost self: *Bartleby*': 'I believe that Bartleby's arrival at the office and his subsequent breakdown into negativity is a mimetic representation of a need to find a nurturant space where he can regress toward the healing of a "basic fault" in the self' (Bollas 1976, p. 226). Although this clinical formulation is like a red rag to a bull to literary critics I am not citing it for that purpose; the essay is a clinical study of the classical kind which openly declares itself and which has considerable explanatory force in terms of unconscious character-motivation. It is after the pattern of Freud's method in his analysis of Hoffmann's story 'The Sandman' (XVII, pp. 227-33), in the course of which Freud argues that the central character is suffering from a castration complex. The point I wish to make is that the limitations of psychoanalytic character-analysis are analogous to the limitations of literary character-analysis. This problem is nicely illustrated by an assertion, couched in contrary terms, by a co-author of another recent book on applied psychoanalytic criticism:

> Fictional characters are representations of life and, as such, can only be understood if we assume they are real. And this assumption allows us to find unconscious motivation[s] by the same procedure that the traditional critic uses to assign conscious ones.
>
> (Kaplan and Kloss 1973, p. 4)

Here too, it is a question of 'mimetic representation'. Neither Bonaparte nor Lawrence (see the next section of this chapter) work on the assumption of a one-to-one equation between fictional characters and flesh-and-blood persons: Bonaparte worked with condensed and displaced figures, and Lawrence with literary stereotypes. There are now new literary developments in psychoanalytic character-analysis, where the oedipal model is shown to work as a triangular structuring force, breaking up dyadic relationships, in the context of a history wider than the subject's personal one (see Girard, Bersani, Tanner, in Further reading). But these follow on from the theories of structuralism and post-structuralism. What we are now looking at in this section is no more literary than psychobiography, though to literary critics it may seem more palatable than Bonaparte's work.

Frederick Crews's book, *The Sins of the Fathers: Hawthorne's Psychological Themes*, came out in 1966. It is a full-length study of Hawthorne's fiction, including the four romances he left unfinished. His argument is that 'Hawthorne's interest in history is only a special case of his interest in fathers and sons, guilt and retribution, instinct and inhibition . . . only by immersing himself in Puritan history could Hawthorne satisfy his interest in buried impulses' (Crews 1966, pp. 29–30). This is to argue, contrary to Lawrence, who only gets a sidelong reference (p. 9, n. 15), that Hawthorne looked at puritan history because he was obsessed with oedipal tensions. Crews does not sufficiently take into account that the puritan culture was itself constitutive of neurosis because of the extreme harshness of its father-figures (as I have argued elsewhere: Wright 1982b). If Crews adopted a more historical perspective himself, he might consider that it was because the puritans were establishing a culture divorced from the checks and balances of the old world of Europe that this culture took upon itself a special intensity of repression: instead of the aristocratic father they left behind, they reinstated a new familial one.

Though this lacuna does not actually invalidate Crews's chosen method of psychoanalysing literary characters it does shed light on the shortcomings of treating literary figures as if they had complexes of their own. In fact it is a worry to Crews to what extent Hawthorne is in control of the return of the repressed in his works. He cannot make up his mind to what extent to give the author credit for the effects his texts display, coming to the impeccable conclusion that Hawthorne is 'ambiguously involved' with his driven heroes 'and that he thereby has an intuitive grasp of their motives' (p. 96). In this respect Crews's critical enterprise was certainly an advance on the then state of Hawthorne criticism and criticism in general, which had absorbed neither Lawrence's intuitive findings in his study of American literature nor Freud's theoretical findings in his study of *Gradiva*. For in the same year as Crews's study there appeared a collection of critical essays, which still in the main carry on both the canonization of Hawthorne and the rigid character/author distinction: 'It is Arthur Dimmesdale and not his creator for whom the "sin" of adultery is the chief issue in *The Scarlet Letter*' (Kaul 1966, p. 2). Nevertheless, Crews's own ambivalent position in this respect raises something of a problem: throughout his study it is never quite clear whether it is Hawthorne or his characters which are in analysis. A sketch of Hawthorne's life is provided in the penultimate chapter of the book, showing him to be something of a classic Freudian case: his father's death at an early age, his lameness, his delicate health, his marriage at 38 to a semi-invalid, his dislike of a maternal uncle, on whom he depended financially. These data are then linked with an interesting argument, that in his late unfinished works 'his entire plots, rather than merely his protagonists, will flee from themes that become more inescapable in symbolism as they become more intolerable to conscious thought' (Crews 1966, p. 115). The return of the repressed gets out of control, Hawthorne can no longer represent the motives of his heroes with sufficient detachment, and hence his art falters.

Though the scope of this study really goes beyond character-analysis (which turns out to be both its strength and its weakness), its main focus is squarely on the motivation of characters in the light of Freudian psychology. They are escapists, unwilling to pass from childhood to maturity. Their sexual obsessions are the driving force of the stories. The plots themselves enact the return of the repressed, in that they 'allow perverse and partial expression to those wishes' (p. 264). The heroes of the stories take refuge in various pursuits, some patently obvious, some not so obvious: strange forest meetings ('Young Goodman Brown'), medical science ('The Birthmark'), botany ('Rappaccini's Daughter'). Crews shows persuasively how the images and symbols are condensations and displacements of the original libidinous impulse: activities whether guilty or innocent, observing witches' sabbaths or tending flowers, become the occasion for the return of the repressed in the form of a neurotic compromise. This aspect of Crews's psychoanalytic criticism is its greatest strength, for it shows character in the making. The weakness resides in Crews's wish to give a total interpretation of each work he considers and over and above this a total interpretation of all Hawthorne's work. In order to do this he takes the *content* of psychoanalysis and applies it wholesale: he displays the plots as oedipal quests, the symbols as typical oedipal symbols, the characters as fixated at various stages of oedipal conflict. He reads Hawthorne as a Freudian allegorist *avant la lettre* (feasible in itself), but in so doing he uses Freud's text as canonical in order to assign to Hawthorne's text a retrospective sanctity of a new kind:

> As Freud put it, the ego is not master in his own house. It is this intuition that enables Hawthorne to reach a tragic vision to understand the inner necessity of everything they [the characters] do, and thus to pity and forgive them in the very act of laying bare their weaknesses.   (p. 153)

Crews's final judgement is that 'Hawthorne must be recognized as a peculiarly narrow writer' (p. 269), for which he blames first Hawthorne, then his method, and finally Freud. Crews has subsequently renounced psychoanalytic criticism (see Crews 1976), and is still renouncing it (see Crews 1980). His latest reasons for rejecting psychoanalysis are that there is no validation to be found in the results of therapy and that such attempts to establish scientific credibility for the theory have proved ineffective. He dismisses the evidence that Freud adduces as mere 'interpretation'. This does not meet the point that where motives and intentions in the individual are concerned it is interpretation rather than strict verifying and falsifying that is called for. Indeed, in his treatment of Hawthorne and his characters Crews was endeavouring to do something analogous to a positivist validation of Freud, whereas whatever there is of value in his study falls within the scope of interpretation, in particular that aspect of his study which deals with a character's investment of his or her desire with whatever offers itself as image in his or her world. This precludes treating all characters as if they were conceived and perceived naturalistically: Crews has ignored Hawthorne's own allegories in projecting his rigid Freudian ones and has thereby taken character out of its fictional matrix. When D. H. Lawrence comes to read Hawthorne, he sees the allegory as an essential part of the fiction.

Psychoanalysis of culture: Lawrence on American literature

Lawrence does not fit neatly into id-psychological criticism, for he opposes his notion of the unconscious to a distorted view of the Freudian unconscious. His misreading of Freudian concepts and the 'post-mortem effects' he displays in the texts (the unconscious coming through) must therefore be taken together, if his relevance to classical psychoanalytic criticism is to be made clear. His writing falls into the category of applied psychoanalysis in so far as its object is to recover the true latent meaning of the work; but unlike the classical psychoanalytic critic he is not interested in the individual psychology or pathology of the authors he investigates. Lawrence's own commitment shows through, to defend the body considered to be the source of all energy and integrity from the oppression of prurient and sadistic puritanism, culturally imposed. Hence he is a psychoanalytic critic of a special kind, for he is launching a critique of psychoanalysis while adopting its essential concern with the placing of the body in culture.

Studies in Classic American Literature (Lawrence 1977) first appeared in 1923. The earlier versions of these essays, all but two of which had appeared in periodicals from 1919 onwards, were collected and reprinted in 1962 under the title *The Symbolic Meaning* (Lawrence 1962); they are more stable than the *Studies* in argument, though less powerful in effect. Lawrence has undertaken a double mission: he wants to investigate the American canon of the nineteenth century in order to reveal the return of the repressed in the puritan consciousness as a whole, 'the dangerous *negative* religious passion of repression, this passion which so easily becomes a lust, a deep lust for vindictive power over the life-issue' (1962, p. 25). At the same time he wishes to 'save' the text from the author: 'Never trust the artist. Trust the tale' (1977, p. 8). In Lawrence's reckoning the author has no control over the return of the repressed. Here he rejoins Bonaparte in asserting that the true meaning of the text resides in its latent content, but he departs from her again because for him 'two blankly opposing morals' are involved: the latent true one of the tale, and the manifest false one of the artist.

What is most interesting about Lawrence's criticism from the psychoanalytic point of view is not just the famous polemic, but that he shows, as Freud does in *Gradiva*, that the very instrument of repression, here the puritan conscience, can become the vehicle by which the repressed desire returns. Lawrence's campaign involves an attack on three related duplicities: first, that of the Pilgrim Fathers, who came (ostensibly) in search of liberty, 'they seemed to seek, not liberty, but a gloomy and tyrannical sense of power. They wanted to have power over all immediate life' (1962, p. 25); second, that of the artist, who produced myths to celebrate the occasion, 'the old American artists were hopeless liars. But they were artists in spite of themselves' (1977, p. 8); and third, that of the reader who (unlike Lawrence) accepted these myths ingenuously, 'we like to think of the old-fashioned American classics as children's books' (1977, p. 7).

In order to understand the thrust of Lawrence's endeavour one has to take account of his assessment of Freudian psychology. Reference will here be made to two extended essays making up one book (Lawrence 1961a and b; orig. publ. 1923), *Fantasia of the Unconscious* and *Psychoanalysis of the Unconscious*. Like so many others of his time, Lawrence regarded Freud as a pansexualist, as one 'who makes sex accountable for everything' (1961a, p. 13). He could not or would not understand Freud's concept of polymorphous sexuality, being himself totally committed to the pure heterosexual genital act. For him 'the act of coition is the essential clue to sex' (p. 12). He thanks Freud only for very small mercies: 'The orthodox religious world says faugh! to sex. Whereupon we thank Freud for giving them tit for tat' (*sic*, p. 13). He will have nothing to do with the Freudian unconscious, describing it as 'the cellar in which the mind keeps its own bastard spawn' (1961b, p. 204). In particular he rejects what he calls the 'incest-craving' of the psyche, which he argues is a conspiracy of culture, 'the mind, that is, transfers the idea of incest into the affective-passional psyche, and keeps it there as a repressed motive' (p. 203). In this respect Lawrence is here oddly in accord with Deleuze and Guattari (see Part IV, p. 162–3), however different the rest of his premises. Lawrence equates the unconscious with a life force, albeit with a special qualification: it is not to be thought of as general but as unique in each individual organism. He believes in a self from the moment of conception; the fulfilling of the unique self is the goal of its life. He will have no truck with any kind of determinism: 'We refuse any *Cause*, whether it be Sex or Libido or Élan Vital' (1961a, p. 13).

Given this view of the unconscious, as 'by its very nature unanalysable, undefinable, inconceivable' (1961b, p. 211), it is hardly surprising that Lawrence sees the Freudian enterprise as a second Fall; the will to know the unknowable becomes a mission of doom. What is the point, he argues, of revealing the unconscious only to prohibit what you find there? He sees in the American conquest of the native an allegorical parallel. The white settlers came to America to find freedom, only to impose their own rigorous laws on the other consciousness, to master it, without making any attempt to absorb the 'otherness' of the new place and its native inhabitants. Their will to know, like the will to know sex, resulted in the wilful repression of all that is joyous and intuitive, what Lawrence calls the mind's attempt to conquer the 'blood' (1977, pp. 91–2). For Lawrence the political repression imposed on the native is like the personal repression imposed on the blood. Though this notion of 'the blood', within its pantheist context, needs to be sharply distinguished from the Freudian notion of the instinctual drives, the essential analogy between Lawrence and Freud holds, in so far as there is a natural force trying to get through and a harsh civilizing force trying to stop it. Hence Lawrence can be seen as an id-psychological critic *avant la lettre*, holding a similar brief to that held by Freud in *Civilization and its Discontents* (1930).

In his *Studies* Lawrence believes he is revealing the latent myths of his writers; he approves of some myths and disapproves of others. The myths of which he approves are those which acknowledge and play out the conflict between the old and the new consciousness, without subjecting the process to an obsessive scrutiny: 'What true myth concerns itself with is not the disintegration product. True myth concerns itself centrally with the onward adventure of the integral soul' (Lawrence 1977, p. 69). Into the category of 'true myth' go Cooper, Melville and Whitman, who all get qualified approval. Into the category of 'false myth' go Hawthorne and Poe, who get qualified disapproval. Since both types of myth are taken as latent within the work, we have here to distinguish between a true myth (integrity) and a false myth ('disintegration product'). This distinction brings in a moral judgement on Lawrence's part, levelled indiscriminately against the author and his characters. He makes no sharp division between the two, but shares out the moral–psychological failures between them. In one sense he therefore disregards the autonomy of the author as the centre of the work, but he does so only in order to reinstate him as the privileged source of a particular type of language, that of 'art-speech', imaginative writing, in his view the repository of truth.

It is the creators of false myths (the 'disintegration product') whose works are particularly prone to the return of the repressed. Outwardly they subscribe to the victory of mind over matter, but inwardly they cannot leave the matter alone. In Poe's work Lawrence sees the murderous impulse to destroy that which cannot be mentally possessed and mastered. The heroines of 'Ligeia' and 'The Fall of the House of Usher', who have been betrayed by their lovers' spiritual obsessions rise up from the grave to get their revenge for having been cheated of life. The sensual rises against the spiritual: 'To try to *know* any living being is to try to suck the life out of that being ... you know your woman darkly, in the blood. To try to *know* her mentally is to try to kill her' (p.76). For Lawrence, Poe is the prime example of one who probes the objects of his love, including himself, to the point of disintegration, 'reducing his self as a scientist reduces a salt in a crucible' (p. 70).

Hawthorne's works similarly reveal for Lawrence the secret triumph of the sensual over the spiritual and he traces this theme directly through from Poe to Hawthorne. He sees Hester Prynne, heroine of *The Scarlet Letter*, as 'the KNOWING Ligeia risen diabolic from the grave. . . . This time it is Mr Dimmesdale who dies' (pp. 95–6). That is, in this case Lawrence sees the male as victim of the repressive process, though he does not return from the dead: what returns are the displaced and perverted forms of desire as intimately related to the repressing force. Hester is compelled by the community to wear the letter A (for adulteress) on her bodice, 'stitched with gold thread, glittering upon the bosom. The proudest insignia' (p. 94). She thereby, according to Lawrence, secretly exults in her fall and is able to go on expressing her voluptuousness, flaunting her sin and her child, while her erstwhile lover, the young puritan minister Arthur Dimmesdale, whose sin is not known by the community, 'has a good time all by himself torturing his body, whipping it, piercing it with thorns, macerating himself' (p. 96). In order to attain its ends, the denied impulse avails itself of the very means that repressed it. This is also the thrust of Freud's analysis of *Gradiva*: 'in and behind the repressing force, what is repressed proves itself victor in the end'. Freud cites 'the typical case of repression in the lives of saints and penitents' and illustrates it by reference to an etching which shows Sin emerging in the very spot where the monk looked for refuge, on the cross itself, where the image of the crucified saviour is displaced by the image of a voluptuous naked woman in the same pose (IX, p. 35).

A similar configuration appears in *The Scarlet Letter* when its Christian hero, accompanied by the beautiful Hester, exposes himself as a sinner to the assembled crowd in the market-place, baring his chest in order to reveal to their horrified gaze the letter A branded thereon:

> 'People of New England!' cried he, with a voice that rose over them, high, solemn, and majestic, – yet had always a tremor through it, and sometimes a shriek, struggling up out of the fathomless depth of remorse and woe, – 'ye, that have loved me! – ye, that have deemed me holy! – behold me here, the one sinner of the world! At last! – at last I stand upon the spot where, seven years since, I should have stood; here, with this woman, whose arm, more than the little strength wherewith I have crept hitherward, sustains me, at this dreadful moment, from grovelling down upon my face! Lo, the scarlet letter which Hester wears! Ye have all shuddered at it! Wherever her walk hath been, – wherever, so miserably burdened, she may have hoped to find repose, – it hath cast a lurid gleam of awe and horrible repugnance round about her. But there stood one in the midst of you, at whose brand of sin and infamy ye have not shuddered!'
>
> (Hawthorne 1978, p. 180)

He who was regarded as holy is suddenly revealed as the greatest sinner, and the mode in which he reveals himself is also that which betrays his passion, a branded A appearing in conjunction with the beautiful woman beside him.

Lawrence attributes effects of this kind to the 'duplicity' of the author; that is to say, like Bonaparte he thinks the author has no control over the return of the repressed. The effects of its return in 'the tale', however, have enabled Lawrence to catch the author out in the act. But in the act of what? The 'post-mortem effects' of Lawrence's own texts are intimately connected with those he displays in his authors. He is a puritan turned on his head, attacking puritanism for its refusal to countenance the pure sexual act in all its plenitude. In his eyes both Freud and the Puritan Fathers are the knowers: his central attack is on that knowledge which invades and inhibits feeling. The 'post-mortem effects' in Lawrence's texts are those of a puritan son engaged with the knowing, incestuous Puritan Fathers. What returns in his texts is the hatred of the father, the 'duplicity' of the author/father, who '*knew* disagreeable things in his inner soul' and 'was careful to send them out in disguise' (Lawrence 1977, p. 89; my italics).

The value of Lawrence's reading is bound up with the effect the text has had upon him. With the help of his reductive formula Lawrence is able to show the way guilt feelings are figured across a number of texts at a particular moment in history. Where Bonaparte extracts a fantasy that is completely private, he detects a myth which is publicly shared, even though the ground of this myth is the Protestant family.

4
Post-Freudian criticism: ego-psychology

Ego-psychological approaches to art strongly oppose the notion that the mainspring of art is a neurotic infantile wish. The endeavour is rather to show that the pleasure of artistic activity derives from a controlled play with infantile material, in the course of which this material is transformed into something publicly shareable. The difference from Freud's theory lies in the view that what is pleasurable is not the fulfilment of an infantile wish, as he believed, but the mere fact of bringing the primary process into play at the ego's behest. To understand what this theory involves in terms of a psychoanalytic contribution, the relationship of the three elements of Freud's second topography needs to be clarified.

In his first topography Freud thought of the ego as entirely equivalent to the conscious and the preconscious; the instinctual energies were confined to the unconscious. In the second topography, elaborated in *The Ego and the Id*, he wants to see the ego as developed out of the instinctual energies, 'from bodily sensations' (Freud 1953, XIX, p. 26, n. 1), and therefore he does not draw a logical boundary between the ego and the unconscious. Similarly, the third element in this topography, the superego, also has an unconscious component. The advantage of the second topography is that the deciphering of the unconscious is not now simply a matter of rigid interpretation, but must take into account the interplay between unconscious and conscious. There is no longer just a force trying to get through and another force preventing it. To begin with, the ego is now seen as in part constructed from the instinctual energies: it connives with them as much as it controls them. In addition, these energies, which Freud now calls the 'id', are also operative in the superego, particularly in their destructive form, directing aggression upon the ego. It is therefore clear that the conscious/unconscious boundary cannot be maintained so simplistically, because the ego must be performing some kind of mediating function, which involves both (pp. 54–7).

Id-psychology, which focused on the instinctual drives, led to a type of psychoanalytic criticism which privileged the private fantasy. Ego-psychology, on the other hand, stresses the managing of this fantasy, and this leads to a type of psychoanalytic criticism which emphasizes the maintenance of identity. The ego-psychologists could derive support from Freud's statement in *The Ego and the Id*, that 'psychoanalysis is an instrument to enable the ego to achieve a progressive conquest of the id' (p. 56), and it is in this sense that they interpret Freud's dictum, 'Wo Es war, soll Ich werden' (translated in the Standard Edition as 'where id was, there ego shall be' (XXII, p. 80)). But what is thereby ignored is the context in which the ego is spoken of as being in the service of the id. The ego is a 'frontier-creature' (XIX, p. 56), endeavouring to facilitate the traffic and trade as much from the external world to the id as from the id to the external world. A dialectical reading of Freud, such as the French Freudians have made, will interpret the 'Ich' as becoming and developing within the id rather than as an 'ego' dislodging it. This allows for negotiations between inner demands and external prohibitions without forcing the 'Ich' to be wholly at the mercy of either. The ego-psychologist reads 'Ich' as 'ego', regarding it as a given identity, strengthened by socialization. He therefore wants all the traffic to be in one direction, namely from the ego as a publicly adjusted identity, towards the id, as having to accept the limitations so imposed.

Aesthetic ambiguity: Kris

One of the earliest ego-psychologists was Ernst Kris, a practising psychoanalyst in America and a former member of Freud's circle in Vienna. His influential book, *Psychoanalytic Explorations in Art* (Kris 1964; orig. publ. 1952), marked a first turning-point in psychoanalytic aesthetics, though Kris acknowledges and makes use of William Empson's contributions in *Seven Types of Ambiguity* (1930), and of Lionel Trilling's essays, 'Art and neurosis' and 'Freud and literature' (Trilling 1964a and b; orig. publ. 1945 and 1947). Kris proposes a theory of creativity in which the emphasis is shifted from the subversive operations of the id to the managing capacities of the ego. Though he retains the analogy of art to dream, this no longer rests on the notion of an unconscious wish that wants to find expression, but depends on the way the unconscious wishes are modified by the preconscious operations of the ego. It should be remembered that the preconscious is everything that is freely and safely recoverable by the ego.

To be consistent and sufficiently secure as a basis for criticism, Kris's view had to be grounded on a psychoanalytic theory which gave pre-eminence to the ego. He therefore had to find some theoretical justification for claiming that the workings of the unconscious can safely be brought within the control of consciousness. Lionel Trilling makes the same point when he claims that, although there is an undoubted similarity between the mechanisms of art and those of the dream, 'the work of art *leads us back to the outer reality by taking account of it*' (1964b, p. 45). Kris sets out to give psychoanalytical backing for this taming of the unconscious, and so he must find in its theory something that can perform the task.

In *The Ego and the Id* Freud speaks of a 'displaceable energy, neutral in itself', which can be added to an impulse and change its quality, say from love to hate. 'The only question is where it comes from, what it belongs to, and what it signifies' (XIX, p. 44). He calls it 'desexualized', but by this he merely means it is not specific to the libido or the aggressive instinct. It can be regarded as an intensifying agent in that whatever it is added to becomes more powerful, but in itself it belongs with no particular impulse. Kris (1964) and another ego-psychologist Hartmann (1964; orig. publ. 1955) take up this notion, calling it 'neutralized' energy. It is important for Kris's aesthetic theory that this neutralized energy can be directed by the ego, enabling it to manage the impulses and fantasies that emerge from the id.

Kris is now able to argue that there is no one-way influence of the primary process in the unconscious upon the secondary process, but he does this by virtually positing a one-way influence in the other direction, in having the secondary process acting upon the primary via the 'neutralized energy'. He maintains that in 'aesthetic ambiguity' the ego is in control and produces a 'multiplicity' of meaning (Kris 1964, pp. 245–59). He makes a new equation between art and dream: the ambiguity found in art, particularly poetry, is like the overdetermination Freud found in the dream-work.

In his chapter entitled 'Aesthetic ambiguity' (written in conjunction with Abraham Kaplan), Kris discusses the different types of ambiguity and states his position with regard to Empson's work. He wishes to relate ambiguity not only to poetry, as Empson does, but more generally to a 'theory of the poetic process' (p. 243). On the one hand he wishes to abolish any rigid distinctions between poetry and prose and between the scientific and the poetic; on the other hand he wants to argue that this need not threaten the standards of interpretation implicit in Empson's own practice and explicit in Empson's concern that the reader may construct the 'wrong poem'. In connection with his seventh type of ambiguity, condensation, Empson speaks of those who 'have enough detachment not to mind what their sources of satisfaction turn out to be' and 'whose defences are strong enough for them to understand them' (Empson 1930, pp. 247 and 248). Both Kris and Empson want to secure the work of art from the unbound energies of the primary process. The problem is how to avoid 'reading into the poem meanings not present to others' (Kris 1964, p. 260). What Kris comes up with is still by and large a traditional view of reader competence, involving: (1) 'standards of correspondence', that is knowledge of the communal symbols on which the reader draws; (2) 'standards of intent', that is knowledge of the artist's sources and intentions; (3) 'standards of coherence', that is the structural unity of the poem (pp. 260–1).

It is clear that what Kris proposes is a relatively safe concept of ambiguity, a plenitude of meanings made up of associations within culture. Any latent ambiguities are safely under the control of the ego: 'creativeness is a relaxation ("regression") of ego functions ... the regression in the case of the ego is purposive and controlled' (p. 253). This is the great slogan of ego-psychology, to which this chapter has been leading. The types of ambiguity Kris lists arise from richness of connotation. In them the competing ('disjunctive') or overlapping ('additive') meanings are all directly interpretable by a public code: 'The word "cat" may be taken to refer to a tabby or a tiger: for the layman these alternatives are disjunctive; a zoologist would construe them as additive' (p. 247). Such 'construings' – a logician's term in itself – show how far Kris is from examining the strategies of the unconscious. At the other end of the pendulum's swing, Marie Bonaparte is at least nearer to an understanding of the possible manoeuvres of the unconscious in taking the cats in Poe's story 'The Black Cat' as displacements for a fantasy and in discussing this fantasy in terms of Poe's ambivalent feelings for his mother. Though reductive, Bonaparte's account admits the subversive nature of desire in language and allows for the possibility that multiple meanings might be created within a work without any reference to any publicly agreed code.

Kris is similarly conservative in his discussion of laughter. He takes for granted that any laughter, because it 'spreads' (that is it is often infectious), becomes a 'social act' (p. 220). This is ambiguous with a vengeance: the 'social act' is just as likely to be one of the undermining of a group unity, aiming at the rejection of social constraints. Indeed, this is implicit in Freud's theory of the joke, seen in particular in his analysis of the obscene joke as a prototype (see Part III). In Kris's case the emphasis is on the ego's control of the instinctual drives: of the rhythmic shaking of the body in laughter he says that an 'archaic pleasure in movement is reactivated and is socially permissible' (p. 225). In the chapter 'Ego-development and the comic' he says that the adult's enjoyment of wit can be 'justified before the superego' (p. 207) and that it is a pleasure that has grown from the child's delight in playing with words. Similarly, Ernst Gombrich calls on Freud's joke theory for a view of play as innocent experimentation (1983, p. 138), arguing that the artist's 'social game', his playing with given historical forms and conventions, involves a combination of preconscious and unconscious activity (for a different reading of Freud's joke theory

see Part III, pp. 137ff.). In both these arguments it is question-
able whether sufficient place is given to laughter and play as
corrective of social convention.

Ego-psychology has left its mark on psychoanalytic criticism
and started it off on another trend. Through its focus on
preconscious processes ego-psychology makes an analogy between the movement of psychic energies under the control of the
ego and the play of language within a cultural context. This has
placed the emphasis on formal devices of art, namely the
varieties of ambiguity, rather than on content. It has therefore
helped to make psychoanalysis literary and respectable, but at
the expense of purging literature of its bodily parts, as Goethe's
angels decontaminated Faust before allowing him to proceed on
his way to heaven.

The dynamics of response: Lesser and Holland

Ego-psychological criticism began by allying itself with Empson and the New Criticism, proclaiming the autonomy of
the text. It sought meanings not in the individual psyche, in
private fantasy, but in the public encodings of the private, in
what was mutually shareable. A reader only counted in this
schema in so far as he was thoroughly institutionalized as
regards 'standards' of 'correspondence', of 'intent', and of
'coherence' (see last section). The concept of the reader has
since been subjected to a more searching analysis. It is a matter
of considerable controversy: 'Is he the "Actual Reader" (Van
Dijk, Jauss), the "Superreader" (Riffaterre), the "Informed
Reader" (Fish), the "Ideal Reader" (Culler), the "Model
Reader" (Eco), the "Implied Reader" (Booth, Iser, Chatman,
Perry), or the "Encoded Reader" (Brooke-Rose)?' (Rimmon-
Kenan 1983, p. 118). The theorists who now follow have
directed attention to yet another species, to what might be
called the Personally Desiring and Aspiring Reader, though in
the case of ego-psychology the second element takes over.

Unlike id-psychological criticism, which was almost exclusively author-centred, ego-psychological criticism begins the
process of analysing the response of the reader. There is a move
from the wish-fulfilling fantasy of the author to the shared
wish-fulfilling fantasy of reader and author, as adumbrated by

Freud in 'Creative writers and day-dreaming' and 'Psycho-pathic characters on the stage'. Author and reader are in collusion: the formal properties of the work disguise the fantasy, allowing the reader a yield of 'fore-pleasure' through his also being able temporarily to circumvent his own repression. In *Fiction and the Unconscious* (1957) Simon O. Lesser moves from the dynamic theory of Freud, of pleasure principle versus reality principle, to the structural theory of *The Ego and the Id*. He argues that form in fiction works in three ways: as an id function it gives pleasure, as a superego function it relieves guilt and anxiety, and as an ego function it facilitates perception, the 'single objective' being 'the communication of the expressive content in a way which provides a maximum amount of pleasure and minimizes guilt and anxiety' (p. 125). Form is here brought into play not in order to do just that – play – which it could hardly do if it were committed to the 'communication of an expressive content', but to reinforce powerful institutional pressures. The dynamics of the work are no longer seen in terms of strategies employed to facilitate the production of pleasure for both author and reader, but as a normative device whereby harmony and balance are maintained. Freud is here turned on his head, because where he saw fiction as an outlet for unconscious wishes, for Lesser 'fiction provides an outlet for idealistic and contemplative tendencies thwarted in our daily experience' (p. 82). The work is now a consolation for the guilt felt at the pleasure of the body having interfered with the higher pursuits of the mind, instead of vice versa. The cleansing operation of the body of the text undertaken by Kris is herewith extended to the body of the reader, himself a Faust on his way to heaven.

Lesser's interpretative procedures amply bear out his belief in the harmonizing text. In his discussion of Hawthorne's story 'The Birthmark' he argues that the hero's obsessive wish to rid his wife of this mark and make her perfect 'represents no more than an extension of a tendency present to some degree in nearly everyone,' that 'at the same time as we recoil we can identify with Aylmer and through him act out some of our secret desires' (pp. 95 and 96). Since the story concludes with the wife's death, the reader, according to Lesser, is forced to recognize the impossibility of Aylmer's demands. This leads Lesser into banalities in no way dependent on the help of psychoanalytic theory: 'Fiction endeavours to gratify as many of our longings as possible, but the very effort to teach us how they can be reconciled with one another and with reality compels it to take cognizance of the ineluctable limits of the human situation' (p. 98). A certain kind of reader is here presupposed, one implied by the text, but this reader is entirely passive, his task consisting of the constructing of 'analogizing fantasies' (compare with Jung – see next section) which, as has been seen, are to be salutarily dismissed. In this presupposition Lesser is conflating an epistemological and philosophical issue with a moral issue within the historical process: of his dictum 'Form allays anxiety' Lesser tries to make out that this is a general aesthetic principle, whereas the fact is that in some historical situations an emphasis on conformity, and in others a challenge to conformity, may be found desirable. The very same work might thus be read from a conservative or a radical point of view, depending on the context. To try to claim that either of these positions is given is to take up a political position, though this is unrecognized in Lesser's argument.

Lesser's *Fiction and the Unconscious* naturalized psychoanalytic criticism in America, rendering it a respectable mode. His style, however, made it more of a sermon than a theory, and thus required a more systematic framework. This has been supplied by Norman N. Holland, initially in his book *The Dynamics of Literary Response* (1968), and later in a series of revisions. It is worthwhile considering Holland's position at some length because it begs a number of important questions regarding readers and reading. His being systematic makes plainer what is being taken for granted.

The early Holland is not far from the orthodox Freudian view as expounded in 'Creative writers and day-dreaming'. His extension of it is that the source of pleasure we get from literature is derived from the *transformation* of the unconscious wishes and fears into culturally acceptable meanings. The text becomes a scene of collusion between author and reader round a 'core-fantasy' shared by both. Holland provides a 'dictionary of fantasy,' following the Freudian phases of infantile development, one or other of which, he claims, determines the way the fantasy is embodied in the text. In accordance with ego-psychology he sees form as having a defensive and adaptive function, by means of which the unconscious wishes get past the censor. He wants to provide a model for the way fantasies move from the level of unconscious to that of conscious meanings, and hopes to found an objective assessment upon it, arriving at an aesthetics of response.

Thus, for example, he claims to detect a core-fantasy in the most recalcitrant of passages. Take, for example, his discussion of the 'Tomorrow and tomorrow and tomorrow' speech in *Macbeth*, which, as he points out, has been criticized for the mixing of its metaphors:

> To-morrow, and to-morrow, and to-morrow,
> Creeps in this petty pace from day to day,
> To the last syllable of recorded time;
> And all our yesterdays have lighted fools
> The way to dusty death. Out, out, brief candle!
> Life's but a walking shadow; a poor player,
> That struts and frets his hour upon the stage,
> And then is heard no more: it is a tale
> Told by an idiot, full of sound and fury,
> Signifying nothing.
>
> (V.v. 18–27)

Holland believes that the power of this speech resides in the evocation of a primal scene, that incident one mythical night when the child fancied it witnessed its parents in sexual encounter and thereby suffered the greatest trauma in denial of the mother and successful rivalry with the father. The 'tomorrows' and 'yesterdays' creeping past are marking the fateful nights between; the 'sound' and 'fury' are the unnameable things heard; the 'brief candle' that must 'out, out' is inevitably the plainest of phallic symbols. The childish wish to express the oedipal hatred is the declaration that the sounds and strutting of the father upon the stage of life 'is a tale / Told by an idiot, full of sound and fury, / Signifying nothing' (V.v. 25–7). One might feel uneasy about the *ad hoc* quality of these attributions; then again one might concede that with Macbeth at the end of his tether such regression to infantile modes of thought is credible. But to what extent does the fantasy contribute to the metaphorical power of these lines, when the latent images of familial relationships ('strutting' actors/fathers) are already closely bonded with the manifest meaning, a king whose symbols of power no longer command respect? The fantasy then is no longer at the core; there is a transformation, but no originary core-fantasy. Moreover, the reader is given a curiously passive role, responding automatically to ubiquitous core-fantasies which can be transformed in random directions.

Holland's latest position is an attempt to shift the focus from text to reader; he now concludes that 'poems do not . . . have fantasies or transform them towards themes – people do' (1975a, p. 110). He no longer views the text as a fixed entity producing calculable effects upon readers ('text-active' theory). Nor does he opt for an interaction between reader and text on the lines of a determinate cause allowing indeterminate effects ('biactive' theory), such as an objective 'meaning' giving rise to varying 'significance' in individual readers (Hirsch 1976). A text, he maintains, cannot be defined apart from readings of it ('transactive' theory). For the 'transactive' process he employs the analogy of a feedback loop, both of which metaphors imply that there are two elements in play, 'feedback' suggesting the continuous alteration of a cause by its effect, 'transaction' suggesting the negotiation of a bargain – a bargain for the reader, as it turns out (Holland 1980).

Holland defines the responses of the reader as essentially those of a search for reassurance, a warding off of anxiety. This security is achieved by the projection of a safe fantasy into the work. The reader 'transacts' with the work, eliciting modes of adaptation and defence which are effective for him alone, since they will be those which arise from his own identity theme. Holland here bases his ideas on a revision of ego-psychology proposed by Heinz Lichtenstein (1961, 1965), who, though he rejects the notion of a self as given from birth, believes in a basic 'organizing activity' (1965, pp. 121ff.) which allows a 'primary identity' to emerge through the infant's interaction with the nurturing mother, this identity remaining basically invariant throughout life. From this Holland argues that the infant, born into the world with a 'general style', establishes an unchanging personal identity through its relation with its mother, which it will bring to bear on all its 'transactions', later including those with a text, assimilating idiosyncratically to itself and thereby strengthening and enriching character. Neither Lichtenstein nor Holland enquire into the social determination of the mother–child unit presumed to have such a formative influence upon this permanent identity. The transaction is described by Holland in four stages: the reader's initial approach to the text ('expectation'), his being selective in what he takes in (mode of 'defence'), his projection of wish-fulfilments (characteristic 'fantasy'), and his translation of them into themes ('transformation'). He coins the word DEFT, an acronym, for this process of identity maintenance. How deft are these transactions of the reader as attempts to put theory into practice?

Holland experiments both with transactions of his own and with those of others, noting the relation between their free associations to a text and their personalities, as revealed in free-association tests (*Five Readers Reading* – Holland 1975b). In his essay, 'Re-covering "The Purloined Letter"' (1980), he makes his own transaction the focus of his criticism, taking the part of both reader and analyst, exploring the history and the features of his personal acquaintance with the text from a first reading at the age of 13. He develops a theme of hidings and discoveries from the text and traces it to his own pubertal fears arising from his concealment of his masturbating from the adults about him. This connects with his enjoyment at the same age of performing conjuring tricks, hiding and revealing being of the essence of such acts. Following from this he sees Dupin as a Prometheus figure, adept at outwitting the father-god, carrying concealed in a magic stalk the fire beneficial to man. Further, the skill of deciphering texts is common to Dupin and to himself as reader; as reader, too, he trusts the knower Dupin, much as the narrator does.

Holland bases the reading transaction on the psychoanalytic phenomenon of transference, which he believes in its general sense to be inescapable ('Why this is transference, nor am I out of it' – Holland 1982). The novelty of Holland's model of reading-as-transference is that the text is the *analyst*, triggering off responses in the reader/analysand, although when Holland becomes the reader/analysand he is at the same time conducting a self-analysis, examining his responses as a reader. He is both patient in transference and analyst in countertransference, examining his responses to his patient/self. His identity-theme perforce must operate in its idiosyncratic way upon the text, just as the patient performs a transference of his familial patterning upon the analyst.

The oddity of Holland's transaction is that he leaves out in theory what he takes account of in practice, the influence of the text on the reader. Hiding and trusting are distinctly inter-subjective themes, because confirmation and correction have to operate across experiencing persons. The persuasiveness of his reading resides in its concern with the rivalry of interpretations, private versus public. Both the 'analyst' Dupin and the analyst Holland are picking out from what is publicly viewed by the forces of law and order something unperceived by these forces. The text as object cannot theoretically disappear into a feed-back loop entirely maintained by a single reader, for this ignores the social nature of language. Language starts from a sedi-mentation of past social congruities of action and desire that have involved the reader with other subjects. As part of this interaction a literary text comes with a most indissoluble tie forever knit with other texts, which contribute to its existence and without which it could not even be read. The writer as much as the reader is in transference with that intersubjective exist-ent, the text, and neither alone can define what is pleasure, what functions successfully, what defences and adaptations are to be brought into play and how tenaciously. While Holland ignores language and textuality in theory, maintaining, astonishingly, that 'psychoanalysis has nothing, nothing whatsoever, to tell us about literature *per se*' (1982, p. 31), in practice he is much given to word-play. 'Skirmishing' with other analysts, Lacan and Bonaparte, he puns on 'a Bone-a-part' and 'the pure-loined letter' (1980, pp. 354 and 358), falling into a Lacanian transference, but without the latter's theoretical commitment to the dual effects that the unconscious gives rise to both at the level of the word and at that of narrative.

His practice, finally, presents a paradox through its own communicability. Throughout his argument there is an unex-pressed presupposition which he has failed to analyse, namely that a reading is a criticism. Holland has inadvertently punned on *reading* which can mean either the private act of reading or a critic's reading as a piece of communicated interpretation. He insists there is a merit in having different readings, but there is nothing in his theory which demands that they be uttered to anyone else, something he takes for granted. To utter transactions is not merely to transact: according to the dictates of his theory Holland should be quietly transacting in private instead of flooding the market with his own, often remarkably persuasive readings. Yet there is no distinction in his theory between the solipsistic transactions of his pure identity-seeking guinea-pigs (*Five Readers Reading*) and those individual transactions which can be rendered intersubjective. A principled as distinct from a merely verbal acknowledgement of intersubjectivity is exactly what is missing from his formulation. A reading-made-criticism enters into a negotiation, and out of that negotiation something concealed but in full view may be cleverly revealed by a Dupin-critic, a reader/analysand-cum-critic/analyst. It is a general weakness of all reader-response theories (not only those which postulate a Personally Desiring and Aspiring Reader) that they fail to ask why readings should be communicated.

What is interesting is that Holland, in his later model of the reading process, reverses the direction of interpretation taken by ego-psychology: where Kris and his co-workers studied the mechanisms of the psyche in order to discover how private meanings were transformed into public ones, Holland now concerns himself with processes whereby public is turned back into private.

5
Archetypal criticism: Jung and the collective unconscious

The only critic so far considered who has taken into account the historical dimension is Lawrence. His aim was not to define the effects of supra-cultural symbols in literature as a whole (the proper field of myth criticism), but rather to make clear the distortions produced by a specific culture upon the psyches of the individual authors within it. Archetypal criticism, on the other hand, pleads for the existence of universal symbols, specific neither to the individual nor to his immediate cultural setting. This insistence on universality is what marks the distinction from Freud's 'typical symbols' which were to be interpreted within a specific cultural context.

Like Freud, Carl Gustav Jung (1875–1961) saw the mind as a centre of conflicting forces, beginning in childhood and following a developmental course throughout an individual's life. His theory of the human personality is built on the concept of a self as the true centre of the psyche which for Jung comprises 'the totality of all psychic processes, conscious as well as unconscious' (Jacobi 1968, p. 5). He rejected Freud's theory of libido as energy underlying the transformation of the sexual instincts, postulating instead a concept of libido as 'an energy-value which is able to communicate itself to any field of activity whatsoever' (*Symbols of Transformation*, 1976, p. 137). For Jung this meant that a flux of undifferentiated energy gets channelled into certain privileged symbols, detached from the workings of language. He calls his developmental process 'individuation', whereby he sees the self in the course of its life experience (but particularly in middle life) struggling on the one hand with archaic images of omnipotent selfhood, on the other hand with the demands made by social norms. He regarded the dreams and fantasies brought by his patients (mainly suffering from schizophrenia) not only as issuing from their unconscious instinctual wishes, but also as creations derived from a common store of 'primordial images' perceived across cultures, 'the inherited possibilities of human imagination as it was from time immemorial', to be found in every individual: 'The fact of this inheritance explains the truly amazing phenomenon that certain motifs from myths and legends repeat themselves the world over in identical forms. . . . I have called these images or motifs "archetypes" ' (*Two Essays in Analytical Psychology*, 1972a, p. 65).

These primordial images, issuing from a 'collective unconscious', collective 'because it is detached from anything personal and is common to all men' (p. 66), manifest themselves in bizarre and extravagant fantasies which threaten to dissolve the boundaries between self and world. The kind of interpretation that takes place in the analytic encounter does not focus on how language means, via condensation and displacement, but on how symbols mean, via the sequences in which 'primordial images' occur. It makes the assumption that images depict something, an inherent meaning, and that there is another meaning on top of what they depict according to the way the analyst and patient relate them. By a process Jung calls 'amplification', the material is subjected to a comparison with analogous symbolic structures from myths, legends and fairy tales. This has given rise to a certain type of criticism which relies on what might be termed 'vulgar' Jungian symbolism in order to trace a sequence of archetypal figures in individual works. The aim of these interpretative efforts, psychological and literary, is the establishment of harmony in the psyche, unity in the work.

In his lecture 'On the relation of analytical psychology to poetry' Jung asserts that psychology can only concern itself with the creative *process*. Like Freud, he does not wish to pronounce on art's 'innermost essence': 'The question of what art is in itself can never be answered by the psychologist, but must be approached from the side of aesthetics' (1972b, p. 65). What does this mean? It is not as humble as it sounds, for it rules out that insights can be derived from science, and makes assumptions about the nature of aesthetics. On the one hand it denies that science might contribute something relevant about social responses to colour and form, on the other hand there is no mention here, as there is elsewhere (1978, p. 82), that the imagination might have a place in science. Kekulé arrived at his theory of the molecular structure of benzene as a result of seeing a mental image of a ring, a (Jungian) snake biting its tail. The relationship between science and art is problematic but it is not one of simple exclusion, as Jung here claims: 'Art by its very nature is not a science, and science by its very nature is not art; both these spheres of the mind have something in reserve that is peculiar to them and can be explained only in its own terms' (1972b, p. 66).

The philosopher of science, Gaston Bachelard, draws on archetypal images precisely in order to challenge the mind's preconceptions regarding a supposed distinction between the familiar objects of the life-world and the special objects of science. He considers that an 'epistemological obstacle' arises from too rigid a separation of imagination and science: the mind ignores whatever endangers an existing organization of thought. It is the very overcoming of this obstacle that allows the advance of new insights (Bachelard 1938). Yet, with Jung, Bachelard claims that the images which facilitate this advance are not personal. For example, the reveries that come from a contemplation of fire are evidence of a pure, even non-sexual, desire for knowledge, undoing the old metaphors by the 'most elaborate transformations' (Bachelard 1968, p. 111). He is also with Jung, whom he cites repeatedly, in seeing a sublimated (desexualized) libido as the energy behind such insights (p. 30). The 'primitive instincts' remain at a deeper level: the impulse towards a disinterested knowledge takes place in an 'intermediary zone' (p. 12), where intuition and scientific rigour can interact, without collapsing into either guideless subjectivity or rigid objectivity. Bachelard conducts a phenomenological inquiry into the communicability of poetic images (1969, 1971), whereby he removes them from the sphere of the personal unconscious.

Jung above all wants to save the work of art from the psychoanalyst's clinical scrutiny, from the equation of art and neurosis. He does this by exalting the creative process as such, as distinct from exalting 'the poet as person' (Jung 1972b, p. 74). In this one might see the beginnings of the dethronement of the author from a central position. The effects of this are limited, however, because Jung replaces one idealization, a personal one, with another, a supra-personal one, in that the poet becomes a mouthpiece for a universal language of symbolism:

> The unborn work in the psyche of the artist is a force of nature that achieves its end either with tyrannical might or with the subtle cunning of nature herself quite regardless of the personal fate of the man who is its vehicle. (p. 75)

To this creative process he gives the name of 'autonomous complex' because it is split off from consciousness. He sees this complex as a central force in the mind, manifesting itself through the archetypes of the collective unconscious. For Jung the collective unconscious is the pure source of art, muddied somewhat by the 'tributaries' from the personal unconscious. The more muddied it is the more it becomes a symptom rather than a symbol. We respond to art the way we do because of the psychological effect of the reactivation of the archetype in us. He slides over the problem of the transmission of archetypes, with the dubious explanation that a *potentiality* for them is anatomically transmitted. Hence he manages to avoid confronting the nature-versus-culture dilemma: are the archetypes in the genes, that is naturally determined, or are they picked up in the course of experience? It is a non-explanation to speak of 'potentiality'; it is like Molière's joke, in which a 'dormitive' property is attributed to opium ('What is the cause and reason for opium producing sleep?' Candidate: 'Because there is in opium a dormitive property' – *Le Malade Imaginaire*).

Archetypal symbols: practice

Although there is therefore a theoretical vacuum behind Jung's grandiose claims, the impulse they have given to the search for the recurrences of symbol has been fruitful for literary criticism, going beyond the reductiveness of vulgar Jungian criticism.

Objectivity in criticism is one of the declared aims of Northrop Frye. He sees in archetypal criticism a possibility for the scientific understanding of texts according to a classificatory system of modes, symbols, myths and genres. The strength of his approach is that his categories can be seen as exemplifying historically established patterns across texts, although he wants to take this patterning as evidence of their value-free objectivity, arising from a common desire to make form. The order of words that we find in literature is structured by archetypes spread out over a series of 'pregeneric' elements, four narrative categories which he calls *mythoi*. These transcendent genres, the romantic (summer), the tragic (autumn), the ironic or satiric (winter), and the comic (spring), are to be seen as 'four aspects of a central unifying myth' (*Anatomy of Criticism*, 1957, p. 192). Conflict supplies the basis (archetypal theme) of romance, catastrophe of tragedy, confusion and anarchy of irony and satire, and rebirth of comedy. Each of these aspects has a succession of phases. In the case of romance the quest-myth is central: Frye singles out four stages, which correspond to his *mythoi*, namely conflict, death, the disappearance of the hero, and the reappearance and recognition of the hero. He sees these as the 'mythopoeic counterpart' of Jung's individuation process where 'the heroic quest has the general shape of a descent into darkness and peril followed by a renewal of life' (Frye 1978, p. 122). For Frye the task of poetry is to 'illustrate the fulfilment of desire' and also 'to define the obstacles to it' (1957, p. 106). Art must project 'the goals of human work' so that desire may be satisfied (p. 115). Frye envisages an apocalyptic end for this desire, an 'anagogic', mystically exalting phase, finding in literature key works, such as *The Tempest*, which self-reflectively concern themselves with poetry's own striving to apply words to the whole of nature via its imaginative projections (pp. 117–19). Though such an ideal completion remains forever unrealizable, it represents the final wished-for union of desire and nature, taking on a symbolic form in which nature becomes the body itself of a divine poetic creator. Art here comes to reflect a nature which is harmonious through and through.

Unlike Jung, Frye does not want to see the archetypes as psychic determinants, seeing this as a slide towards subjectivity. Maud Bodkin, on the other hand, in her book *Archetypal Patterns in Poetry*, prefers to found archetypes upon 'emotional tendencies', configurations of which she sees persisting over time as subjective realities 'in the minds of those who are stirred by the theme' (Bodkin 1934, p. 4). The reader is linked to the writer by these common patterns (p. 8), a biological and social inheritance (p. 25). In the chapter 'The Ancient Mariner and the rebirth archetype', having testified to Coleridge's extreme variation of mood, from inert failure to create to vigorous creative impulse, she tries to account for these variations in terms of archetypal patterns: stagnant water equals lassitude, and wind equals recovery and activity. She draws many mythical and biblical parallels where breath stands for rejuvenation and takes from this that the poet is using a universal symbolism. She sees the reader drawn into a communal experience and proposes a reading practice whereby he is told to dwell upon the poem, 'wander with it, muse, reflect and prophesy and dream upon it' (p. 29), an analogous process to Jung's 'amplification'. This might be looked upon as a step towards reader-response criticism: the reader has access to the power of fantasy in the form of archetypal patterns.

Frye and Bodkin are together in stressing the communicability of such symbols. Frye maintains that there is no private symbolism, 'the "onlie begetter" of Shakespeare's sonnets . . . was not Shakespeare himself . . . but Shakespeare's subject' (1957, p. 98). Here he accords with Jung: 'It is not Goethe that creates *Faust*, but *Faust* that creates Goethe' (Jung 1972b, p. 103). Frye is with Jung in so far as Jung's emphasis on the communal aspect of the creative process and on the work of art undermines the favoured view of the artist as an original genius and instead makes him a medium for the transmission of archetypal myths and images. The poet 'is at best a midwife, or more accurately still, the womb of mother nature herself: her privates he, so to speak' (p. 98). Frye's mode of criticism leads to an understanding of recurring verbal structures in literary works, creating the possibility of a systematic reading, as distinct from a criticism which applies a set of psychic categories in order to identify recurring themes. Frye himself meanwhile observes: 'I am still often called a Jungian critic, and classified with Maud Bodkin, whose book I have read with interest, but whom, on the evidence of that book, I resemble about as closely as I resemble the late Sarah Bernhardt' (Frye 1981, p. 16).

Archetypal symbols: theory

A major theoretical weakness is to turn what are undeniable historical recurrences, contingent patterns detectable within cultures, into some given absolute realities, autonomous and all-pervading. Bodkin began by ostensibly intending to test Jung's theory but she is not far into her book before she is taking 'primordial images' for granted. With Frye, she makes an unargued conflation of mere occurrence with objectivity. She places a great deal of weight on the fact that images recur, but why should such recurrences necessarily lead to 'penetrating significance' rather than monotony? Bodkin here regards the very appearance of archetypes as self-justifying, unlike Frye, who is interested in revealing a conceptual framework without explicitly saying that it guarantees aesthetic value.

Tempting as it may be to feel that such recurrence removes arbitrariness from the symbol, Frye is on unsure ground when he makes convenient links between natural successions such as the seasons and the cultural meanings assigned to them into 'literary universals'. Repetitions in nature, such as the rising and the setting of the sun, can hardly be taken as evidence of a unity found in nature, one it is poetry's task to imitate. It is dubious to assert on these grounds that there is a universal core, that 'some symbols are images common to all men', for instance, food and drink, the quest, light and darkness, sexual fulfilment (Frye 1957, p. 118). Bachelard, who makes similar claims for the symbolism of the four elements (1971, pp. 176ff.), asserts that 'imagination is the true source of psychic production' (1968, p. 110), but nowhere gives an analysis of what this central concept of imagination is. A similar assumption can be seen in Bodkin when she speaks of a 'mediating process' between lived experience and awareness; she produces no characterization of this mediation, except to say that imagination is at its core (Bodkin 1934, p. 7).

In making the archetypes rise neither from the individual nor from an immediate historical culture, archetypal criticism has made the concept float free of all human genesis. Frye addresses himself to the problematic relationship of desire and culture. First, desire is idealized as a demiurge which informs the human patterns of labour upon nature but is in turn aseptically untouched by them. Frye does not want to reduce it to the 'simple response to need' of the animal (1957, p. 105), nor will he accept any definition with respect to particular intentions. When he defines it as 'the energy that leads human society to develop its own form', desire is still being kept separate from human society. Second, what desire produces is idealized. This is a kind of paradoxical corollary of the above, for the archetypes that Frye catalogues as corresponding to four natural 'recurrences', for example the Romance, with its unchanging dramatis personae, are also idealized, transcending history. Where, for instance, does Frye consider the relation of the epic hero of the quest to the feudal/tribal warrior? Neither Jung nor he question the expectations of social role which produces this kind of hero. If the influence of social forms upon desire remains out of the enquiry, the influence of desire upon those forms will remain equally mystifying, especially if rigidified into universal and objectively accessible symbols. There is, finally, no dialectical relation between desire and the forms in which it appears.

To make archetypes objective, 'autonomous verbal structures' (Frye 1957, p. 110), is to exclude the operations of intersubjectivity at the start of the enterprise. To turn the communal into the universal, either in Frye's manner by treating its forms as supra-cultural, or in Bodkin's by lodging them in psychic determinants, or in Bachelard's, who manages to do both at once, is to sidestep the problem of the relation of human bodies to those societies which mould them. This disinclination is traceable back to Jung, who sees the unconscious as a common reservoir of highly charged symbols rather than as something that has its ground in a particular body, the character of which must come into the equation.

PART II

6

Object-relations theory:
self and other

Where ego-psychology was concerned with the psychic mechanisms which mediate the relationship between the ego and the id, and the consequences this has for the individual work and the individual reader, object-relations aesthetics is interested in the psychic processes which mediate the relationship between self and world, and the consequences this has for the formal aspects of art. This concern widens out into an investigation of what psychoanalysis might have to contribute to understanding what goes on between the artist and his medium, the critic and his art-object. The focus thereby moves from what happens within the psyche to what happens between one psyche and another. I shall first examine the theory of Melanie Klein, and then give an account of its impact on art criticism. I shall go on to the theory of D. W. Winnicott, with an account of its consequences for an understanding of aesthetic illusion.

Fantasy and reality

In the work of Melanie Klein (1882–1960) the instincts of the body and the tensions and conflicts they give rise to again become a central concern. Although in her theory she takes a great deal for granted, she cannot be accused of ignoring the birthpangs of a self in a human body subjected to the mouldings of experience. In this respect Klein's work marks a return to Freud and offsets the impact of ego-psychology. Klein allows the unconscious its due place in the interaction of the infant's (Latin: *in-fans*, 'non-speaker') body with the external world, which it has at first no means of distinguishing. It is this interaction that establishes 'object-relations', the structurings 'projected' outwards and 'introjected' inwards which form the pattern of a self's dealings with the world, including other people. Projection is a process whereby states of feeling and unconscious wishes are expelled from the self and attributed to another person or thing. Introjection is a process whereby qualities that belong to an external object are absorbed and unconsciously regarded as belonging to the self. The infant thus creates an ideal object for itself by getting rid of all bad impulses from itself and taking in all it perceives as good from the object.

The critics to be considered in this section make use of particular features of Klein's theory, especially those concerning what she calls 'part-objects', an aspect of this process of projection and introjection. Their aesthetic theories will be the better understood if Klein's concept of a development in the child from an inadequate perception of things and persons about it to a viable one is explained in some detail.

The term 'object' is not to be taken only in its usual sense of a thing, but is extended to persons, though without any pejorative implication. Objects, for the child, are not at first clearly delimited and secure in their separateness as they are for the adult. The reality of the external world has to be worked for, beginning with 'part-objects'. These are what an adult would perceive as parts of other things or persons but which the child invests with powerful fantasies both pleasing and frightening. In particular, the child will in fantasy invest a part of something with the characteristics of a person, the result being that it will waver between love and hate towards this 'part-object'. At the core of Klein's theory is an awareness that good and bad can alternate and coexist within a single concept, an insight that has much wider implications than those for child development, since the same ambivalence could be claimed to infect all our attempts to apprehend the world in terms of self-favouring images. The relevance to art is immediate, for it too is concerned with waverings between acceptance and rejection, satisfaction and denial.

In the course of her work with very young children Melanie Klein observed how their feelings for reality were structured by certain fantasies to do with the child's relation to the mother's body. The fantasies played out were often of a sadistic and destructive nature, concerned with an experience of the mother's body as a container full of dangerous and threatening objects. Why was this so? Following Freud, Klein affirms the dualism of death instincts and life instincts from the very beginning of life (see Part III, p. 143–4, for a definition; for a full examination of this controversial issue within Freud's meta-psychology see Laplanche 1976). In this respect Klein remains within the bounds of an id-psychology, but she departs from Freud in asserting that a rudimentary ego is present from the beginning, capable of certain defensive strategies designed to protect a pre-symbolic, pre-linguistic self, whose theoretical status is far from clear, since it seems to have a primitive notion of its own sex.

Klein believes that this rudimentary ego becomes exposed to the destructiveness of instinctual aggressive urges. The anxiety produced within the organism causes the primitive ego to split. The infant defends itself by means of projection, expelling the bad, and introjection, absorbing the good: the breast, its primary object, is experienced as a 'good object' and a 'bad object' in turn. According to Klein, the infant can adopt one of two 'positions'. She uses the word 'position' rather than 'phase' in order to emphasize the fact that the infant can move from one to the other and back again, a possibility that remains throughout life. These positions need defining here, because, as will be seen, in the view of Kleinian critics they are relevant to the relation of the artist to his medium and the audience to the work of art. In the first of these two positions, the 'paranoid–schizoid', the infant lives in fear of the 'bad' breast as an imaginary persecutor punishing it for its aggressive attacks. This is accompanied by an idealization of the 'good' breast in which the infant mentally abolishes the 'bad' breast and sees the 'good' breast as never failing to yield satisfaction to its demands. When the infant learns to perceive the mother as a person, it is possible for it to take up the 'depressive' position. Because it fears that it has caused the mother injury, it is filled with guilt and regret. It thus comes to have the urge to 'make reparation'. For followers of Klein the depressive position plays a crucial part in the creative process.

The movement from one position to another hinges upon the ability to invest fantasy with symbol, and in Klein's clinical practice one can find examples of how this is to be done. To escape from being at the mercy of fantasy, some measure of symbolic control has to be achieved. A key article 'The import-ance of symbol formation in the development of the ego' (1977; orig. publ. 1930) shows how Klein views the beginning of symbol formation and illustrates the central place she assigns to fantasy in the course of development. (The article is discussed in Lacan 1978, pp. 90–3, 107–16, for its relevance to his 'mirror-stage'.) If Freud's case-histories read like novellas (Timms 1983), then Klein's might be said to read like an interminably serialized, unusually bizarre Gothic novel:

> The first time Dick came to me, as I said before, he manifested no sort of affect when his nurse handed him over to me. When I showed him the toys I had put ready, he looked at them without the faintest interest. I took a big train and put it beside a smaller one and called them 'Daddy-train' and 'Dick-train'. Thereupon he picked up the train I called 'Dick' and made it roll to the window and said 'Station'. I explained: 'The station is mummy; Dick is going into mummy.' He left the train, ran into the space between the outer and the inner doors of the room, shut himself in, saying 'dark' several times. I explained to him: 'It is dark inside mummy. Dick is inside dark mummy'. . . .
>
> During the third hour, however, he also, for the first time, looked at the toys with interest, in which an aggressive tendency was evident. He pointed to a little coal-cart and said: 'Cut.' I gave him a pair of scissors, and he tried to scratch the little pieces of black wood which represented coal, but he could not hold the scissors. Acting on a glance he gave me, I cut pieces of wood out of the cart, whereupon he threw the damaged cart and its contents into the drawer and said, 'Gone.' I told him that this meant that Dick was cutting faeces out of his mother. He ran into the space between the doors and scratched on the doors a little with his nails, thus

showing that he identified the space with the cart and both with the mother's body, which he was attacking. He immediately ran back from the space between the doors, found the cupboard and crept into it.

(Klein 1977, pp. 225–6)

This 4-year-old psychotic boy is unable to relate to real objects in a useful way because he takes them all to be embodiments of his dread. Klein's theoretical explanation is that the boy's anxiety is so great that he cannot make an adequate symbolic 'equation'. In normal development there is a sufficient quantity of anxiety (not an excess), leading the child to transfer from the original organs of interest, the parents' organs, to other objects, which it identifies with them, a process which causes it to move on as they come in turn to provoke anxiety. The brute interpretations which Klein offers the child, that the station is the mother's body, which he wishes to penetrate if only the father were not in rivalry with him, encourages the boy to structure his rudimentary fantasy into an early oedipal sub-system. She tells him what to play and he plays it, or as Deleuze and Guattari have it: 'Say it's Oedipus, or you'll get a slap in the face' (1977a, pp. 44–5; and see Part IV, p. 164.)

Klein's aims are first and foremost therapeutic: the alleviation of anxiety situations to prevent them becoming fixation points for psychosis. She shows the necessity of symbol formation in both the schizoid–paranoid and depressive position, without in either case giving an account of the relationship of symbol to language. The effect of the mother's fantasies on the child is never theorized and hence Klein's attribution to the child of a very early knowledge of its parents' sexual organs is not given any principled foundation: the interaction between the child's fantasies and a prior structure of desire, that of the mother and her history, has been developed by the Lacanian child analyst, Maud Mannoni (1970, 1973). Unlike Klein, Mannoni does take account of the effect of the mother's unconscious on the child, which brings back into the argument the social dimension it has lacked.

Through structuring their fantasies in play Klein enabled her young patients to gain access to the unconscious and establish a relation between the self and the object world. What both her theory and her practice amply demonstrate is that fantasy is a precondition of any engagement with reality. Unfortunately this radical insight, which could lead to a better understanding of the ambiguous perception of objects (implicit in Freud's 'The uncanny'; see Part III), has been neglected by those of her followers who have developed the aesthetic implications of her theory, moving mainly in the direction of ego-psychology.

Object-relations and aesthetics

Freud saw art as a privileged means of attaining instinctual pleasure. In order to achieve this end without suffering fear or guilt the censor had to be caught unawares: the successful strategies of the artist in getting an audience to share the pleasure was what Freud called the artist's 'innermost secret' (Freud 1953, IX, p. 153). Object-relations aesthetics starts out from a different premise: art is seen as a privileged means of relating to an object. Far from deriving any 'innocent' pleasure from this encounter, artist and audience are deeply implicated in a process of attrition and contrition. For Kleinians aesthetic pleasure resides in the creating and perceiving of an object whose integrity has been fought for (see Segal 1977; orig. publ. 1955). Guilt is assuaged rather than circumvented.

The prototype for the aesthetic interaction both as regards the artist to his medium and the audience to the art-object is the (unconsciously) felt encounter between infant and mother. The medium of the artist becomes the mother's body; the separating out of the bodily self from the primal object is the central mode of experience. The creative act repeats the experience of separating from the mother. It can take place in the context of either of the two Kleinian positions, the schizoid–paranoid or the depressive, according to whether the artist is experiencing his objects as fragmented or integrated. Although Kleinians regard the depressive position as providing 'the mise-en-scène for aesthetic creation' (Stokes 1978, p. 222), the artist will invest his medium with the fantasy appropriate to his continuing stage in desire. The schizoid–paranoid position is one swing of an oscillation between identification with the breast and separation from it, which initiates, according to Klein, all objectifications. The theory can therefore claim to account for two types of aesthetic experience, one which one might see as harmonizing, the other as rebellious. In either case, however, the emphasis is on the conservative pole of the experience:

> Art of whatever kind bears witness to intact objects even when the subject-matter is disintegration. Whatever the form of transcript the original conservation or restoration is of the mother's body.
>
> (Stokes 1978, III, p. 326)

> Insofar as a good pictorial space ... is inherent in any painting, one could say that it represents the minimum content of art, an enriching experience of envelopment and unconscious integration ... the work of art acts as a containing 'womb' which receives fragmented projections of the artist's self.
>
> (Ehrenzweig 1970, p. 185)

In both cases the unconscious is seen as investing the *form* of the art-object through the interaction of artist and medium. 'The image in form' and 'the hidden order of art' are key concepts respectively of Adrian Stokes (1902–72), painter and art critic/historian, and Anton Ehrenzweig (1909–66), lecturer in art education and writer on aesthetics, both of whom have developed the implications of object-relations for the theory and criticism of art. The starting-point of each is the relation of an individual's bodily experience to those cultural objects we value for their aesthetic appeal, though the direction taken is somewhat different.

Ehrenzweig sees this relation as a problem concerning the perception of all objects. He raises the issue of how objects come to be selected for perception in the first place, because he sees it as crucial for an artist, and for the creative individual in general, to be able to return to a state of primal sensing. He was initially interested in opposing gestalt psychology for its postulation of a firm and stable structure in perception: he maintains that such structure has to be learnt, that in the beginning perception is uncertain in its ranging over a field of view, and that, however reliable mature perception may be, early sensing is fluid and unstable. Vestiges of it are still accessible to us in dreams, in mental imagery, and in the hypnagogic visions that occur in the twilight state between dream and waking (1970, pp. 100–1). He argues that gestalt psychology makes too ready an assumption that simple organizations, the so-called 'good gestalts', are inevitably selected from the beginning, and, by a fortunate coincidence, happen to correspond to the external objects of most use to the developing child. As Ehrenzweig points out, the objects it selects are hardly immune to libidinal interest (pp. 26–34).

According to Ehrenzweig, the ego can throughout life get rid of existing categorizations through a process he calls 'dedifferentiation', whereby it 'scatters and represses surface imagery' (p. 34); that is to say, it will dispose of the mundane sortings of experience which fail to satisfy the id. A change of repression is involved in the form of a new mediation between id and superego. Ehrenzweig argues that when the ego has been the servant of the superego for too long the ego collapses, or 'decomposes', as he puts it, and falls back on the id for sustenance, getting new sensory evidence, new material for imagemaking (pp. 230–1, 283–5). He maintains that the decomposing of the ego is not necessarily a regression, that 'far from being autonomous of the id, the ego's perception is constantly at the disposal of unconscious symbolic needs', but without being at the id's command (p. 274). He thereby explicitly opposes Ernst Kris, who does not give the unconscious a sufficiently constructive role in the creative process, thinking of it as essentially primitive and as striving towards regression to earlier fantasies (see Part I). Ehrenzweig postulates a developing unconscious which turns 'disruptive' effects into 'constructive' ones (p. 273). He has a concept of 'unconscious scanning' (pp. 46ff.), whereby the ego and id together sort from an undifferentiated field of experience. It is a process analogous to proof-reading, where rational expectations have to be suspended if the break in the figure is to be perceived.

Ehrenzweig postulates a developing productive id which can alter perception for the public good. Creativity results from an interplay between conscious ordering and unconscious scanning which can forever reorganize the old images. The true order is thus not at the level of the ego *per se*: that is why he entitles his book *The Hidden Order of Art*. He argues that there is in all art a tension between conscious surface gestalt, a kind of secondary revision, and a hidden sub-structure, the part played by the primary process. In modern art, however, there is an open conflict between the two. In some cases there is an 'extreme dissociation of the surface and depth functioning', as for example, in action painting, yet this kind of art too is not exempt from a hidden order which 'redeems' its 'near-schizoid' character (pp. 81-2). However, this presents a challenge to the viewer, who is implicated, for his own good it seems: 'A modicum of surface fragmentation is always needed in order to bring into action the usually starved low-level sensibilities' (p. 80). He too has to join in the scanning process, learning to proof-read with an open mind, so as to detect the new gestalt, the hidden sub-structure, and be relieved of his anxiety. One might here make an analogy in reverse with a reader confronted by what Roland Barthes calls a 'writerly' text (Barthes 1975): where Barthes turns a 'readerly' text (a classic by Balzac) into a 'writerly' one by breaking it up into fragments, Ehrenzweig turns 'writerly' texts into 'readerly' ones by finding a hidden order.

So how does he do it? Ehrenzweig sees the artist as having to go through an initial psychotic phase, in that the essential process of dedifferentiation involves the destruction of links with reality. But whereas the schizophrenic's inability to tolerate the 'ambiguity' of dedifferentiation makes him resort to self-destructive splitting in order to be omnipotent, to be in as many places as possible, the creative individual must get beyond this fixation point. Otherwise he will, like the sorcerer's apprentice in Goethe's poem, hack the broom to bits with each bit becoming a new broom continuing the destruction, while he fails to gain magic control (Ehrenzweig 1970, p. 132). This first phase, the projecting of fragments, corresponds to Melanie Klein's schizoid–paranoid phase. For the second phase, however, Ehrenzweig departs from Klein. Instead of the depressive phase (which he reserves for a final phase which may or may not come about) he postulates a 'manic–oceanic' phase, where 'creative man prepares, as it were, in his work a receiving "womb", the image of a benevolent mother figure, to contain and integrate the fragmented material' (p. 204). This state is not to be regarded as regressive, but as the re-experience of a primal state which enables the artist to integrate the fragments within the flux of experience, on an 'unconscious undifferentiated level':

James Joyce's splinter language is of this kind. His fantastic word conglomerates are not just violent compressions of language splinters, but establish counterpoints of dreamlike fantasies that run on below the surface and link word clusters into an unending hypnotic stream.   (p. 132)

Thus the most 'writerly' of texts is turned into a 'readerly' one. Joyce can, of course, be read either way; the comparison is made to let each position provide a context for the other.

For Ehrenzweig every artist is initially a schizophrenic (not a neurotic as in Freud) before the chaotic fragments of his material have been assimilated in the unconscious, but he has no satisfactory explanation of how this comes about. He has a tendency to speak of the unconscious as providing a new 'coherence' of itself, as if a true order, already established within the primary process, can be drawn into alliance with the ego's systems and refurbish them. The 'depth coherence' of 'oceanic envelopment', which gives Cubist painting 'a hypnotic, almost mystic quality' draws us into 'the manic womb of rebirth' (pp. 135–41); the schizophrenic mysteriously lacks this 'depth coherence' and is logically therefore 'incoherent'. Since it is this very coherence for which an explanation is called for as the *sine qua non* of creative achievement, we are here stuck, as with Jung's archetypes (though Ehrenzweig favours Frazer's account of 'poemagogic' images (pp. 194ff.)), with another non-explanation. However, despite his concern to stress the redemptive pole of sensuous experience, Ehrenzweig does acknowledge the central relevance of the material of bodily perception, whereas aestheticians, from Plato onwards, have usually been suspicious of it.

The manic–oceanic blissful encounter that Ehrenzweig stages between artist and medium, spectator and art-object, is repeated in reverse form in the experience of the Barthesian reader/writer seeking ecstasy in *The Pleasure of the Text* (Barthes 1976). For in both there is involved a celebration of the senses ('drifting occurs whenever I do not respect the whole' (Barthes 1976, p. 18)). Where Ehrenzweig's artist gathers up his fragments within the 'containing womb' of his projected vision, Barthes is making the text of pleasure serve as a 'fetish object' (p. 27), splitting it into parts ready for the exchange consumption of perverse fantasies. What for Ehrenzweig is a yielding to priority, a return to authority, is for Barthes a transgression, the archaic desire of one 'who plays with his mother's body' (p. 37), dismembers the text, perversely enjoys schizoid sensations without any attendant persecutory effects. The model of the artist/spectator 'sucked and enveloped . . . inside the picture plane' (Ehrenzweig 1970, p. 133) mystically partaking of a new identity has its radical counterpart in the *jouissance* of the Barthesian reader/writer pursuing unabashed his polymorphous–perverse non-identity within the fragmented body of the (mother) text. It is true, however, that Barthes' theory allows for a double reading, a 'contradictory interplay of (cultural) pleasure and (non-cultural) bliss' (Barthes 1976, p. 62). And with a different emphasis this is also true for Ehrenzweig.

For Kleinians the two essential poles are the schizoid–paranoid and the depressive phase, but for Ehrenzweig, as already mentioned, the depressive phase is not so central. It is not the origin of creativity (that is the attempt to regain the whole mother), but the result of the non-realization of the vision, when the unconscious linkages do not translate themselves into surface coherence. Unity and coherence still obtain, however, in the 'hidden order'. In Ehrenzweig's view the truth of art is to be found in a coherent 'substructure' which redeems the fragmentation of the surface gestalt.

Where Ehrenzweig was concerned with the unconscious exploration of bodily experience as such, Adrian Stokes is concerned with the sensations aroused when the body – and the self within it – relates to the object-world, either in contemplation of what is separate and self-sufficient or in an attempt to merge with and absorb what is before it. This applies equally to the relation between artist and medium and to the relation between spectator and art-object. Stokes wishes to stress that the imagery of this double experience resides in the form of the created object, wherein an expressiveness may be detected, though not as readily as in subject-matter as such. Form itself is representational and what it represents is the mode in which the unconscious fantasy of the artist/viewer invests the medium/art-object according to which of the two orthodox Kleinian positions is the prevailing one, the schizoid–paranoid (which

Stokes sees in its merging rather than in its splitting moment) or the depressive:

> Our relationships to all objects seem to me to be describable in the terms of two extreme forms, the one a very strong identification with the object, whether projective or introjective, whereby a barrier between self and not-self is undone, the other a commerce with a self-sufficient and independent object at arm's length. . . . the work of art is *par excellence* a self-sufficient object as well as a configuration that we absorb or to which we lend ourselves as manipulators.
>
> (Stokes 1978, III, pp. 151–2)

There is in Stokes a quite specific ethical commitment: the quality of the artist's/viewer's aesthetic experience and its lasting value, as regards both the creation of art and the criticism of it (one assumes), depend on the degree to which the 'otherness' of the medium/object has been allowed for.

In his early writings Stokes discusses the ways in which the stone of the Renaissance seems to respond to the artist's fantasy, depending on whether he is carving or modelling (1978, I, pp. 29–80 and 181–259; orig. publ. 1932 and 1934). In his later writings he uses the same terms, but no longer in their specific technical sense: carving and modelling now define the two most general ways in which the artist might relate to his medium, extending to the visual arts. The 'carving' mode respects the integrity and separateness of the medium, symbolizing the whole object and the integrated ego; the 'modelling' mode functions in reverse, in that the individual forms are more sharply distinguished, epitomizing the part-object relation and the unintegrated ego, enveloping the spectator (1978, I, pp. 237–9).

A virtuoso performance of Stokes's actual criticism can be found in 'Stones of Rimini' when he discusses the Tempio Malatestiano reliefs. He develops the spectator's attention to the details of the contrasts in the marble between the swirls of wave-drapery and the firm outlines of limb and mountain, not neglecting to hint at the power of sexual challenge in those waves, inhabited by angry dolphins and fierce-jawed sea-monsters (1978, I, pp. 250–5). In all of this, however, he totally disregards the historical matrix for this energetic conflict which he sees as harmonizing and presumably integrated. In 'Form in art' he writes: 'we can always discover from aesthetic experience that sense of homogeneity or fusion combined, in differing proportions, with the sense of object-otherness' (1977, p. 407). By this he means that the sense of unity with the object is balanced by an acknowledgement of its uniqueness.

But the confident matching of the disjunction of these two modes of creating and viewing with an analogous opposition of forms, carving and modelling, is by no means given: to assume so is to ignore the social context of this sensuous object called the work of art. Although Stokes specifically asserts that all works of art 'must reflect typical concatenations of experience, of endeavour, in the milieu in which the artist and the public live', thus allowing for changes in style (1978, III, p. 230), he wants at the same time to hold to a given attachment to these modes as sensuous forms. He thereby neglects the social and historical ground from which these forms issue and fails to explicate how certain thoughts, feelings and expectations attach themselves to them. Take the love of stone as evidence of a value placed on the sensuous and subjective side of the aesthetic, that is to say the actual bodily experiences of colour, shape and texture, and Stokes can be credited with a correct emphasis upon form. But in failing to show how its significance is dependent on context, he is working with an idealized, a-historical (though not, of course, an unhistorical) creator and viewer.

The flaws of the object-relations theories of aesthetic response come out all the more markedly when these theories are applied canonically, as in Peter Fuller's book, *Art and Psychoanalysis*. He argues that the 'constant' appeal of the *Venus de Milo*, 'relatively speaking' (Fuller 1980, p. 126), is due to the fact that at one moment in history (the Greek moment) the figure is sensuously idealized as whole and perfect (emphasis on reparative aspect because of that perfection), and at another moment in history, the Romantic moment, it is sensuously appreciated as mutilated and imperfect (emphasis on both schizoid–paranoid and reparative aspect, because the mother, attacked in fantasy, has survived). While his development of the historical fortunes of the statue is very suggestive, there is a lack of an adequate account of its aesthetic appeal, such as Stokes provided in his discussion of the Tempio reliefs. Where Stokes and Ehrenzweig have offered extensions to the theory of the sensuous features of art, Fuller takes over the theoretical place already assigned to such features whenever they engage his attention. He contents himself with validating his interpretations by freely quoting from a wide array of orthodox texts of the object-relations school, combining them to suit his purposes. This citing of authority (which includes two Marxist critics, Sebastiano Timpanaro and Arnold Hauser) has two consequences. One is that Fuller takes over the essential place of the biological (from Timpanaro's materialism) without pursuing the attendant problems. The other is that he makes a genuflection towards a historical explanation (Hauser's mention of the appeal of ruins and torsos as a Romantic symptom), yet brackets off the question why this should be so (p. 129). Nowhere does he undertake a rigorous analysis of the relation between the biological and the social. Granted that the body as 'biological' is virtually a 'constant' over two millennia (evolution being a slow process compared with cultural change), this does not make the mother-and-child dyad into a 'biological constant'.

Playing and reality

The character of the mother-and-child dyad and the particular patterns of development that it follows have been the concern of a paediatrician and psychoanalyst whose theory is of immediate relevance to art, and especially to the presence within it of illusion. D. W. Winnicott's (1896–1971) empirical discovery regarding a young child's use of a favoured soft object raised the question of the kind of interplay that was going on between inner and outer world, between fantasy and reality. Where Klein worked with the content of fantasy as revealed in the young child's play, Winnicott understands the role of fantasy as leading to illusion and a certain structure of play. He designates an 'intermediate area of experience', in which the child sorts out body parts from non-body parts and in doing so creates 'transitional' phenomena and objects (*Playing and Reality*, 1974; the key article came out in 1951). It sucks and hugs a soft cloth or object. Sucking and rolling it up makes it like the breast and the child ignores what is not the breast, what is different. It is able to suspend disbelief (for the object is not what it really wants) and make use of illusion in order to test out which parts of experience are under its control and which are not, in Winnicott's words what is 'me' and what is 'not-me'. The transitional object is a form of defence against separation from the mother. The capacity to *play* with illusion is what distinguishes this experience from the fixed delusion which may later turn a transitional object into that permanent security prop, the fetish (Greenacre 1970), both in the Freudian sense (it disguises the actuality of the lack) and in the Marxian sense (it functions as a commodity that supplies human want). Winnicott is ultimately concerned with the child's ability to use objects in what one could describe as a non-exploitative way.

Where Klein's narratives partake of the Gothic, Winnicott's might be regarded as having an absurd Beckett-like quality. The heroine in the account that follows is a little girl called 'the Piggle', who is being treated for night-terrors and general disturbance following the birth of a sibling.

Piggle: Now the Winnicott baby has all the toys. I'll go to
          Daddy.
Me: You are afraid of the greedy Winnicott baby, the
          baby that was born out of the Piggle and that loves
          the Piggle and that wants to eat her.

She went to her father and tried to shut the door as she left. I heard the father working overtime in the waiting room trying to entertain her, because (of course) he did not know where he was in the game.

I told the father to come into the room now, and the Piggle came in with him. He sat in the blue chair. She knew what must be done. She got on his lap and said: 'I am shy.'

After a while she showed her father the Winnicott baby, this monster she had given birth to, and it was this that she was shy about. . . . Then she started a new and very deliberate chapter in the game. 'I'm a baby too,' she announced, as she came out head first onto the floor between her father's legs. . . . She went on being born from father's lap onto the floor, and she was the new baby and I had to be cross, being the Winnicott baby that came out of the inside and was born out of the Piggle – and I had to be very cross wanting to be the only baby. . . . There came a new development. She was now having a different way of being born out of the top of the father's head. [footnote: 'Being conceived of, i.e., born as an idea in the mind; wanted. D.W.W.'] It was funny. I felt sorry for the father and I asked him if he could stand it. He replied: 'O.K., but I would like to take my coat off.' He was so hot. However, we were able to finish at this point, because the Piggle had got what she came for.

(Winnicott 1977, pp. 28–31)

In the above scene, as directed by Winnicott, the Piggle is trying to place herself with regard to the new (Winnicott) baby that she has created with the help of the therapist. (One might see her as testing out her use-value as against her exchange-value. Is she valued as a subject (as her self) or is she merely an object which has been reproduced for the satisfaction of superior agents?) Both the 'objects' she uses, the father/progenitor and the therapist/baby-sibling, are joining in as the child re-enacts her separation from the mother and re-creates herself in play. The self is here itself a transitional object, testing out its reality, not in a private fantasy, as was the case with Klein, but in an intersubjective structure of play: 'the object, if it is to be used, must necessarily be real in the sense of being part of a shared reality, not a bundle of projections' (Winnicott 1974, p. 103). All the participants are aware that they are taking part in a serious game: the Piggle 'knew what must be done', starts 'a new and very deliberate chapter', and knows when to finish it; the father knows he has a part to play even before he knows what it is; the therapist is both amused and sorry for the father, but no whit less involved. There is a nice irony in the way that the father is being implicated in the transference by having to act out the birth for which he was responsible. There is a metonymic shift from mother to father and a shift in time: the illusion is created that the father is the mother, a former time is now, and the Piggle is a new baby. The child is able to tolerate objects towards which she feels ambivalent instead of being at the mercy of them.

It is this intersubjective structure of play which aestheticians have taken up. There are, however, certain presuppositions underlying object-relations theory which need close examination precisely because they are inevitably and unnoticeably transferred into the aesthetic theories that base themselves upon it. The object, however it is viewed, whether as a transitional object or as a familiar object, is considered to be already singled out, separate, with clear boundaries. If the transitional object is to be taken as a paradigm of some sort for art and culture in general, this unexamined premise will, for all the emphasis on play, import into all forms of creativity and interpretation a prejudice for objects assumed to be ready for human recognition. The Surrealists, in particular, set out to challenge this prejudice. Objects flow into and out of each other's limits: watches melt (Salvador Dali), birds blend with leaves or mountain peaks (Magritte). It is not only in Surrealist art that this is the case, for it happens without the artist's conscious intention: in Millais' *The Return of the Dove to the Ark* (1851) a dove can be seen as a breast, kissing as suckling. Although Winnicott allows meaning to change, he does not consider the possibility of objects blending and flowing, as do the Surrealists.

The concept of the transitional object has attracted the attention of critics and aestheticians precisely because it is analogous to the play of illusion in art. In illusion, as in the Millais picture, objects can overlap. Winnicott does not see that the unconscious has the power to invade these boundaries. He writes of 'the *paradox* involved in the use by the infant of what I have called the transitional object' and asks 'for it not to be resolved' (Winnicott 1974, p. xii). This is a symptom of a certain theoretical blindness on his part. To rest on paradox is to assume the recognition of objects before they have been differentiated, a positivist habit. There is an inconsistency in his holding to the transitional object in an undefined space between 'inner and outer' and his calling its existence a paradox. Winnicott is a paediatrician talking in terms of 'me and not-me', A and not-A, to mothers and logicians, mothers that are currently tempted into buying tiny garments with 'me' stitched on in a prominent place ready to tuck their child's 'I' inside.

Alfred Lorenzer and Peter Orban point to 'Winnicott's untenable separation between the self and the outer world *before* the formation of the transitional objects and transitional phenomena' (Lorenzer and Orban 1978, p. 749). They argue for the sequence to be reversed, that transitional objects be seen as steps in the development of a subjective structure. Winnicott, they suggest, is not clear about how the self arises from the undifferentiated experiences; he talks of 'an intermediate area of *experiencing*, to which inner reality and external life both contribute' (Winnicott 1974, p. 230), whereas Lorenzer and Orban say the converse: 'the inner and outer do not *make up* this intermediate area; instead they *differentiate themselves out of it* . . . into transitional objects and phenomena' (Lorenzer and Orban 1978, pp. 474–5). It follows that such differentiation will be subjective and variable, that the boundaries of objects can be argued about. The ambiguous (permanently transitional) object is thus produced out of experience that is historically determined, not out of units assumed to pre-exist, such as a mother-and-child dyad.

The problem of accepting the mother–child dyad as a constant transfers itself to a certain use of D. W. Winnicott's theories to which he himself points. He extends the trust necessary between mother and child to that between individual and society. The play with transitional objects, which takes place in an intermediate area he calls 'potential space' (1974, p. 126), becomes by continuous development the creative use of cultural objects: 'Cultural experience begins with creative living first manifested in play' (p. 118). What is not clear is where this creativity with objects slides into a common acceptance of them, as can be seen in what follows.

An attempt to use Winnicott for a theory of culture has been made by Richard Kuhns, who endeavours to base a philosophy of art on psychoanalytic theory, taking the development of the ego as the critical principle. He contends that the ego achieves growth through fictional play with transitional objects, reaching a communal stage with 'cultural objects', performed through public 'enactments' (art, ritual, ceremony): 'culture is a tradition of enactments' (Kuhns 1983, p. 53). Freud, he argues, ignored tradition from the ego point of view, concentrating on the art-object as highly 'cathected' (invested) with personal emotion. Kuhns regards art as a highly cathected *cultural* object. The viewer's response to the artist's use of tradition (his countertransference to the artist's transference) will be a source of ego-strength. Culture is the domain of ego-functioning: cultural enactments are part of the maturational process and therefore have a profound influence on individuals within that culture, in the stages of both primary and secondary socialization (both play and culture in a 'potential space'). Cultural objects are transitional objects because they are shared. Through them the relation between self and object (that is the object in a mundane sense) is mediated. What is not clear is how the child's transitional object turns into the existing object, or what the distinction is between a cultural object ('enacted') and an object in a mundane sense (p. 63). Kuhns assumes a favoured trajectory for the transitional object, dividing art-objects from mundane objects, designating a play area where one can harmlessly pursue illusion in order to adapt creatively to a traditionally given order of existing objects, thereby stabilizing the self.

This assumption is particularly evident when he comes to propose a theory of tragedy (pp. 104–13). Kuhns claims that he is Aristotelian in his approach to tragedy. He links Aristotle's catharsis to Freud's concept of 'splitting', defined as the ambivalent taking up of two different attitudes, owing to 'a conflict between the demand by the instinct and the prohibition by reality' (Kuhns 1983, p. 109, citing Freud 1953, XXIII, pp. 275–7). The conflict between the two and the impossibility of reconciling them is brought into focus; the mingling of pain and pleasure so produced effects the cathartic relief. This uncertain mingling makes the tragedy into a transitional object: as the child has conflicting experiences (fear and relief) with its transitional object, so too does a spectator with tragedy, and, just as the child proceeds to a mature and confident handling of reality via his play with the object, so the spectator is able to ameliorate the tensions between private sexual need and public reality. The honorific word 'reality' is confined to the public political world; as applied to the inner, the unconscious, it is conspicuous by its continual absence. Objects viewed from the standpoint of private sexual need remain fictional; reality belongs with the public object. Kuhns thus contradicts his attempt to keep ambivalence in the argument: tragedy becomes tamed to an experience which will enable spectators to refashion unreal inner needs in the mould of the real public and political system.

Potential space and the field of illusion

The theory implicit in Winnicott's practice is actually better than the one he explicitly holds. The use of the 'squiggle game', where analyst and child take it in turn to draw a squiggle for the other to make into an object (Winnicott 1974, p. 19) shows a pragmatic understanding of playing. Analyst and child play a game of rival interpretations of the random squiggle in front of them, making their own partial selections according to free associations. The semiotician Julia Kristeva and the psychoanalyst and writer André Green have a better theoretical understanding than Winnicott of what is involved in the process.

For Kristeva play begins at the meeting-place of nature and culture, a play that is productive of all objects and persons, including that of mother and child. Her theory of play is relevant to art both in its explanation of the importance of signs and symbols and in its showing how bodily experience provides the material for that use. Both these aspects concern that which resides in the margins of language. Moreover, her examination of the pre-linguistic stage in the infant shows the importance of these margins for the use of language thereafter. Kristeva believes that something like play begins before the self comes into being. Nature asserts itself in the infant's body, before any self has made its appearance, as unorganized pressures of desire, constituting what she calls a *chora*, a 'receptacle' of as yet undirected experience, a space prior to the infant's entry into a sign-system (Kristeva 1980, pp. 281–6). These currents of experience have their own rhythms and patterns, but do not yet have any consistent relation to need. Through sudden linkages, produced by the gatherings and releases of tension – one might say, not unlike Wordsworth's 'chance collisions and quaint accidents' (*The Prelude*, Book I) – the infant comes to laugh. There is the fun of play in passing from 'fright' to 'peace' (Kristeva 1980, p. 285), when an illusion, the result of some chance concept-experiment, shows itself a joke: the father, say, was *not* throwing the infant away – only up, to be caught again in safety. Sometimes the infant has the joke turned against itself, as when the 'good-enough mother' (Winnicott's concept, cited somewhat ironically by Kristeva), allows it some disillusionment, helping it to free itself from over-dependence, 'scoring a point' on her own account, but easing the moment with laughter (p. 282). This is a complement to Klein: Kristeva's child chuckles its way into selfhood, Klein's, a sensitive soul from birth, beats its own breast. In Kristeva's modification of Klein both these may be moments in the beginnings of the self; there can be a synthesis of thesis and antithesis.

These jokes and disillusionments prepare the way for the next stage: 'Winnicott's "potential space" elaborated by a "transitional object", perfects the necessary conditions for semiotic functioning and transition to language acquisition' (p. 286). Semiotic functioning depends upon the *chora*, the private experience of the bodily drives, which has a key part to play in the learning of language, in enabling the child to participate with some equality in the fun of meaning. The zest of experimentation, the *chora* disrupting the order, does not cease at some critical point at which language becomes mature and complete; the pre-symbolic is as active as ever. The implications of this reading of Winnicott are radical. The potential space is a place from which to challenge the parents' language, to be, one might say, a 'bad-enough child', a concept notably absent in Winnicott. Kristeva's theory is general enough to apply to male and female subjects alike, but it leaves open the revolutionary potential of the semiotic, pre-symbolic 'child', since the poetic destruction of the order of language by no means guarantees its being carried over into the political sphere (on this point see White 1983, pp. 16–17; for a feminist critique see Gallop 1982, pp. 113–31).

Another theorist concerned to keep the interaction between persons, their intersubjectivity, in the forefront of theory is the French psychoanalyst André Green, closer to Winnicott's practice than to his theory. Drawing explicitly on object-relations theory and combining it with other Freudian theory, including that of Lacan, Green has extensively explored the correspondence between the analytic encounter and that of writer and reader, extending it to the parallel relationship of producing and consuming in all the arts. His focus is on there being two conscious and two unconscious minds at work in any such interaction. In the analytic situation both analyst and analysand are operating with hypotheses about self and other. A negotiation about them can go on, and it is one that affects and develops both, a double dialectic. The analyst and analysand elicit speech and gestures from each other which have not existed before, because they grow out of the relations between the two, the 'I' and the 'me' on both sides, the 'I' being the subjective play (like Winnicott's squiggle), the 'me' what the other side picks up (the modification): 'What the analysand communicates is an analogue, a double of the effect produced on his own bodily, affective, and intellectual experience by the patient's communication' (Green 1978a, p. 180). This takes place in a potential space in which the nature of the illusion is left unrealized for the time being.

Green sees that there is an ambiguity on both sides of the writer/reader communication which is analogous (though not homologous) with what goes on between analyst and patient. In each case two subjects are engaged in the mutual production of a transitional object, the analytic 'text' and the literary text, both an illusion of agreement. The literary text, unlike the patient, cannot be subjected to further cross-questioning, but there is material in the figures of the text that can be worked on like an analysand's associations. What alters, 'overflows', is the *re*-reading done by any interpreter (Green 1978b, p. 277), who brings to bear upon the text his lived experience, which is 'outside the sentence' (p. 281, Green quoting Barthes 1976). This experience is first and foremost affective: the analyst–interpreter seeks to interpret the emotions the text awakens in him. Green describes this encounter as 'trans-narcissistic', a concept which avoids the past id-psychological approach that fantasy alone is a pre-text for writing and reading. Fantasy has a *double* effect, because conscious and unconscious on both sides are involved, each with its own perspective. To the degree that the encounter fulfils a private wish it is narcissistic, but since this inevitably involves confronting another's unconscious, the wish is thereby modified, and this transcends the narcissism of the single subject.

In his book, *The Tragic Effect* (1979), Green extends his theory to account for the emotional effect of tragedy: the 'potential space' becomes tragic, a place for misrecognitions. Green discusses the affective drama of Artaud as a prototype of the modern theatre, for it is with the insights that modern drama offers that we can go back to tragedy proper. Artaud's insistence on the 'physicality of signs' makes us forcefully aware of the unconscious bodily aspect of utterance, bursts the bounds of ordinary speech and shocks the spectator out of all passivity, so that 'the intelligibility of the spectacle is no longer, as in the past, related to its emotional resonance' (Green 1979, pp. 9 –10). This goes directly counter to the theory of Aristotle, who had no place for the uncontrolled unconscious. Nevertheless, Green contends, Aristotelian recognition (the passing from ignorance to knowledge, involving an emotional change) has not been banished from the stage: what has happened is a change in what is recognized. The post-Freud theatre is a 'theatre of desire, a theatre of the primary process'. It shows the characteristic processes of the unconscious as revealed by Freud. Green argues that the central unconscious concern is with the Oedipus complex, in particular its failures. It is the psychoanalytic critic's task not merely to proclaim the bad news, but to examine the process of veiling that hides the oedipal dynamic within the immediate structures of the play. Tragedy resides in the blindness of the protagonist who is as much involved with surface understandings as the 'naive' spectator. What is at stake is not just the blindness of a deceived consciousness but that of a consciousness out of touch with the unconscious. It is in this double view that the transitional nature of the play-object shows itself, in this case as a 'tragic effect': there are misrecognitions both by the characters within the play and by the spectator. Neither Hamlet nor the spectator knows, for instance, why Hamlet cannot get to the point of killing his uncle. The play-object is not what it appears to be.

Green sees the critic as one engaged in the play of the veiling/unveiling process. One of the three tragedies on which he practises his theory is *Othello*. Where Freud said that, until he examined *Hamlet*, no one knew the source of its fascination (VII, pp. 309–10), Green is virtually saying the same for *Othello*. He maintains that this play has always been considered not quite satisfactory, despite its obvious power to arouse strong emotion. Like Freud, in his essay 'Psychopathic characters on the stage', Green holds that the spectator is able to get pleasure from drama (in particular tragedy), because his attention has been diverted:

Between what Shakespeare presents to our senses and what he allows the unconscious to say there stands the difference that Freud aims to decipher. What must be restored is the thing that was offered on the stage, aimed to divert rather than to rivet the spectator's attention. What took place on the other scene must be the object of another reading, with the help of another type of link between its signifying elements, uttered according to another mode of scansion, marked by another punctuation, expressing a discourse that resists verbalization, being itself a veiling of a discourse, without which there would be neither tragedy, hero, spectacle nor spectator.

(Green 1979, p. 135)

The veiling is thus essential to all the constituents of the tragic experience, since action is at the mercy of drives of which the subject is unaware.

Green's general argument in the book is that aesthetic pleasure resides in the simultaneous arousal and control of the drives. Arousal is possible because of diversion of attention: there is fear, but the reason is not known. What controls the direction of the drive in *Othello* is the cultural expectation of jealousy: a mundane assumption, that a man is jealous of a woman as object of desire, provides a screen, but the force is rather envy, that of the position of a subject in the social structure. The jealousy disguises the envy of a subject who is refusing castration. To refuse castration is not to accept the repression of the Father, to cling to a narcissistic view of one's power and freedom. Green wants to distinguish between that level of understanding which accepts Othello as a warrior-hero subjected to a conventional challenge to his honour, reacting with 'simple jealousy', and that level which detects both Othello and Iago as governed by envy of the Father, the power of the Venetian state. Both are alienated, one by race, the other by rank, from the envied image of Cassio, the favoured Venetian. The envy binds desire narcissistically to the power-structure with the result that both aim at the death of Cassio and project elsewhere, upon Desdemona and Emilia, (homo)sexual jealousy of Cassio which conceals their Father-hatred. This is not *simply* saying that Iago and Othello desire Cassio homosexually. It is attributing the source of that desire to envy and explaining the jealousy with regard to the women as, for both of them, a transformation of that envy. It is not an analysis that looks for historical explanations for the centrality of that concern in a play produced in the late Renaissance; Green, in fact, dismisses Iago's relations to Machiavelli with the remark that his function (in being motivated like Othello, with an imperious castration complex) 'far exceeds that contemporary interest' (p. 121). What is significant for Green is the castration complex in general, not the historical form it takes. What he is investigating in the three tragedies of his choice is 'the other side of the Oedipus complex' (p. 32), always present in some form, where a firm identification with the 'right' parent (for a man the father, for a woman the mother) is undermined by an identification with the parent of the opposite sex.

The strength of Green's practice here is that it manages to account for strong emotion in terms of a rhetoric in the text. According to his theory there is a latent private fantasy (denial of castration) and a manifest public one (the desire to possess a woman), which interact in a potential space, a field of illusion, where two fantasies commingle in a desire for possession. Where previous critics linked the castration complex with a universal structure in the author's mind, Green neither brings in the author nor analyses a single character as being subject to the complex, but shows instead how the configuration of characters stages the castration complex in terms of a set of shared power-relations. Pleasure resides in the characters being put through anguish while the spectator can mingle pleasure and pain through a double identification: a conscious imaginative one miming the jealousy-pattern, and an unconscious imaginary one miming the narcissism-pattern.

In his criticism Green makes characters and past 'naive' readers into analysands, reading falsely, while he, being both analysand and his own analyst, reads correctly. This would seem to reflect a similar problem in psychoanalysis itself in its assignment of intersubjective rights to the analysand in theory, while there remains the question of his being able to take them up in practice. Would he be, as in Winnicott's theory, already, as child, himself inscribed in 'potential space'? Green is an expert analyst, but he has, as with a formal session, brought his analysis to closure. For all the subtleties of his interpretation, to which no summary can do justice, the text has been frozen into a single stable ambiguity. What is missing is what is left out of any totalizing reading, not only a psychoanalytic one: an engagement with the text rather than with the characters. The text ought to be in potential space. He has not shown up any labour in the text as indicative of the conflict between the two meanings. He, for instance, underestimates Othello's desire to be a successful warrior and a victorious general to the point of omitting the clear evidence in the play that he was. Othello's doubting his fulfilment of the role is no disproof of his fulfilment of it. The rivalry in the illusion is of two real desires. This leaves open the question of the text as a whole (the rhetoric *of* the text as opposed to the rhetoric *in* the text), which would include within it this lower-level character-conflict, relating it to the text's own history – why, for instance, it has been valued as a 'good object' for so long.

In Winnicott's case the practice was better than the theory; in Green's case the theory has been better than the textual practice. He saw the intersubjective principle in Winnicott's practice, but he imported into his own critical practice a totalizing view. The task of praxis is to unveil the gap between theory and practice.

Green has brought together object-relations theory and French theory, linking fantasy, play and intersubjectivity. Negotiation of meanings takes place through illusion, where the double-match of conscious orderings and unconscious experience can be tested out for the degree to which they satisfy desire. The intentions of authors and readers are subject to this negotiation in the 'potential space' of reading/writing. Emotion is involved on both sides of the negotiation, and it is Green's strength that he acknowledges this in both theory and practice. The dialectic, however, may be prevented from advancing where it fails to allow for language reaching out to more than the analyst–analysand, author–reader duo.

PART III

7

Structural psychoanalysis: psyche as text

The psychoanalysis of Jacques Lacan (1901–81) could be said to found itself on the failure of theory to match practice. Winnicott drew attention to play and illusion in the child's engagement with the world, but ignored the relation between the identifications of objects and the accession to language. Objects, even when viewed as 'transitional', are not necessarily permanent and unchanging. Nor are subjects, the term used by French theorists in order to avoid connotations of selfhood and personhood, for this would be to anticipate discussion of how selves come into being. Language has put its network upon the world: the part illusion plays in its workings as a result of the split between conscious and unconscious cannot be ignored. Lacan's Freudian revolution is the systematic claim that the unconscious is more than the source of primal instincts linked at random to ideas and images. Lacan rejects this randomness. Conscious and unconscious are asymmetrically co-present: the inner structure maps the outer conceptualizings. This mapping is above all governed by linguistic experience.

Psychoanalysis and language: Lacan

Lacan begins with the infant in an amorphous state, with no boundaries to its experience of sense or of need, as a jumble he punningly calls 'l'hommelette' – *homme-lette*, 'little man';

omelette, 'shapeless mass' of egg (Lacan 1977b, p. 197). To mark the initial stages of separation Lacan returns to Freud's early concept of the ego in the latter's paper 'On narcissism' (Freud 1953, XIV), and to the key metaphor of narcissism, that of the mirror. For Lacan there is a mythical, and sometimes a literal, moment of a mirror-stage (Lacan 1977a, pp. 1–7), in which the infant makes an imaginary identification with its reflection in a mirror. Lacan explores and widens the implications of the narcissistic metaphor. The child looks in the mirror and is delighted by several qualities of its own image simultaneously. Whereas before it experienced itself as a shapeless mass, it now gains a sense of wholeness, an ideal completeness, and this all without effort. This gratifying experience of a mirror-image is a metaphorical parallel of an unbroken union between inner and outer, a perfect control that assures immediate satisfaction of desire. Lacan calls this pre-linguistic, pre-oedipal stage the realm of the 'Imaginary'. He takes the infant to be modelling itself upon the mother, since that is the first being with whom it has interaction. But this model is an illusion, since the mother is thought, like the mirror-image that follows its every movement, to respond to every impulse. The mirror-image is 'a homologue for the Mother/Child symbolic relation' (p. 196).

What is imagined in particular is a primitive belief typical of this stage, a belief Lacan terms the 'Desire of the Mother' – a double genitive referring to both the mother's desire and the desire for the mother. First, the child imagines itself to be the desire of the mother in the sense that it is all that the mother desires ('desire' taken as a metonym for what is desired, much as we use 'wants' as a noun for what is wanted). The child becomes all that would satisfy the mother's lack, in psychoanalytical terms becoming the 'phallus' for the mother, all that would complete her desire. The mother herself has suffered deprivation, by division from her own mother, and by denial of her own father, and can thus be drawn into a collusion with the child that it will assuage the lingering pain of those separations. Second, the 'Desire of the Mother' is the child's own desire for the mother, as that part of its experience which has been prompt to satisfy its needs. Hence it too is drawn into this fantasy of completion. Since repression is neither experienced nor acknowledged, there is, according to Lacan, no unconscious at this stage.

Both of these aspects of the 'Desire of the Mother' combine to keep the child's ego-concept in a profoundly illusory state. The absence of a gap for the child between a concept and its application is a proof of the concept's inadequacy; the ego-concept has never been tested in use. The gap appears with the initiation of the child into the order of language, what Lacan calls the 'Symbolic Order'. The structures of language are marked with societal imperatives – the Father's rules, laws and definitions, among which are those of 'child' and 'mother'. Society's injunction that desire must wait, that it must formulate in the constricting word whatever demand it may speak, is what effects the split between conscious and unconscious, the repression that is the tax exacted by the use of language.

Lacan makes appeal to the linguist Ferdinand de Saussure, who viewed the sign as split into two parts, a signifier and a signified. A signifier is typically a word-sound, recognized by being heard as different from others within an expected range. A signified is a concept, singled out from an originally undifferentiated continuum of thought. The link between them is entirely arbitrary, for any sound can be linked with any concept. Once bonded in use, however, the combination is secure, as firmly bonded together as the two sides of a single sheet of paper (Saussure 1977, p. 113; orig. publ. 1915). Saussure expresses the combination by the formula $\frac{S}{s}$ where S stands for the signifier and s for the signified. Lacan begins his critique by throwing doubt upon the security of the combination. He gives an example where what appears to be the same signified, namely a door, can be marked with two different signifiers, 'Ladies' or 'Gentlemen'. This sly example brings out what critics within linguistics had already pointed to, namely that Saussure ignores the problem of reference, the process whereby parts of the world come to be referred to as things or persons. Illusion can enter the sign-system because the identification of the signified depends upon human judgements, which can, notoriously and justifiably, differ. The Saussurian security is here removed: a hidden gap opens up between signifier and signified, the bar no longer a bond, but a division.

For Lacan the most general effect of this division is the

assigning of gender roles. He treats the fact of having a male or female body as irrelevant before the division: without language there is neither gender nor gender-oriented desire. Once inserted into language the subject becomes at once 'discordant' with it:

> There is nothing in the unconscious which accords with the body. The unconscious is discordant. The unconscious is that which, by speaking, determines the subject as being, but as being to be crossed through with that metonymy by which I support desire, in so far as it is endlessly impossible to speak as such.
>
> (Lacan 1975, in Mitchell and Rose 1982, p. 165)

Language places the subject in the chain of words which binds it to one gender or another, but the force of the unconscious can subvert that definition. .

To indicate the dominance of the Father's signifier over the signified, Lacan inverts Saussure's formula, putting the signifier, S, on top, and the signified, s, under the bar: $\frac{S}{s}$. This also metaphorically suggests the place of unconscious desire as beneath the range of the conscious level of language, out of sight and unnoticed, yet able to shift unpredictably. In an endeavour to clarify this shifting 'under the bar' Lacan speaks of an interaction between the Imaginary and the Symbolic in their operations upon what he calls the Real. The Real for Lacan is the given field of brute existence over which the Imaginary and Symbolic range in their rival attempts to control: one can say that it is that to which all reference and action have relevance, but which can only be handled through signifying practices. This contested field he conceives as a Möbius strip (a band of flat paper with one twist in it, making two sides into one) where Imaginary and Symbolic ambiguously meet. The strip is like the Real; the ambiguity of the side(s) represents the conflict between Imaginary and Symbolic. This is the place where illusions occur, for example, where the ego-ideal (the mirror-image) interacts with the Father's definition of the subject, as compared with the way the subject envisions itself in its relation to the mother. In a diagram (Lacan 1977a, p. 197; see also n. 18) he marks a cross-hatched area between two parts of a square: in this grey area the Imaginary sees a signifier one way, the Symbolic another, splitting conscious from unconscious.

This double view upon the signifier produces effects of ambiguity. Words are turned in meaning, are 'troped' upon, most notably in metaphor and metonymy. Lacan borrows again from linguistics, this time from Roman Jakobson, who argued that these two tropes were the prime constituents of language (Jakobson and Halle 1956). For Lacan metaphor and metonymy are linguistic formulations of what Freud discerned in condensation and displacement, although the parallel is not exact (see p. 23–4). Unconscious desire can mistake one appearance for another *similar to it* and be led to substitute one signifier for another; or it can shift from one thing to another *found with it*, discerned as being more significant for desire, so producing a metonym. Such metaphorical and metonymic effects are constantly at work in language without speakers being aware of it.

Lacan sees an identity between language-forms and the response to repression: the dictum 'the unconscious is structured like a language' is more than an analogy, for the unconscious is born to be no more than its linguistic birthmarks. The fact that every word indicates the absence of what it stands for intensifies the frustration of this child of language, the unconscious, since the absence of satisfaction has now to be accepted. Language imposes a chain of words along which the ego must move while the unconscious remains in search of the object it has lost.

Lacan likens the pattern of metaphor to what happens when the Father's Law, the 'Name-of-the-Father', replaces the 'Desire of the Mother'. He quotes a line from Victor Hugo's 'Booz Endormi' (1977a, p. 156):

> His sheaf was neither miserly nor spiteful.
> (Sa gerbe n'était point avare ni haineuse.)

The sheaf, metonymic itself for all the fertility and fruitfulness of harvest, stands as a metaphor for the potency and generosity of Boaz, the old Testament patriarch, making clear his role as father and provider in that which grows tall, giving love to his wife and his people. The providing father, offering a delayed satisfaction, is on this account able to say 'No', to demand that delay, to exact that repression. The 'Name/No-of-the-Father'

(Lacan's pun – *Le Nom-du-Père/Non-du-Père*) is thus substituted for the 'Desire of the Mother' (p. 200; on this parallel see Muller 1979, p. 44). Where the Desire of the Mother was a lure, the metaphor of the Father's word becomes a kind of trick, playing with an interanimation of the old desire with a promised, forever deferred satisfaction of that desire. The Saussurean bar takes on a temporal dimension: the object is not lost, but merely delayed – for how long in future time, he who is patient enough to learn to speak the Father's 'non' will discover. This implies an incessant referral of the subject from one signifier to the next: the absence of one can only be replaced by another, equally marked with absence. The phallus is transformed into the symbol of patriarchal law (Boaz's 'sheaf' made out to be never 'miserly' and 'spiteful'), whereas it is a signifier of loss, the result of the split caused in the subject upon entry to the Symbolic.

The Father's words, those definitions out of which the object-world is ready-made for the child, are thus fraught with illusion. This is a new development in Freudian theory: every single utterance, spoken or written, is invaded by the unconscious. Lacan's own style, frustrating for the reader, continually mimes this illusion by means of puns, innuendos and outrageous conceits. It is by no means clear whether the theory is thereby shown to be undermined or validated by his own practice in writing or speaking (on this point see also Bowie 1979, p. 149).

Although Lacan thus argues for every single utterance being invaded by the unconscious, the overriding impression is that the Imaginary and the Symbolic are by no means given equal status, that Lacan is disinclined to give the unconscious any power to correct the order which has created it. To say this, however, is to take insufficient account of the very problems posed by the theory, a theory which tries to split in the abstract what cannot be conceived as split in the concrete. In his late seminars Lacan tried to address himself to the problem of the relationship of his three orders. He became increasingly interested in the image of the Borromean knot (three rings, no two of which actually intersect, but which are kept knotted together), and he saw this as analogous to the relation of his three orders: if one ring is cut, all three fall apart. This gives no pre-eminence to any one of them, and makes any alteration, to say the least, unpredictable. One might here take Beckett's brief play, *Not I*, as an illustration of what happens when the rings fall apart. The central focus of *Not I* is a mouth, picked out by a faint light from the rest of the face, frantically voicing disjointed words and phrases. The Imaginary (the body's experience) is being severed from the Symbolic (the speech of the subject), producing not an illusion, but a delusion of a part-object (a mouth) in the Real, desperately searching out sensory experience:

> when suddenly . . . gradually . . . all went out . . . all that early April morning light . . . and she found herself in the . . . what? . . . who? . . . no! . . . she . . . found herself in the dark . . . and if not exactly . . . insentient . . . for she could still hear the buzzing . . . so-called . . . in the ears . . . and a ray of light came and went . . . came and went . . . such as the moon might cast . . . drifting . . . in and out of cloud . . . but so dulled . . . feeling . . . feeling so dulled . . . she did not know . . . what position she was in . . . imagine! . . . what position she was in! . . .
>
> (Beckett 1973, p. 2)

Mouth is reliving the trauma of the primordial moment when the body senses its split from the Real. This experience can neither be included in the Imaginary, the realm of illusory wholeness, nor can it be part of the Symbolic, the domain which grants a conditional identity. The traumatic moment can thus return in psychosis as the experience of the 'fragmented body', unique for every subject, remainder and reminder of this fracture, appearing in art as images of grotesque dismemberment – Lacan cites Bosch (Lacan 1977a, p. 4). Language both reveals and conceals the fracture. For Lacan, narrative is the attempt to catch up retrospectively on this traumatic separation, to tell this happening again and again, to re-count it: the narrative of the subject caught in the net of signifiers, the story of *The Purloined Letter*, the story of the repetition compulsion.

Lacan, literature and the arts

What, then, are the implications and applications of Lacan's theory of the subject for literature and the arts? Lacan's own example of critical practice is not to be taken as exemplary. It is nevertheless essential to an understanding of what is new in psychoanalytic criticism. Although his treatment of Poe's story is not itself a form of deconstructive criticism as variously understood by literary critics, it can be seen as playing a part in sustaining such a criticism. Even when taken as a form of applied psychoanalytic criticism (Derrida 1975), its emphasis on text-structure takes it beyond the well-trodden domain. My first purpose is therefore to explicate it as a form of textual criticism. My second purpose is to use Lacan's 'Seminar on "The Purloined Letter"' (1972; orig. publ. 1966) as a point of departure for more general critical issues, namely its implications for the reading-process (the unconscious as a reader) and, analogously, for the seeing-process (the unconscious as a viewer), and the relevance the latter has for a criticism of the visual arts.

The traditional Freudian psychoanalytic approaches to literature examined so far have centred on the analysis of the personal psyche, whether this was the author's, the character's, the reader's, or a combination of these. The new psychoanalytic structural approach centres on the workings of the text as psyche, based on the theory that the unconscious is structured like a language. As *Gradiva* was for Freud an allegory of the return of the repressed, in the form of specific imagery, Poe's 'The Purloined Letter' is for Lacan a symbolic repetition of a structuring fantasy, his linguistic version of the repetition compulsion. The story is seen as an allegory of the supremacy of the signifier over the subjects it brings into being, the way they are forever at the mercy of the repressive differences exacted by the structure. The traumatic entry into language enforces the repetition by the unconscious of its own creation. Lacan's reading of the story concentrates on a repeated scene, only loosely connected with the mundane events, yet inadvertently structuring their dramatic import.

Poe's tale concerns the double theft of an incriminating letter, initially sent to an exalted personage Lacan calls 'the queen'. Caught unawares by the entrance of the king, she leaves it lying innocently on the table. Enter Minister D, who takes in the scene at a glance, steals the letter in full view of the helpless queen and the unsuspecting king, and leaves another in its place. The queen engages the prefect of police to recover the letter. When, after a systematic search of the minister's apartment, he fails to recover it, he calls in Dupin, an amateur detective. Dupin reckons that the minister, like the queen, would leave the letter unconcealed as the best way of hiding it: thus he finds it, dangling from the mantelpiece in a card-rack, and, arranging a distraction, he steals it, leaving another in its place.

I have explored more fully elsewhere the various analogies to the psychoanalytic process (Wright 1982a); here I am only concerned with the bare structure of the repetition and the mode in which it is enacted. For Lacan the story is structured round two scenes, which he calls 'primal scene' and 'repetitive scene'. There is a change of locale and a repetition of a pattern involving three protagonists: scene 1 in the royal boudoir, with the king, the queen, and the minister; scene 2 in the minister's apartment, with the police, the minister, and Dupin. There is a parallel operation: the minister/Dupin takes the letter that the queen/minister leaves unguarded, while the king/police are oblivious. It is this repeated structure, rather than the theft itself, which interests Lacan:

> Thus three moments, structuring three glances, borne by three subjects, incarnated each time by different characters.
>
> The first is a glance that sees nothing: the King and the police.
>
> The second, a glance which sees that the first sees nothing and deludes itself as to the secrecy of what it hides: the Queen, then the Minister.
>
> The third sees that the first two glances leave what should be hidden exposed to whomever would seize it: the Minister, and finally Dupin.
>
> In order to grasp in its unity the intersubjective complex thus described, we would willingly seek a model in the technique legendarily attributed to the ostrich attempting to shield itself from danger; for that technique might ultimately be qualified as political, divided as it here is among three partners; the second believing itself invisible because the first has its head stuck in the ground, and all the while letting the third calmly pluck its rear.
>
> (Lacan 1972, p. 44)

A glance, a look, are here open to illusory reinterpretation:

the letter is precisely what is not seen (by some) and seen differently (by others). In each case the possessor of the letter is made to stand helplessly by while the theft takes place. Each time the letter is appropriated, the subject is captured by the signifier, for which the real letter stands: a love-letter whose content is never revealed, a metaphor for desire, and a pun on the common metonym (letter for letter). 'Falling in possession of the letter – admirable ambiguity of language' (p. 60) is falling into transference, repeating the illusion of the completeness of the sign. The winner is now himself locked in the Imaginary; the loser realizes he has been. Dupin as analyst has a better understanding of the transferential structure of language and its effects. If a subject tries to deny the difference (retains the letter), there is a loss of contact with the Symbolic, hence of determined identity, even gender. The minister has turned the envelope inside out and addressed it to himself 'in an extremely delicate feminine script' (p. 65): the signifier is floating away from him. Sexuality (guaranteed only by difference) and textuality (the language system) are thereby equated, for each depends on a signifying system.

Lacan's reading of Poe's story, his purloining of the letter, has implications for the reading and writing process in general. The triangular structure within the text has shown itself to continue outside. Jacques Derrida has overtaken Lacan's reading (Derrida 1975), to be overtaken by Barbara Johnson in turn (Johnson 1977). The text (the letter) is not the property of a single subject, neither author nor reader. Lacan's disrespectful dismantling of Poe's story has revealed a new figure in the text, something hidden in full view as one reads. The reader/writer is an ostrich burying his head in a book.

The scenes as Lacan describes them are enacted in silence. What structures the uncanny repetitive movements are three glances: the characters are caught out by a look of desire. For Lacan desire is lodged to a degree in all that is seen, every observer taking his object-world for granted, but since the unconscious is inscribed in that desire there will always be a mis-seeing, a *méconnaissance*. Unconscious and repression, desire and lack – this dialectical opposition is present in every visual recognition. The pattern is exaggerated in the perversions: the exhibitionist seeking a perfect confirmation of his desire in the imagined desire of the other; the voyeur finding all his desire in his own looking, afraid to accept the Symbolic Order's dictum that it is not to be found there. Both perversions are denying the uncanny duality of all looking, all objectifications. Lacan identifies a 'scopic drive' for this lodging of desire in looking, a subject's search for a fantasy that represents for him/her the lost phallus. He calls the part of the object round which this fantasy is developed *objet petit a* (see 'Of the gaze as *Objet Petit a*' in Lacan 1977b). Freud was aware of such a drive, but stressed mainly its perverse aspects, whereas Lacan extends it to every act of seeing. The eyes, as one of the modes of access for libido to explore the world, become the instruments of this drive. A drive is not just pleasure-seeking, but is caught up in the signifying-system, characterized by the subject's first entry into that system. For Lacan this happens when the child learns to signify the presence and the absence of the mother. The sexual drive is now deflected from the child's primal object, the mother, into seeking an object always out of reach, to be found only by discovering its trace as an absence in every signifier. This signifying process comes to affect all looking, every recognition at once a finding and a failure to find.

Lacan explains this absence – that the fantasy is always missing from what is seen, that its absence looks through its wished-for presence – in the following way: 'When, in love, I solicit a look, what is profoundly unsatisfying and always missing is that – *You never look at me from the place from which I see you*' (Lacan 1977b, p. 103). The lover is narcissistically projecting an image of a desire that magically completes his own, that looks at him from the place where he wishes her to be; the absence breaks through the fantasy for he finds that she 'never looks at him from the place in which he sees her'. The 'place' is where he has placed her in field of the scopic drive, and she is discovered to be not there. The reality does not correspond to the wish, for her desires must be reckoned with. Lacan adds: '*what I look at is never what I wish to see*' (ibid.).

The eye is not merely an organ of perception but also an organ of pleasure. There is a 'dialectic of the eye and the gaze' (p. 102) – 'the eye' as caught up in the Symbolic Order and 'the gaze' as pursuing a narcissistic fantasy – for every object, subjected as it is to the scopic drive, partakes of the conflict between Imaginary fantasy and the demands of the Symbolic, the desire of the Other.

'I feel a great personal connection with Surrealist painting,' says Lacan, following on from his paper, 'Of structure as an inmixing of an Otherness prerequisite to any subject whatever' (Lacan 1970, p. 197). René Magritte's notorious picture *The Rape* is a case in point of an 'inmixing of an Otherness' as a dialectic of the eye and the gaze. The subject of the picture is apparently a face, framed in what is clearly a woman's hair, styled in what was then a consciously fashionable manner. It turns out, however, that the eyes are nipples, the nose a navel, and the mouth the pubic hair of a woman. If the cultural frame (the woman's hair) is ignored, the naked torso is plainly seen, hidden in full view. The picture is a metaphor for any gaze, signifying desire and an invasion of the other's desire ('The Rape'). The face, framed for culture by the hair, becomes fully sexual, a metaphor for desire being operative in everything. The face not being hidden is indicative of the public (not the pubic) personality, here unmasked, unveiled as the private(s). The (symbolic) eye (the painter's) has disturbed the (narcissistic) gaze of the viewer by turning the illusory eye in the picture into a nipple via a visual pun which removes the blindfold and makes the viewer see the ubiquity of the libidinous. He is caught out by his own looking; his eyes see themselves seeing themselves. This undermines the false idealization of the face, for it reveals that the body is operative at the level of the gaze. Only the fashioned hair gives the contextual clue that relates the cultural to the sexual.

Lacan's concept of the dialectic of the eye and the gaze undermines that view of art which takes it to be an imitation of life. There is no comparison of a representation with a putative reality: mimetic art is still presenting a fantasy, a favoured view of reality. There is no pure seeing. Lacan takes the artist to be saying: 'You want to see? Well, take a look at this!' (Lacan 1977b, p. 101). Art, says Lacan, combines a lure of the gaze (the *trompe-l'oeil*) and a taming of it (the *dompte-regard*). It tames because 'it encourages renunciation' (p. 111), calming the spectator by the turning of his gaze-fantasy into another look, in which there is the simultaneous awareness of desire and lack. The work of repression is acknowledged by the artist/spectator, in Lacan's view. In Freud's view of art as sublimation, for both artist and spectator the sexual drive is redirected into sociable acceptable goals, but neither are aware of the repression that brings this redirection about.

As an illustration of the lure and the taming, Lacan cites Pliny's anecdote concerning the rivalry between the two Greek painters, Zeuxis and Parrhasios (pp. 103 and 111–2). Zeuxis painted some grapes and thought he had triumphed when they were so lifelike that birds came to peck at them, taken in by the resemblance. Parrhasios, on the other hand, painted a picture of a curtain, and Zeuxis, on coming to look at it, wanted to see what was painted behind it. Now Parrhasios was gleeful because Zeuxis had been taken in. Ernst Gombrich, who also discusses this tale, rightly points out that 'poor Zeuxis' was easily fooled because the likelihood of the painting just being of a curtain was extremely low, and therefore the representation need only be of the most rudimentary quality (Gombrich 1977, p. 173). Lacan (who translates the Latin *linteum* ('curtain') as 'veil') makes a point similar to that of Gombrich but for a different reason. Neither in the case of the birds nor in the case of the man need the representation be exact: the birds would require only a crude stimulus to be taken in and it is not through a mimesis that the man was deceived. He was not taken in by the veil-as-representation, as he would have been had he imagined it to be a real present veil, but his gaze was lured into searching for the fantasy by the fascination of presence beyond absence. Parrhasios has triumphed for he not only did what Zeuxis did – produce a mimesis – but he performed a further sleight-of-eye, his eye seducing Zeuxis' gaze.

The victory of eye over gaze puts into question that theory in which imagination's task is pure disclosure, in that the ideal, the hidden picture, was shown to be not hidden but absent. The victory, however, is not meant to be one-sided, for the artist knows – and shows the spectator that he knows – that he himself suffers the same lack. He is not just an exhibitionist; he invites the spectator to share, not inner harmony, but desire and lack, not to compete in desire (as to who has the most immediate access to that harmony), but mutually to sustain a renunciation of a *fantasy*.

Lacan's thinking on art has not been developed in the field of art criticism, but his theory of the lure of the Imaginary has been adopted in a critique of the cinema. Christian Metz is a theorist and critic who has made systematic use of a combination of Freudian, Kleinian and Lacanian theory to account for what in his view is the peculiar fascination that the film has for the spectator, as the medium most appropriate for the luring of the gaze, and more successful in evading the Symbolic than other arts. The cinema, a field for the scopic drive, situates the spectator in a certain relation to objects such as Melanie Klein described, a relation which corresponds to Lacan's Imaginary. It is up to the film industry to induce 'filmic pleasure' rather than 'filmic unpleasure' by presenting its product as a 'good object', granting what is desired. The cinema lures the ego through being an image of its mirror-self; the screen is ready for narcissistic looking, a mirror for mirroring, thus a double of its double (Metz 1982, pp. 2–4). It is a Lacanian mirror in which the ego pursues its favoured image of itself, imagining that it is inserted into the Symbolic Order. There is no recognition of the screen as mirror-image, because the spectator is deluded into identifying with the camera. The 'all-perceiving subject' is an omnipotent eye, constituting the film within himself, in a pure act of perception (p. 48).

In stressing the importance of the look, Metz considers fetishism, voyeurism and exhibitionism, perversions of the sexual drive that underlie the 'scopic regime' of the cinema, and in these he finds its unconscious roots. Cinema is a series of substitutes that at one and the same time disavow that there is any lack, yet betray that there is because the absence of the (lost) object is conceded by the very nature of the photograph. The fantasy-objects within the film relate desire to the political economy (as in advertising; see the use of Lacan in Williams 1978, pp. 60–6); it is in the interests of the film industry to keep this relation close. Hence it is essential for the fiction-film to erase the traces of its steps, to hide its lure and its means of production in the 'referential illusion' (Metz 1982, p. 185). In studying the language of the cinema Metz uncovers these traces. He is the critic/analyst occupying the place of Dupin in Poe's story, understanding the Symbolic, while the spectator is the minister caught in the Imaginary. The impurities to be found both in pure entertainment and in the purest of texts are shown most clearly in the film, scene of the specular, site of seduction *par excellence*. The film is the letter, signifier of desire, a spectator-trap, as Poe's story was revealed to be a reader-trap, both inside and outside the text.

The relation between psychoanalysis and literature has changed as a result of the new developments in French psychoanalysis. Whereas the deliverances of classical psychoanalysis were used towards providing interpretations of actual texts, the effect of Lacan's work has been to revitalize literary theory. With the help of such new theoretical understanding, approaches may indeed be made to actual texts, but it is as a result of the light they cast upon language and communication that they are most valuable. Lacan's 'Seminar on "The Purloined Letter"' (1972) is central to the (non-) application of his theory to literature, having implications for both reading and writing. It elicits something from one text that can be extrapolated to authors, readers and texts in general.

The lure of all texts lies in a revelation, of things veiled coming to be unveiled, of characters who face shock at this unveiling. From the detective story with its piecing together of clues by an all-seeing Dupin, to the romance with the discovery of the hidden heroine or hero, 'great expectations' are subjected to sudden reversal. Oedipus the would-be detective expects to read the letter according to his narcissistic dream of kingly knowledge, but finds what is unveiled is his blindness. It is not only the characters who are beset by illusion: writer and reader find a lure and pleasure in the letter in which their unconscious is embodied. They can each play Dupin and minister upon each other. One can have his desire while the other lacks, and vice versa: hence Lacan's claim that desire and lack are together shared by them both. In the pursuance of his desire, which is also the desire of the Other (that is, as specified by the Symbolic Order) the reader may explore the ground of images beyond what the text may *apparently* control. The Symbolic may be subverted, but only to the extent of seeing a hitherto unperceived figure, one hidden in full view. Image study in the past was made to subserve interpretation, often pursuing a so-called universal meaning. For Lacan new meanings are the shifts of desire in language, the question being whose desire shall purloin the letter.

But the answer cannot be entrusted to an agreement between

two subjects, caught as they are in a specular relation. Psychoanalysis and the reading process (both inside and outside the clinical situation) require the awareness of the Other as a checkpoint. The grey area, the Möbius strip over which the purloining takes place, is unlike that of Green's or Winnicott's aesthetic play for two, because the power of the letter, of interest to kings and the police, implies an Other for both of them, not a transcendental signified, but language, of which it is not the case that only two can play. Lacan does not want analysis to become 'the relation of two bodies between which is established a phantasmic communication' (Lacan 1977a, pp. 90–1). The space of interpretation is not merely 'potential', because the interpretative play has to come to terms with the Real (brute nature in self and world and their history), not only the Possible. This complicates the implication of any act of reading and writing, for it indicates that modern psychoanalysis may have a *general* task to play in theory, and not a particular one with regard to some lower-level problem. Instead of enlisting the critic as analyst/archaeologist digging for a repressed signified (Freud's main project in *Gradiva*), it involves the critic as analysand/rhetorician, attentive to the workings of the text (Freud's project in slips and jokes). What is wanted is not a spade, but a pen.

The turn of the reader/writer

The 'turn' of the reader/writer is here used in a double sense: first, because it is their turn to be considered as a site where meaning is produced and where the distinction between them is no longer a hard and fast one; and second, because with the influence of Lacan's definition of the unconscious as structured like a language, the phenomena of transference in reading become all-pervasive, the structures of desire in language turning (in the sense of affecting) reader and writer alike.

The division I have made between 'structural' and 'post-structural' is not a neat historical one. Lacan, for example, is equally part of the post-structural enterprise. The division I am making is based on a practice of reading, in so far as it concerns psychoanalytic criticism. In one case (this section) the focus is on the reader in the text, both text of life and literary text, both determined by history and hence already written before the subject arrives on the scene. It is the reader who is transformed rather than the text. In the other case (next section) the capture of the reader is not taken as final. She can by a dialectical play move the text on to a new meaning, undermining its old power and deriving new power by exposing the text as self-contradictory. Lacan's procedure is to challenge the misreadings of past readers of Freud, by focusing on Freud the semiotician as distinct from Freud the humanist (Ernst Kris), or Freud the biologist (Sulloway 1979); Jacques Derrida's procedure is to subject Freud's texts to the same scrutiny as any other text, reading Freud's revolutionary discoveries against him, using the very transferential structures that Freud discovered in language to undermine *his* system. Freud's texts too are at odds with themselves and cannot be frozen into a metapsychology.

In either case the reader/writer distinction is no longer valid because making sense of the sign system implicates both: each is caught in the net of signs, is up against language. Reading, writing and criticism are part of a continuum whereby readers write in the act of reading and writers are shown to read in the act of writing. Barthes and Balzac are jointly implicated when the story *Sarrasine* is turned into *S/Z* (Barthes 1975; on this very point see Johnson 1978, p. 9: 'The difference between literature and criticism consists perhaps only in the fact that criticism is more likely to be blind to the way in which its own critical difference from itself makes it, in the final analysis, literary'). Texts can be made to turn upon themselves, meaning both less and more than the writer may have intended. The psychoanalytic concept of transference in its extended form (which I will recapitulate as I proceed) has changed the way in which the production of meaning is to be conceived. The examples about to be discussed are Roland Barthes's *A Lover's Discourse* (1979) and Shoshana Felman's 'Turning the screw of interpretation' (1977): both focus on the dilemma of the reader/lover in transference, albeit in different ways. Barthes is the reader of his own writing, self-consciously displaying the various effects of transference, and it is in this sense that he is performing a higher-level psychoanalytic criticism. Felman, while making a spectacular advance and attack on previous psychoanalytic criticism, is more orthodox in so far as she is working on the text of another writer.

A Lover's Discourse nicely illustrates the collapsing of the reader/writer/critic distinction. In his introduction Barthes explains both his detachment from and involvement with the persona of the book:

> In order to compose this amorous subject, pieces of various origin have been 'put together'. Some come from an ordinary reading, that of Goethe's *Werther*. Some come from insistent readings (Plato's *Symposium*, Zen, psychoanalysis, certain Mystics, Nietzsche, German lieder). Some come from conversations with friends. And there are some which come from my own life.
>
> (Barthes 1979, p. 8)

The 'I' of the text is both a person and a scene. 'I' is a problematic word; in 'To write: an intransitive verb?' (1972) Barthes examines its use. He wishes to show that a writer is not speaking from the position of a spontaneous bourgeois subject (the transitive 'I write the book'), but is rather subject to the system that places him, inseparable from his act, defined by the system (the intransitive 'I write'). To elaborate this he invents an image from grammar. Culture produces an illusory 'passive' *I*, the nature of which is wholly externally defined. The experiencing self produces an illusory 'active' *I*, the source of action appearing to be a pure ego without origin. The truth is half-way – a 'middle voice', Barthes' pun, since the voice is the very thing that is in question. He thereby shows a Lacanian sensitivity to the power of language over the body, for the pronoun 'I', 'the *je* and what is deprived of the mark *je*' (1972, p. 144), is one of the most powerful tools for the subjugation of meaning. There is that in the body which is not represented by 'je' in the ears of others, thus being deprived of expression.

In *A Lover's Discourse* the Imaginary is given a 'je' which will not fit the body. The lover is gagged by the Symbolic, yet trying to utter through forcing the Imaginary to follow the bourgeois signifier. The particular constraints forced upon the lover are the 'figures' that make him one (the 'fragments' of the discourse), not to be understood in a rhetorical sense. The figures are episodes, characteristic of a romantic lover's experience, self-enclosed courses of thought and feeling, rituals, obsessive fancies, to which the lover is bound: 'A figure is established if at least someone can say: "That's so true! I recognize that scene of language"' (1979, p. 4). Barthes wishes to offset the seductive influences of the figures of love, the chapters of cultural narrative imposed upon the subject, 'the *love story*, subjugated to the great narrative Other, to that general opinion which disparages any excessive force and wants the subject himself to reduce the great imaginary current' (p. 7). To make it impossible for the figures to fall into a conventional narrative he deliberately eschews an order of development by putting them in alphabetical order, a gesture of unlearning the ABC. To put something in alphabetical order that has some other order is deliberately to disturb it: the body's alphabet becomes the clearer as the culture's alphabet becomes blurred. Culture's version of the alphabet would have made the narrative flow. Nevertheless, he wants to sensitize the reader to the structure of these influences, however random they appear. It is not so much an individual psychology he is interested in, but the cultural fabrications, the traps there are for beings of passion. He notes the irrational swervings and sudden reversals which fail to break out of the given figure, as if the body was still showing its powers of resistance while helpless within the order, 'I am a Daruma Doll, a legless toy endlessly poked and pushed, but *finally* regaining its balance, assured by an inner balancing pin' (p. 141). This is part of a fragment under the title *This can't go on*. The titles and marginal notes have an effect he describes as 'à la Brecht', encouraging an alienation effect at the same time as an identification. The reader is to recognize the familiar schemes of emotion, the conventional sequences of thought, in order to distance himself from them. Hence the lover/writer and the critic/reader continually intersect.

The Barthesian lover does not have access to these alienation effects, safely tucked away as they are in titles, sub-titles and marginalia. He has to do the best he can, and this includes modelling himself on others. He needs a book to tell him how he feels. One might see him as having the same problem as E. T. A. Hoffmann's readerly/writerly cat:

I decided that as a youth of erudition I should come to a clear understanding of my condition and began immediately, although with effort, to study Ovid's *De arte amandi*, as well as Manso's *Art of Loving*; but none of the characteristics of a lover given in these works seemed to fit me properly. It occurred to me suddenly that I had read in some play that an unquestionable spirit and a neglected beard are specific characteristics of a lover. I looked in the mirror. Heavens, my beard was neglected. Heavens, my spirit was unquestionable.

Since I now knew that all was correct with the way I was in love, my soul was comforted.

> (Hoffmann 1969, *The Life and Opinions of Kater Murr;* orig. publ. 1820/1)

In *A Lover's Discourse* a voice speaks about the romantic novel *The Sorrows of Young Werther* in which a lover makes the description of his love all but a full-time occupation. Although Barthes' lover is struck only by Werther's passion for a woman he may not possess, it is worth noting that Goethe's epistolary novel revolves round a lover who also reads. He models himself on a Greek poet, Homer – in the spring and summer – and on a Celtic bard, Ossian (an impersonation of an impersonation, since the 'bard' was Macpherson) – in autumn and winter.

Barthes reads psychoanalysis. He knows that love, even and especially romantic love, is transference love. In the artificial hot-house conditions of the psychoanalytic encounter the old, the primal love, is reactivated, without having to wait for the right 'figure' (in Barthes' sense) to turn up. In order to delineate the scope of Barthes' reading/writing enterprise one might distinguish three levels of transference in *A Lover's Discourse*. In all three reader and writer are jointly involved. The first two levels involve them in their capacity as readers/analysands, that is as 'innocent'; the third level involves them in their capacity as critics/analysts, that is as 'knowing'. Only at the third level is the reader/writer a critic able to reflect on the effects produced by the text. This may be seen as analogous to those fluctuating stages in the psychoanalytic encounter in which analyst and patient are working through resistances.

The first is the Imaginary level, where the amorous subject addresses the (absent) mother. Here the archetypal lover/reader is the infant looking for links in the world/text which will bridge the gap left by the primal experience of separation. It is to be noted that Barthes sometimes adopts the benign perspective of Winnicott, at other times the dire perspective of Lacan, so that the concept 'Imaginary' is not purely Lacanian. In the figure 'Waiting', for instance, the lover knows that he is playing with reality (Winnicott's book is cited in a footnote). Waiting by the telephone for the 'call' of the beloved is like waiting for the mother to reappear:

> The being I am waiting for is not real. Like the mother's breast for the infant, 'I create and re-create it over and over, starting from my capacity to love, starting from my need for it': the other comes here where I am waiting, here where I have already created him/her. And if the other does not come, I hallucinate the other: waiting is a delirium.
>
> (Barthes 1979, p. 39)

This is a non-pathological form of playing out one's lack (with the sound of a voice), taking place in a moment prior to the constricting definitions of language. Other moments can only be endured by making a fetish of the play-thing. The figure headed 'The ribbon' designates a Lacanian moment, where the amorous subject becomes fixated upon every object the loved one has touched, as though it was a part of that body:

> Werther multiplies the gestures of fetishism: he kisses the knot of ribbon Charlotte has given him for his birthday, the letter she sends him (even putting the sand to his lips), the pistols she has never touched. (p. 173)

Werther's kissing the ribbon is not simply kissing something that metonymically stands for Charlotte, for the lover is kissing what metaphorically – through its being a sign of absence – can stand for what the Mother lacks. This is no benign transitional object enabling the lover/infant to effect his separation, but a pursuit of something he is unwilling to surrender, his narcissism. In the case of the transitional object the play is a game for two in which narcissism is modified by encounter with that of another: in the case of the *objet a* (Lacan is here alluded to) the fantasy pursued erases the beloved, who is repeatedly 'stifled' beneath the 'massive utterance' of the lover's discourse (p. 165, 'I am odious'). This theoretical distinction is not to be blurred (as is the case in Gregory Ulmer's otherwise excellent and fuller account of transference in Barthes' work; see Ulmer 1980, p. 71), since it marks two different ways of envisaging loss.

The second level of transference is that in the Symbolic, where language castrates by continually referring the lover to suitable cultural models, the 'permitted' mode of love already referred to. (In *The Pleasure of the Text* Barthes undermines the whole procedure by proposing to make the entire text into a fetish, fragmented and gaping, made to yield ecstasy – *jouissance*). Just as Werther needed someone to point out a lovable woman to him (Charlotte is committed to Albert before Werther arrives on the scene), so the Barthesian lover needs the book. The fetishistic quality of many of Werther's own actions reflects back on the helpless adoration the voice confesses to, since he specifies similar fetishes he finds 'adorable'. It is a fantasy based on a fantasy, of a narcissistic love of one unable to shake off the mother's image.

The third level of transference is that of the critic, who is both analysand and analyst. This joint function has already been discussed in the theory of André Green and in an example of Norman Holland's practice. In the present case a Lacanian model of transference is implied in that *A Lover's Discourse* is not just a matter of a pact between two subjects. Readers love texts, as Barthes shows in *The Pleasure of the Text*, and the *Lover's Discourse* demonstrates how that love can be a distorting infatuation, with the self caught in the existing, unsuspected signifying chain. Here is a writer giving the writer's game away in a game of his own, the writer's game being that of entrapping the narcissistic reader in a collusion of which even the writer is not fully aware. In showing how a text captures a reader Barthes enables *his* reader to escape capture both from transference and from the ideology that has contributed to it. He thus goes further than Lacan and further than Green. On the one hand he shows how 'writerly' texts set out actively to disturb the 'naive' reader's transference; on the other hand he shows how 'readerly' texts may be thawed from their classic crystallization in a discourse in which writers, readers and critics endeavour to prevent the fixation of the text, its freezing back into ideology.

In her article 'Turning the screw of interpretation' (1977) Shoshana Felman is concerned precisely with keeping the text open and on the move. Like Barthes she reveals the transference of which lovers and critics are unaware, both as readers within the text and as readers of the text. The story she investigates is Henry James's *The Turn of the Screw*. She shows how the discourse of the critics is caught up within the transferential structures of the story so that one set of unwitting analysands (the critics) are merely repeating the antics of another set of unwitting analysands (the characters). The act of interpretation ('turning the screw') links literature and psychoanalysis in a joint and hazardous enterprise, since both set the process of transference going, unbeknownst to naive and sophisticated readers alike, who believe there is a meaning there to be disclosed.

The setting of the story is a large country house, where a new governess takes charge of two young children in the absence of the owner, their uncle. She is aided by the housekeeper, Mrs Grose, and hindered by what she takes to be the 'ghosts' of two past servants, who appear to visit at intervals. The critical debate that Felman investigates centres around whether the governess is trying to save her charges from evil (the ghosts exist) or whether the governess is hopelessly neurotic (the ghosts are a projection of her repressed passion for the absent master). In a hundred-page virtuoso performance Felman shows the efforts on both sides to be doomed, already anticipated by the canny/uncanny textual strategies she uncovers:

> The reader of *The Turn of the Screw* can choose either to *believe* the governess, and thus to behave like Mrs Grose, or *not to believe the governess*, and thus to behave precisely *like the governess*. Since it is the governess who, within the text, plays the role of suspicious reader, occupies the *place* of the interpreter, to *suspect* that place and that position is, therefore, *to take it*. To demystify the governess is only possible on one condition: the condition of *repeating* the governess's very gesture. The text thus constitutes a reading of its two possible readings, both of which, in the course of that reading, it deconstructs.
>
> (1977, p. 190)

Or perhaps we should say, Felman deconstructs, because, like Poe's Dupin, she 'knows *what to repeat*' (Johnson 1977, p. 496).

She is the analyst, anticipating the capture of her analysand–readers, neatly turning their very misreadings against them, while making James, Freud and Lacan work for her own reading strategy, by citing them out of context, as part of a general intertext:

> I didn't describe to you the purpose of it . . . at all, I described to you . . . the effect of it – which is a very different thing.
>
> (Felman 1977, p. 94, citing James, *The Sacred Fount*)

> The unconscious . . . is most effectively misleading when it is caught in the act.
>
> (Felman 1977, p. 199, citing Lacan)

In Lacan's model of transference the analyst is 'absent' in order that the analysand may do the analysing, refusing the place assigned to him as 'subject presumed to know', playing 'dummy' instead (Lacan 1977a, p. 229). Similarly, there is a master who will not play, both within the story (the owner of the house to whom the governess addresses letters), and outside the story (the author of the text who is addressed regarding the meaning of his tale). 'The Master's discourse is very like the condition of the unconscious as such: Law itself is but a form of Censorship' (Felman 1977, p. 145). Hence, quotes Felman, making the object-language of the text act as her meta-commentary, ' "The story *won't* tell," said Douglas; "not in any literal, vulgar way" ' (p. 106). The literal is the vulgar (what Barthes calls the 'prattling text' (Barthes 1977, p. 5)), because it nails signifier to signified, stopping the production of meaning, closing up the gap that is the unconscious, the 'won't tell'.

Felman gets down to the rhetorical functioning of the text, its deferring of meaning through figures of desire, 'how' the story means, rather than 'what' it means (Felman 1977, p. 119). The Jamesian metaphor of seeing is enlisted as a metaphor for transference, in that it becomes part of a chain, seeing–reading–interpreting–viewing through the eyes of the unconscious, links by which meaning is transferred and agonized over: 'What it was most impossible to get rid of was the cruel idea that whatever I [the governess] had seen, Miles and Flora [the children] saw *more* – things terrible and unguessable and that sprang from dreadful passages of intercourse in the past' (Felman, p. 158, citing James). The business of passing on the story involves both the actual transferring of a manuscript, and the transference of love between the couples who pass it on, and this in turn requires the exchange of looks: ' "Yes, she was in love . . . *I saw it, and she saw I saw it*; but neither of us spoke of it" ' (Felman, p. 132, citing James; her italics). The manuscript, since it was sent through the post, had (presumes Felman) an address on it: the story of the governess is a letter and a story about letters. Hence 'letter' becomes a metaphor of the manuscript of the story and of the narrative as a whole, sent to the reader. There is thus a parallel between the letters in the story we and the characters never get to read and the story as a whole which defeats our reading, but which nevertheless determines a story (for the readers in the text) and a history (for the critics in the world). The governess begins as detective and ends up as criminal, grasping a dead child. The reader begins as analyst and ends up as analysand, reactivating his past traumas. Instead of the reader getting hold of the story, says Felman, the reading effect is that of the story getting hold of readers, catching them out in a fiction of mastery.

This is an exemplary psychoanalytic reading, pursuing the interrelationship of psyche and text, without either one mastering the other, as was the case with classical applied psychoanalysis. Yet there are a few questions one might like to raise, which are not easily met. Where is the writer's transference in all this? James's repression is praised by Felman, but not analysed: 'James, like the Master in *The Turn of the Screw*, doesn't want to *know* anything about it' (p. 205); 'James's reader-trap' is 'a *trap set for suspicion*'; (citing James) 'an *amusette* to catch those not easily caught' (p. 188). Why is James out to catch readers? And why are we, with Felman, so gratified to be inscribed and comprehended by the text, for in the end we are no wiser than any other poor dupe that misreads, 'as we see the very madness of our own art staring back at us . . . the joke is indeed on us; the worry ours' (p. 207). But what if the governess, Mrs Grose, the children, the 'undead' servants, previous duped readers, James himself, do not like the place assigned to them in 'the text', and are waiting, like the characters in a fairy tale, to be finally disenchanted, freed from the game of servants and masters? It seems almost as if Felman, in her desire to put psychoanalysis and literature on an equal footing, had reintroduced (repeated) the hierarchies of master and slave in her reading. The text lies in wait, ready to occupy the subject. The scene of reading has become the story of the capture of the psyche.

Post-structural psychoanalysis: text as psyche

Derrida and the scene of writing

Unlimited ink has by now been spilt on Derrida's project. His sustained attack on the western metaphysical tradition is grounded in a notion of writing as devalued and repressed by that tradition. The main culprit singled out is philosophy with its desire to fasten words upon the world once and for all. What is at stake is not just writing with the letters of the alphabet, but any activity which sorts out the world into differing units. In the previous section the focus was on reading and writing as interdependent activities to the extent that both involve a continuing act of interpretation that is never final. Derrida's deconstructive approach to reading is already implicated in the critical practice of Barthes and Felman, but the Lacanian emphasis was more on the way both readers and writers were determined by the text, were being written by the very text they thought they were reading. To that extent Lacan reigned over Derrida.

Lacan stresses the supremacy of the signifier in determining subjects in their acts. But for Derrida the signifier is not so supreme, and it is in pursuit of that argument that he substitutes and resubstitutes a set of terms of his own devising. These terms, to name only the most persistent, 'writing', 'trace', 'differance', 'dissemination', are designed to show the way any text undermines itself. Writing at once represses and reveals desire ('writing

is unthinkable without repression' (Derrida 1978, p. 226)).
Words, whether spoken or written, are subject to 'différance',
differing from and deferring any transient fixation of meaning.
Derrida refers to this process as the sign being 'under erasure',
the rubbing out being performed by past memories ('traces') in
the unconscious, 'archives which are *always already* transcrip-
tions' (p. 211), not copies, but unconscious interpretations. In
Derrida's reading of Freud (to which I will be turning) the
unconscious, through memories non-verbal as well as verbal,
thus becomes active in the production of meaning, its traces
being present in every word. Whereas for Derrida the unconscious is a weave of pure traces, for Lacan the unconscious is
structured like a language. So wherein lies the difference? One is
saying that the unconscious is operative in language all the time
(seeing text as psyche). The other maintains that the entire
unconscious is structured like a language (seeing psyche as
text). It is a marked distinction of emphasis rather than a
radical disagreement. Lacan places the emphasis on language's
imposition of a mould which creates the unconscious, Derrida
places it upon the unconscious's ability to escape the mould.
Derrida is nearer to certain modifications made by followers of
Lacan, in which the unconscious, 'rather than a language, is the
very condition of language' (Laplanche and Leclaire 1972,
p. 178).

The disagreement may in part be attributable to the difference of their interests, which makes it difficult to enlist them in
the same venture, the investigation of the theory of the text.
Lacan as a psychoanalyst uses texts as illustrative material for a
theory of the genesis of the subject in relation to language (what
makes a *subject* being his primary concern). Derrida as a philosopher looks at texts in order to undermine their power over
subjects (what makes a *text* being his primary concern). This
may be illustrated by their analyses of two literary texts,
Lacan's reading of 'The Purloined Letter,' and Derrida's reading of Kafka's parable 'Before the Law'. Where Lacan reads Poe's
story as an allegory of the supremacy of the signifier, subjects
being at the mercy of the law that made them, Derrida reads
Kafka's story as a parable of a failure to exert one's freedom
through the law, the point of the story being that the law is there
for you. There is a pun in the title: 'before the law' can mean

either prior to the law (you are the legislator), or up in front of the law (it legislates over you). In Kafka's story the man from the country allows the doorkeeper to bar the way, only to find out just before his death that the door had been there for him alone (Derrida 1982).

What Derrida derives from his reading of Freud is not only a deconstruction of Freud's texts but a self-reflection upon the very activity of deconstruction itself. It is Freud's discovery of the unconscious which has prepared the way both for a theory of textual deconstruction and for a deconstruction of the mode of that discovery. For Derrida, Freud becomes a Derridean *avant la lettre*, paradoxically, by showing this very idiom to be a mere figure of speech/writing. There is no 'before the letter': the subject *is* the subject of writing, both its product (as already written) and its producer (as rewriting the written). In describing the perceptual apparatus in terms which illustrate this double movement, 'Freud performs for us the scene of writing' (Derrida 1978, p. 229). The metaphors of which Freud avails himself describe a graphic system of representation; Derrida pursues these images of writing through a series of texts spanning thirty years:

> From the *Project* (1885) to the 'Note Upon the Mystic Writing-Pad' (1925), a strange procession: a problematic of breaching is elaborated only to conform increasingly to a metaphorics of the written trace. From a system of traces functioning according to a model which Freud would have preferred to be a natural one, and from which writing is entirely absent, we proceed toward a configuration of traces which can no longer be represented except by the structure and functioning of writing. (p. 200)

That is to say, Freud's neurological metaphors, such as 'breaching' (*Bahnung*), can retrospectively be seen to perform the movements of writing, instituting 'differance' among a set of resistant neurones that 'breach' and thus record the traces in response to external stimuli, these traces continually left in the memory. They are not to be conceived of as emerging pristine at some future date. According to Freud they already exist loaded with feelings of fear and desire, but are open to further interpretation (as his example of 'Emma' shows (Freud 1953, I, pp. 353–4)). Like the dream-thoughts in Freud's theory of dream interpretation they cannot be directly transcribed, but have to be 'reproduced' *nachträglich*, after the event.

It is from Freud's 'Note upon the mystic writing-pad' that Derrida is able to develop the full potential of the metaphor of the psyche as a writing machine, one with a potentially disruptive element built in it. The 'mystic writing-pad' is a child's plaything, still common today, used for rapid notes that can be quickly erased to enable later ones to be written. One writes with a simple stylus upon a celluloid surface under which is a piece of paper in loose contact with a waxen pad. The writing appears because of the temporary adhering of the paper to the wax.

Freud detects three particular analogies between this writing apparatus and the perceptual apparatus, to which Derrida draws attention: (1) the celluloid corresponds to the protection that the psyche institutes for itself against an excess of stimuli from without; (2) the fact that the paper is re-usable represents the endless capacity of the perceptual system for responding to sensory stimuli without becoming overloaded in any way; (3) the impressions that actually remain on the underlying wax – 'legible in suitable lights', as Freud puts it (XIX, p. 230) – stand for unconscious traces which remain hidden in the unconscious. Derrida fixes upon the writing metaphor, especially through the third analogy, which brings out the continuous interaction of those hidden traces with the succeeding script. The unconscious is thus active at complex and profound levels as the marks of repression are inscribed. Blurrings and obliterations take place beneath the concealing paper. Derrida sees the possibility of the unconscious as thus active in all experience with the signifiers of the repressive order, a pointer to the deconstructive potential of all reading, which is only a form of rewriting, becoming 'legible in certain lights'.

One aspect of the model is singled out by Derrida for its inadequacy. In using a material metaphor for the psyche, Freud is omitting its spontaneity. Freud's use of the metaphor of writing points to what he has omitted: that the effects of history in experience must take the investigation outside that of a narrowly physicalistic psychology. The metaphor that Freud would finally have to cast away once his neurological theory had been achieved betrays the reason why this cannot be done. He did not see the significance of his own metaphor: that the unconscious is actively productive in the signifying system. The discoverer of the unconscious has had his own writings examined for their unconscious effects. Freud saw the mind as being inscribed upon by what it perceived. Thus a mechanical image of the brain was inadequate in itself to account for the influences of history.

As a general conclusion Derrida proposes that it is time for the signifier and all the forms involved in the construction of the signifier to become the focus of attention in order to resist the logocentric fixation upon plausible but illusory signifieds. The unconscious is hypersensitive to the signifying machines of repression. Derrida quotes Freud as noting the link of pen and penis, writing on white paper and sexual penetration, and praises Melanie Klein for her revelation of the way school activities – we might rename the three Rs as Reading, Writing and Repression – show the presence of strong unconscious investment. The teaching of reading and writing is in both method and content the establishment of the channelling of desire, and sexuality will invade them both. Derrida especially notes the ambivalence of Klein's good and bad objects co-present in the equipment of writing, an uncanny mingling, 'writing as sweet nourishment or excrement, the trace as seed or mortal germ, wealth or weapon, detritus and/or penis etc.' (Derrida 1978, p. 231). This is the theme of deconstruction itself – is literature a 'wealth' generously spread for readers or a 'weapon' to be used against the author-ity? Is writing the chief instrument of repression or is it the means by which the symbolic may be subverted?

The return of Freud: jokes and the uncanny

This double question marks the return of Freud in this book, in that it will be the occasion of reading him with a difference. He will be read not as in Part I for the content of his theory, but for the 'uncanniness' or 'canniness' of his writing, that is according to the way his writing reveals or conceals unconscious intention. Jokes and the unconscious go together, for the uncanny works

like a joke, and the joke partakes of the uncanny: both participate in the double movement of the return of the repressed and
the return of repression. On the one hand, both can appear to be
a reassurance that desires will be satisfied; on the other, both
can be an unexpected denial of what was hoped for.

One might sum up the Freudian development followed so far
by seeing id-psychology as focusing on the return of the repressed, ego-psychology on the return of repression, and
object-relations theory as uneasily trying to reconcile the two.
Deconstructive readings of Freud try rather to reveal the
tension, to elicit the contradictions that disturb fixed logical
categorizations. Jonathan Culler's summary makes this abun-
dantly clear:

> Freud begins with a series of hierarchical oppositions: nor-
> mal/pathological, sanity/insanity, real/imaginary, experi-
> ence/dream, conscious/unconscious, life/death. In each case
> the first term has been conceived as prior, a plenitude of
> which the second is a negation or complication. Situated on
> the margin of the first term, the second term designates an
> undesirable, dispensable deviation. Freud's investigations
> deconstruct these oppositions by identifying what is at stake
> in our desire to repress the second term and showing that in
> fact each first term can be seen as a special case of the
> fundamentals designated by the second term, which in this
> process is transformed. Understanding of the marginal de-
> viant term becomes a condition of understanding the sup-
> posed prior term. . . . These deconstructive reversals, which
> give pride of place to what had been thought marginal, are
> responsible for much of the revolutionary impact of Freudian
> theory.
>
> (Culler 1983, pp. 160–1)

Both Freud's full-scale investigations into *Jokes and their Relation to the Unconscious* (1905) and his more tentative enquiry into
'The uncanny' (1919) have provided ample material for such
deconstructive reversals. I shall begin with an account of
Samuel Weber's reading of Freud's *Jokes*, because here the joke
served as a pivot for a most searching investigation into the
corpus of Freud's work, one centrally concerned with recovering the Freud that got lost in translation. In *The Legend of Freud*

Weber sets out to show 'the conflictual dynamics of the unconscious' (1982, p. xvi) at work in the very theory of the unconscious itself. He argues that the duplicity Freud detects in the ego's attempts to systematize the external in response to its narcissistic desires will erupt in that theory itself. Although Freud's metapsychological writings betray a tendency to underestimate the force of the unconscious (the crucial texts picked out are 'Project', *Three Essays* and *Beyond the Pleasure Principle*; see, for example, Laplanche 1976), it is ironically his being drawn to the joke that points the way to the proper estimation of that force.

As was seen earlier, ego-psychology assumes that the pleasure gained from the joke is due to its bringing about the play of energies in the psyche, for the ultimate benefit of the rational ego, which emerges refreshed and fortified. Deconstructive criticism of Freud, however, finds in his theory of the joke (1905) an anticipation of his theory of narcissism (1914), with a consequent shift of emphasis (Mehlman 1975; Weber 1977, 1982). The ego is no longer seen as a force that synthesizes and stabilizes, but as an ego committed to the affirmation of its illusory power.

Weber's *Auseinandersetzung* with Freud's joke theory ('analyzed into its components – that is, *auseinandergesetzt* – the word designates a process of decomposition or analysis'; used by Freud, and by Weber against Freud (Weber 1982, p. 24)), centres on his challenge to the distinction Freud upholds between the 'innocent' joke of pure pleasure and the 'tendentious' joke, the joke with a purpose. Before proceeding with Weber's analysis I need to clarify the organization and general presentation of Freud's argument.

Freud distinguishes three stages in the evolution of the joke, arising from a basis of primitive play. The first is at the level of the child's delight in games of recognition, which often manifests itself in verbal play, for 'children, who, as we know, are in the habit of treating words as things, tend to expect words to have the same meaning behind them' (VIII, p. 120). The pleasure of such recognition, Freud maintains, does not come from a sense of power but from a saving of psychic energy. This saving is in itself enjoyable (Weber presumes it 'saves' the effort of discriminating), so according to Freud 'the games founded on this pleasure make use of the mechanism of damming up only in order to increase the amount of such pleasure' (p. 122). This pretence of frustration on the child's part, making the play not quite so innocent, is a throw-away insight that should perhaps be rendered unto Freud.

The second stage of the joke's development moves it from the level of play to that of the 'jest' (*Scherz*). It entails making a concession to the growing demands of the intellect, which is not content to rest on the absurd chiming of words. There is a meaning, but it is of no consequence: 'the meaning of the joke is merely to protect that pleasure from being done away with by criticism' (p. 131). What distinguishes the jest from the joke proper (*Witz*) is that it is 'non-tendentious'; it has no axe to grind – its sole purpose is to give pleasure.

The third stage, then, is the joke proper, the 'tendentious' joke, in which there is a distinct purpose, taking the form of challenging either a person or social inhibitions of all kinds. There are two forms, the hostile and the obscene, the first giving the opportunity to express 'aggressiveness, satire, or defence', the second 'serving the purpose of an exposure' (p. 97). The verbal play is now working in conjunction with this tendentious purpose. Freud envisages this type of joke as embedded in a three-person situation. The teller requires a listener as 'ally': the first and third person are thus linked in being in an alliance against the second person or object, the butt of the joke. As a prototype of the tendentious joke Freud cites the example of 'smut', the dirty joke, where the first and third person are enabled to share an imagined mastery over the forbidden and inaccessible sexual object, the woman, allowing a discharge of frustration in a seduction whose imaginary nature partakes of a fancied reality through being publicly shared (pp. 97–102). The alliance is confirmed by the spontaneous laughter in which the complicity of the third person in this mutual release of tension (the 'saving' of psychic energy) is made obvious to both. This 'economy of psychical expenditure' involves a double pleasure, the verbal play itself, which is the core (*Kern*), and the pleasure of lifting the inhibition, which is the casing (*Hülle*) (p. 138).

This is the point around which Weber organizes his *Auseinandersetzung* with the joke theory. His deconstructive intent is directed particularly at dismantling the distinction between the 'innocent' core and the 'tendentious' casing. Weber sees Freud's continual stress upon the playful aspect of the joke as negating a narcissistic desire, which takes the form of reducing all that is alien in the external to the sameness of unity. Even a rhyme exemplifies a determination to erase difference and establish sameness, as Weber puts it, serving 'the interests of the narcissistic ego bent upon reducing alterity to a variation of identity' (Weber 1982, p. 98). The example that comes to my mind here is a well-known post-Freudian Jewish joke which employs a Jewish practice of using a rhyming tag as a dismissive gesture, one that denies difference. It is about the Jewish mother, who, on being told about the Oedipus complex, says 'Oedipus-Schmoedipus – What does it matter as long as he loves his mother?' In the very rejection of the classification she is exemplifying the actual narcissistic idealization which it defines. The play on words can hardly be defined as innocent.

The joke is thus not merely a comforting collusion in which a temporary relief is effected from the demands of repression, but a place of conflict. Weber begins his unravelling of Freud's distinction by examining the position of the third person, the listener. He finds that it is curious, in that it combines a spontaneous unconscious element, namely the laughter itself, with a desire for complicity with the Other ('the third person'). There is an ambivalence in the 'third person' of the joke, for though, on the one hand, it represents the spontaneous breakthrough of the id in that bodily phenomenon of laughter, on the other, it partakes of the superego, which characteristically voices its demands in the public grammatical third person. The narcissistic confidence in the 'continuity of Self and Other' is reassured by the Other's complicity. The first and third persons are fused – id and superego become identical in the illusion of the joke. The third person is that nameless Other who is listening to you; the laughter is an id-confirmation of a superego agreement. The 'classical' double-bind (the way Freud sees the father's command to the son) in the superego's command to the ego – 'Be like me! Be yourself!' – is thus apparently resolved (p. 107).

The teller thus seeks a complicitous laugh for his tampering with the law. The readiness of the hearer to provide such a laugh, however, exposes him to being caught out by an unscrupulous teller. There are jokes which capitalize upon the joke situation itself, exploiting the hearer's willingness to challenge the taboo. Weber considers the most narcissistic of jokes to be the take-in joke or shaggy-dog story, in German *Aufsitzer* (metaphorical origin 'to straddle', literal meaning 'to dupe' (pp. 80–2)), mentioned by Freud in a footnote as 'idiocy masquerading in the form of a joke' (VIII, p. 138). The *Aufsitzer* is a joke on the hearer, who has been duped into the expectation of a 'good joke', namely one in which he is invited to join in the challenge to the taboo, but he is himself 'had', for there is no satisfaction to be gained. The teller enjoys a sense of control over the hearer, who has now betrayed himself in his readiness to break the taboo. By means of this trick the ego is able to 'install' the superego, without having to give up its narcissistic desire for a would-be-safe identity (Weber 1982, p. 107).

The border between the private and the public definition of the self is precisely one where the joke of the gap between theory and practice can go several ways at once, for there is more than one theory of that practice. Hence the joke cannot be seen either solely as a challenge to authority (Bakhtin's view of laughter; Bakhtin 1968), or as a 'social act' (Kris's view of laughter). It is neither solely 'weapon' of liberation from repression and oppression, nor solely part of the 'wealth' of nurturing culture (see Derrida above on 'writing'). Texts, and theories about texts, are always at the mercy of subversion from whatever direction, private or public, as Weber's deconstruction of Freud has illustrated. Freud's theory of the joke leads to 'the Joke of Theory' (Weber 1978, p. 28). It shows 'that what had been thought marginal' (see Culler above), here the shaggy-dog story, can lead to a redefinition of the general term 'joke'.

There is a link here with the uncanny, in that it too can be looked upon as a failure of theory in practice. This is certainly the burden of the many critical readings of Freud's essay in so far as he makes use of E. T. A. Hoffmann's story 'The Sandman' as a prime example. An early reading of this essay (Prawer 1965) pronounced Hoffmann to be master of the uncanny compared with Freud's rendering of him. This is still endorsed, but with a difference: take Freud's performance in the essay overall and he is reinstated as Hoffmann's equal. There have been at least nine recent readings of Freud's essay, all showing in various ways the unmistakable imprint of Lacan and Derrida, some of which I shall be citing. The general view is that it would indeed be a mistake to let Freud's analysis of Hoffmann be the last word on the uncanny. What is interesting is precisely the inadequacy of his interpretation, and how this inadequacy has produced a whole series of after-effects. As was the case with the stories of Poe and James, Hoffmann's tale and Freud's essay is yet another 'case' of a transference-story *par excellence.*

The consensus of critical readings of Freud's essay has it that 'The uncanny' (1919) reveals the founder of psychoanalysis in the grip of a repetition-compulsion and there is a general eagerness to display the effects (for a reading which makes this the central issue, see Cixous 1976). On the one hand, it is argued, Freud's paradigm for the uncanny, E. T. A. Hoffmann's story 'The Sandman', becomes a prime example of the return of *repression*, because Freud edits out its uncanny potential. On the other hand, Freud's essay as a (w)hole is held up as a prime example of the return of the repressed, because what is left out of the story returns to haunt the essay. Here, then, there is a failure of theory in practice, in that Freud represses the uncanny in Hoffmann, yet allows it to appear in his own text. How does this come about?

The notion of the repetition-compulsion is at the centre of what is probably regarded as Freud's most controversial work, *Beyond the Pleasure Principle,* published in 1920, one year after 'The uncanny.' The compulsion to repeat was seen from the beginning as one of the commonest symptoms of neurotic behaviour, taking the form of obsessive rituals, recurring dreams, patterns of relationships, and manifesting itself, as has been shown throughout this book, at the level of transference. It was the need to find an explanation of such repetition phenomena 'beyond' the pleasure principle (because they were unpleasant) that led Freud to revise his earlier instinct theory and posit 'death instincts' in opposition to 'life instincts', for he could not deny the intensity, which he called 'daemonic', in such repetitions, which was closer to hate than to seeking after libidinal satisfaction (XXI, p. 119). The death instinct, arising from the organism's wish to return to a desireless stable state, can take the form of seeking to destroy, and in alliance with the sexual instincts (here associated with the life instincts), of a will to power, to sadistic or masochistic aggression (XIX, p. 163). The notion of a death instinct is not a comforting one, since it is a threat to the ego's narcissistic desire for omnipotence, and hence immortality, and yet, as it works in conjunction with the life instincts, it will keep desire circling round its (lost) object instead of becoming fixated on the self. It is this uncanny movement that critics have discerned in Hoffmann's and Freud's text.

Hoffmann's story is a complex narrative, beginning with three letters and continuing with a third-person narrator, who makes intermittent appeals to the reader. The plot concerns the fortunes of a student, named Nathanael, who is suffering from a haunting childhood memory, to do with a lawyer named Coppelius who used to come to the house on a mysterious errand, and whom the boy associated with the grim nursery tale of the 'Sandman', a bogey figure who threatens the eyes of children. Nathanael recalls how on one occasion he is caught spying and is manhandled and nearly blinded by Coppelius. The dreadful memory is revived by a visit from a seller of spectacles and telescopes, named Coppola, and by a figure associated with him, the Professor Spalanzani. Nathanael is caught between the desire for the latter's daughter, Olympia, and the girl to whom he is betrothed, Clara. Olympia turns out to be a mechanical doll and is torn to pieces before his eyes by the two men. A further incident, in which a variety of motifs combine, causes him to jump to his death.

In my retelling of the story I have deliberately dwelt on some features Freud left aside: the narrative complex and the repetition of violence. Freud's reading subordinates everything to a single thematic motif: the hero's fear of losing his eyes as equivalent to his fear of being deprived of his sexual organ. The threat of castration within the story is seen as actual. Nathanael is afraid of castration as a *real* event, believing that the dreaded figure of the Sandman has returned to punish his childish curiosity by robbing him of his eyes (penis). Freud notes a repetition: Coppelius (Sandman 1), Coppola (double of Sandman), and Spalanzani (double of double) arrive on the scene each time Nathanael is with a woman. The uncanny effect,

Freud argues, refuting the psychologist Jentsch, is only peripherally due to the blurring of life/not-life in the doll: there is 'no doubt' that the uncanny feeling 'is directly attached to the figure of the Sandman, that is, to the idea of being robbed of one's eyes' (XVII, p. 230).

Freud's essay is far too long and rambling for an adequate summary here (for an attempt to trace its peregrinations see Cixous 1976 and Weber 1973), but an outline may be appropriate. The essay is divided into three sections whose subject matter overlaps, so I will merely indicate its nodal points, letting Freud state his intended mode of procedure, which already contains his conclusion:

> Two courses are open to us at the outset. Either we can find out what meaning has come to be attached to the word 'uncanny' in the course of its history; or we can collect all those properties of persons, things, sense-impressions, experiences and situations which arouse in us the feeling of uncanniness, and then infer the unknown nature of the uncanny from what all these examples have in common. I will say at once that both courses lead to the same result: the uncanny is that class of the frightening which leads back to what is known of old and long familiar.
>
> (XVII, p. 220)

The first course involves tracing the connotations of the words *heimlich* and *unheimlich*. Here Freud finds that the distinction between them is not as exclusive as it may appear, but that the *heimlich* contains within itself a secret, in that the word signifies on the one hand the familiar and domestic, and on the other what is concealed and hidden, the two meanings coexisting: 'Thus *heimlich* is a word the meaning of which develops in the direction of ambivalence, until it finally coincides with its opposite, *unheimlich*' (p. 226). The second course involves taking a more tortuous path, one that branches out in two main directions. Freud is concerned with a close scrutiny of a variety of uncanny phenomena, and he proceeds by way of free association. In the first instance this leads to Hoffmann's 'Sandman', its uncanny effects – not so much the life-like doll, but the hero's fear of losing his eyes to the Sandman; the motif of the double as the primitive man's 'harbinger of death', the compulsion to repeat, the dread of the 'evil eye' as part of an animistic world view: 'the *unheimlich* is what was once *heimisch*, familiar; the prefix 'un' is the token of repression' (p. 245). The other direction Freud takes leads to the testing of this insight and the assuaging of a number of doubts, involving the role of repression in producing the uncanny. When do such bizarre motifs as dismembered limbs, being buried alive, death and the return of the dead, produce an uncanny effect and when do they not? And, at last, the crucial move from psychology to aesthetics, what is the distinction between the uncanny of immediate experience and the uncanny of fiction?

The core of the problem is the way the uncanny lies on that problematic boundary between fiction and reality which Freud has a positivistic leaning to keep firmly apart. It posed something of a problem for him when he found the 'primal scene' not to be a real event, but a retrospective interpretation (see 'From the history of an infantile neurosis', XVII), hence a fiction. He found the same principle to be in operation with the child's understanding of sexual difference, for only *nachträglich* did it infer that in the female there is a 'missing organ' to account for ('Some psychical consequences of the anatomical distinction between the sexes', XIX), another fiction. Freud's essay circles round the notion of the castration complex, which he sees as the source of the uncanny in Hoffmann's story. Having thus learnt that there is fiction in truth, as it were, Freud is bent on discovering the truth in fiction.

So what do the critics do with Freud? Again there is a certain critical consensus and it concerns both what Freud leaves out of Hoffmann's tale and what he leaves out of psychoanalysis. The two are related, for each is a consequence of the other. Freud's reading is neither an adequate literary reading nor an adequate psychoanalytic one. Hoffmann's story has a better account of the uncanny in it than the one Freud gives, both as regards literature and as regards psychoanalysis. But most interestingly, what Freud leaves out of Hoffmann transferentially strays into his long and rambling essay.

Freud's omissions regarding literature can be summarized as follows (some are particularly acutely argued for by Hertz 1979, within a Bloomian framework, and by Kittler 1977, within a Lacanian/Foucauldian one). Freud has ignored the narrative strategies and textual devices employed (consciously/unconsciously) by Hoffmann. 'The Sandman' is in fact remarkable for the way it can be made paradigmatically to illustrate what psychoanalysis has to do with text structure. The return of the repressed works at the level of narration, plot and figuration. First, as regards narration, there is a narrator, not mentioned by Freud, who speaks of his desire and implicates both reader, author and character: not only the narrator, but also the hero has trouble in beginning. The way the story – finally – begins is via a 'feint in the direction of epistolary fiction', three letters whose 'real'/'fictitious' status is cunningly deployed by Hoffmann (Hertz 1979, p. 306), and totally ignored by Freud. Second, as regards plot, the story does not enact the return of the repressed solely in the figure of the Sandman. What is repeated is not only a content but a structure, a structure of delay, and what is delayed is death. This is the function of the repeated and different scenes of dismemberment, the unscrewing and re-screwing of the child Nathanael's limbs in the spying scene, the violent death of the father, the tearing apart of the doll, Nathanael's brains dashed out on the pavement. The plot thus performs a detour to death. Third, as regards figuration, this is perhaps the level at which the effect of the uncanny is most clearly perceived (for a brilliant analysis, on which I am here drawing, see Hertz 1979). To restore colour to fading images is to invest with desire. Both the narrator and Nathanael have trouble in describing the brilliant colours of their inner vision and feel impelled to add ever more colour to the narrative, to keep alive the images which torment them (and by further extension the reader), to stop them from fading, to play and replay the compulsive fantasy. Hence the images of glowing grains of coal, dazzling eye-glasses, blood-red rays, bleeding eyes, warm glances, soul-scorching words. Such figures of repetition (disregarded by Freud) are at their most uncanny when they are seen as '*merely* colouring, that is, when it comes to seem most gratuitously rhetorical' (Hertz 1979, p. 301), for at that moment one does not know what it is that is doing the turning.

But Freud's sins do not end here, for there are also his omissions as regards psychoanalysis. In his insistence on the equation of eyes and penis he has coloured everything with the fear of literal castration, the loss of the male sexual organ: it is 'the violent and obscure emotion' excited 'by the threat of being castrated' that 'gives the idea of losing other organs its intense colouring' (XVII, p. 231). He thereby overlooks the point that eyes are the most powerful organs of desire and ignores the relation between perception and desire, in particular that moment when the child 'perceives' what the mother 'lacks' (Weber 1973). The eye, therefore, takes on a special significance because it bears such a threat to desire, both for its role in this discovery and as an organ of perception, itself part of the satisfaction of desire. Loss of eyes becomes a metaphor for the dismembering of the self-image and subsequent loss of identity. Any adequate psychoanalytic reading would thus have to account not only for the return of the repressed in the form of the Sandman as Oedipal Father, but also in the form of Clara (and Olympia) as objects of desire which fail the hero, both in their own right (Clara refuses Nathanael's suffering, his 'text' – his poem; Olympia turns out to be an automaton), and by dint of his own blinded narcissism. The theory of narcissism, as one critic notes, is uncannily relegated by Freud to the status of three footnotes (Rubin 1982). In his reading Freud leaves out, represses, everything that Hoffmann allows to emerge, above all that which is a blow to narcissism. Hence the motif of Olympia as uncanny double is reduced to 'Nathanael's feminine attitude towards his father' (XVII, p. 232), or to an anthropological curiosity (alluding to Otto Rank). The double, once a comforting spare soul, became, at a later stage of civilization, 'a thing of terror' (p. 236). Freud makes no mention of the repeated images of death. He tries to re-automatize the uncanny, where Hoffmann de-automatizes it by letting death return (Meltzer 1982).

Freud produces an explanation for the uncanny in *experience*, as a resurgence of an infantile complex, or as a reviving of an animistic mode of perception, or both, but he has none for the uncanny in *fiction*. Fiction has more resources of the uncanny, but I was the first to explain it, says Freud, without saying it. What he has left out has returned as a supplement in his own text. Freud, in his essay, has 'disseminated' castration, in an infinite play of substitution (Derrida 1982, p. 268), by borrowing fiction – Hoffmann's story, plus a variety of literary examples and allusions – knowing (fearing) that there were supplementary resources to be found there, that fiction is required as a supplement to life. As he spins out his own narrative he seems to need more and more fiction in order to keep the uncanny off, perhaps hoping, like that archetypal storyteller Scheherazade, that death may be indefinitely postponed. In the course of his narration, however, Freud displays the very things he left out of Hoffmann's text: images of death and dismemberment, anxiety regarding priority (like the narrator in Hoffmann, who wants to be 'original'), the unbinding operations of the primary process. Death, the final castration, the uncanniest thing of all, can only return in fiction.

But it is castration that makes possible the play of substitution: though the Father says 'no' to desire, the unconscious can get by. Thus, paradoxically, ambivalently, the failure of the object is both a blow to narcissism – a re-experience of primal lack – and a sign that the old rule for defining that object cannot hold and a new one must be substituted. Both objects and human desires undergo change. What Jean-François Lyotard calls the 'unpresentable' makes a sudden emergence out of the 'artifices' of the old objectifications, putting them in question; something is 'happening' which defies representation and conceptualization but which is unmistakably present nevertheless (Lyotard 1983, p. 338; and also lecture at Cambridge, 'The sublime and the avant-garde', 12 March 1984). The experience of the uncanny is an unconscious realization that such a change has come about. The breaking of existing categorizations can take the form of a disturbing fixity in behaviour and perception, repetitions obsessively held to, that evince their purposelessness, their irrelevance to desire. Bergson has noted how we are amused by self-defeating automatisms in another's behaviour. The winding-up of the doll Olympia in Hoffmann's story becomes comic by its clear metaphorical designation of that very source of the comic – that the subject is no longer guided by his own desires. The old mode of behaviour (what Freud calls the feminine attitude to the father) is no longer workable as a self-image, yet rigidly adhered to, out of fear. In literature, uncanny automata, mechanical dolls, machines out of control, become powerful metaphors for this inability to adjust one's objectifications or else for the rigidity of the existing order. The uncanny is the illusory aspect of all objects brought home to us:

we cannot rely upon them as leading to the satisfaction of desire. The surrealists took the failure of the category as a central theme of their manifestos. Surrealist art specializes in the uncanny object, the watch that melts (Dali), the pipe that proclaims 'Ceci n'est pas une pipe' (Magritte). The uncanny object brings home to us that all objects are in some sense 'transitional objects' (Winnicott), or in Klein's sense, 'good' and 'bad' at once, involving a sudden shift of desire.

Literature and the arts can present us with forms of the uncanny that life cannot, because the writer/artist has more access to illusion. He can contextualize as he wishes, choose whatever frame he likes (Magritte), discuss illusion (Hoffmann). Whereas in life one is at the mercy of repetition (the repeated detour to the brothel Freud relates in 'The uncanny'), the artist can play with the repressed. It is here that the uncanny rejoins the joke. Both the trickster and the artist can 'turn' the listener/reader and make her participate in a shift of desire. The result can be the changing of the old categorizations: the text may be reinterpreted, the painting reframed, the poem re-written, indefinitely.

The uncanny and the joke have here been dealt with at length because they throw more light on literature and the arts than Freud's avowed positivist researches into the subject. Investigation of the uncanny has shown once again how a marginal term (something on the borders of aesthetics and psychology) can reveal itself as a special example of what is most general.

Bloom and the return of the author

> I offer a special case of the anxiety of influence as a variety of the uncanny. A man's unconscious fear of castration manifests itself as an apparently physical trouble in his eyes; a poet's fear of ceasing to be a poet frequently manifests itself also as a trouble of his vision.
>
> (Bloom 1975, pp. 77–8)

The anxiety of influence is Harold Bloom's version of the return of the repressed. In the context of post-structuralist theory it also marks the return of the author, who, in 1968, was declared to be dead by Barthes (see Barthes 1977). The author has risen from the dead and demands recognition, but his demand is made from the site of the poem itself and is addressed only to the elect: that is to say, a chosen poet/critic feels himself overcome by 'election-love' (Hebrew '*ahabah*; Bloom 1980, p. 51), as if a divine gift was bestowed on him. The gift turns into a powerful fixation, which Bloom sees as analogous to the Freudian moment of primal repression: the unconscious of the young poet ('ephebe') becomes imprinted by that of the poetic father-figure ('precursor'). This sets off an intertextual rivalry, which is the Bloomian version of transference, implicating both poet and critic. Not only does the ephebe (mis)read the precursor but the critic (mis)reads the ephebe–precursor relationship. (I shall be developing Bloom's concept of 'misreading'.) Criticism is thus what Bloom calls 'a rhetoric of rhetoric', a double misreading.

The challenge of a newcomer to the work of an established poet takes essentially the form of a turning of his meaning, a troping. This arises from the newcomer's reactions of defence against the strong paternal assertion, for each major trope identified by classical rhetoric can be matched, according to Bloom, with certain psychic defences (taken from Anna Freud's catalogue; Anna Freud 1966). If one maps Bloom's theory on a deconstructive reading of 'The uncanny', one can observe the end-process of what a later poet does to an earlier one. Freud is rated by Bloom as 'the strongest of the poets' (Bloom 1982, p. 144). The readings I discussed in the previous section saw Freud under Hoffmann's spell, suffering anxiety as regards death-as-castration. In Bloom's terms this would translate into a threat to his poetic strength and his priority. The final stage in which the anxiety of influence makes a newcomer into a 'strong' poet is marked by the moment when the precursor's image-structure appears uncannily in the newcomer's poem, as if it were now his. It is uncanny, because early and late have become reversed (the trope of *metalepsis*, in Latin 'transumption'). The defence mechanisms put in play are introjection (of the precursor's images) and projection (their reappearance as the newcomer's). The resultant 'revisionary ratio' (the changed relation between precursor and newcomer) is given the name *apophrades*, the return of the dead (1980, pp. 101–3; for a full and remarkably clear account of Bloom's map of 'misprision' – six defences, corresponding to six tropes, combined into six 'revisionary ratios', and finally paired into three 'poetic crossings' – see Leitch 1983).

The uncanny return of the precursor makes the latecomer seem to be the true author. It has been noted that 'Freud has hardly anything to envy in Hoffmann for his "art" or "craftiness" in provoking the *Unheimliche* effect' (Cixous 1976, p. 547). By the strength of his poetic will Freud has thus triumphed over time and death, for he has successfully troped against the precursor's id. According to Bloom, 'tropes are necessary errors about language, defending ultimately against the deathly dangers of literal meaning' (Bloom 1975, p. 94). Literal meaning is death because the movement of desire has been stopped. One might say that Goethe's Faust could only join the angels by a swerving away from literal meaning (the use of a subjunctive instead of an indicative). He got to heaven by turning a meaning, thus troping (tricking) his way to immortality, at the same time allowing Goethe to swerve from tragedy via a good joke.

Bloom reads Freud 'antithetically', that is as one strong poet reads another strong poet, against the establishment. According to Bloom's theory of misreading, this means reading him through his precursors as *Bloom* sees them, through Goethe, Shakespeare and Schopenhauer, etc., and not through Charcot, Janet, Helmholtz, etc., as Freud might fancy, or through Hegel, Nietzsche and Heidegger, as Lacan chooses to (Bloom 1982, p. 91). Since misreading is essentially *reading-through*, the result will always depend on the mediating influence. Hence my reading of Freud's reading of Hoffmann through Bloom is not the same thing as Bloom's reading of Freud's reading of Hoffmann through Goethe, Shakespeare and Schopenhauer.

So what does the antithetical Freud look like? Bloom claims that in the essay 'The uncanny' (from which it seems impossible to get away) Freud stumbled upon a psychology of the Sublime. But he only stumbles, because he can only see the dire aspect of the uncanny. He thereby chooses to ignore a well-established philosophical tradition of what Bloom calls the 'negative Sublime'. The classical emphasis on rule and order was gradually overtaken by the ascribing of the loftiest value to great feeling, instead of great thoughts. This allowed for feelings of terror to mingle with awe, via a narcissistic illusion of omnipotence.

Freud himself succumbed to the negative Sublime and was trapped in its illusion of control, 'the pride of an originator who could say "I invented psychoanalysis because it had no literature", or even more ironically: "I am not fond of reading"' (pp. 206–7). Freud's 'strong' reading of 'The Sandman,' Bloom argues, consists precisely of such a misreading of the Sublime, because he reduces the uncanny to an infantile and archaic complex. This makes him blind to the mode whereby the canny turns into the uncanny, that is by an act of the poetic will. I take it that he means that Hoffmann figures excessively to hide the repressed, namely the return of death. It is the not-naming that counts, and which results in what Bloom in another context calls an overdetermination of language and an underdetermination of meaning. Freud repeats this configuration in transference to Hoffmann: the figural is a defence against death. The Sublime, as Bloom will argue, is the overcoming of the catastrophe of death, or rather of being born into death.

Bloom's Freud is thus very much the literary Freud. Bloom makes 'The uncanny' the occasion to link a group of Freud's metapsychological texts, concerned with the concept of defence, in order to argue for a 'catastrophe theory' of the imagination ('Freud and the Sublime', in Bloom 1982). These texts are for Bloom essentially about what happens when a poet/self (Bloom operates with selves rather than subjects) arrives on the scene, only to find his place already taken, the poem already written. He can only snatch victory from defeat by rising sublimely to the occasion. *Beyond the Pleasure Principle* overcomes the catastrophe of a drive that aims at death. 'On narcissism' overcomes the catastrophe of falling in love with the self. 'Negation' allows repressed images to get through by means of a misconstrual. *Inhibitions, Symptoms and Anxiety* provides a panoply of psychic defences, a veritable rhetoric for the psyche to defend itself against anxiety. 'Analysis terminable and interminable' provides the anxiety that leads to 'enabling fictions' (p. 115). Bloom does not forget the body: anxiety is unpleasure. Giving birth to poems is to relive the primal anxiety. Repression produces the rhetorical strategies for overcoming anxiety and is thus the necessary condition for producing poetry. The Sublime is the outcome of repression, not of sublimation, because the energies are sexual and have not lost their desire-quality: the canny imagination produces poems.

It produces in particular what Bloom believes to be the dominant lyric form of what he grandly calls 'post-Enlightenment literature': the 'High Romantic Crisis-poem' celebrates the triumph of the poetic will. For Bloom it marks not only the birth of an individual poet, but also that of a poetic genre. It seems as if the Romantics had to overcome the rules of their neo-classical Fathers to follow (Mother) nature, the point being that they do *not* follow nature, and hence one might also see it, as Bloom does not, as a rebellion against the Mother. For Bloom, poets after Milton have to be 'strong' to fight against the tradition, competing against one another, instead of labouring in the service of representation. Inspiration no longer comes from nature but from another poet. For instance, Bloom cites four lines from *The Auroras of Autumn* by Wallace Stevens, one of his strongest poets:

> Out of the window,
> I saw how the planets gathered
> Like the leaves themselves
> Turning in the wind,

and comments, 'Stevens, out of his window, sees his own (and Shelley's) trope; the gathering planets are *like* the leaves turning in the wind. This giant perspectivizing shrinks the cosmos to one autumnal metaphor' (Bloom 1977, pp. 378–9). Poets/selves when they look out of the window do not engage in a pure act of seeing: what the poet sees is his own trope and that of another's. The view is obscured by representation itself, as in Magritte's picture, *The Human Condition*, where a canvas carrying the outside landscape obscures the view from inside.

According to Bloom, the meaning of a poem is another poem. 'The freedom to have a meaning of one's own ... is wholly illusory' (Bloom 1979, p. 3). It is an illusion to be achieved against a prior plenitude of meaning, a meaning already 'authorized' by another. There is no benign play here: enter the 'bad-enough-child', not catered for in D. W. Winnicott's system, the poet-son who takes up a 'strong' stance in a space not so 'potential', a battleground already occupied, where a space for the imagination has to be cleared perforce. Since for Bloom poems are relational events, since his intertextual theory of poetry is so clearly object-relational, depending as it does on feats of introjection and projection, it is odd that he seems not to have made any reference to the British object-relations theorists. He is a great converser with other critics/analysts, and in the essay on Freud discussed he holds converse with Derrida, Lacan, Laplanche, Anna Freud, Jung, Rank, Wollheim and Norman O. Brown, to cite just a few, but there is no mention of Winnicott or Klein. It is ironical that Bloom gives Anna Freud a key place in his canon, dedicated as her work is to unquestioned ideals of maturity, while Melanie Klein, with her feeling for the wayward and aberrant, is ignored. It is true that there are marked differences from Bloom, suggestive in themselves. Where Klein's reparation springs from a capacity to mourn, for Bloom the creative will is precisely the refusal to mourn. Yet the 'revisionary ratios' and 'poetic crossings' of the Bloomian ephebe look uncannily like the 'agonistic' movements (to borrow a term from Bloom) of the pre-oedipal Kleinian infant. Klein is herself a strong reader of Freud and merits a strong reading in turn. But perhaps this is already what has happened, since such readings can take effect without the reader's awareness. For the Mother has been displaced by the Father: the progenitors of the infant/ephebe have been shuffled. Bloom, with undaunted mettle, brings forth men-children only.

So where does Bloom finally stand in terms of theory in practice? He has provided a virtuoso critical practice which is workable and which makes room for the critic as brother-poet. This practice gives access to the tradition in renewed form, for it is to be won, in the Faustian sense, by effort and struggle. Most ingeniously, there is always an author-in-crisis, belated, wounded and mortal, and there is always a prior plenitude of meaning to struggle against. Thus the author returns, but with a difference. Bloom has brilliantly wedded the old orthodoxy with the new: there is a typology, but its archetypes are unstable; there is textuality, but it is the doing of persons, and not only that of the random effects of language; there is an author, but he is a pseudo-author; there is a myth, but it is grounded in psychology.

Yet there is something oddly self-validating about his practice: nothing is ever produced to upset the theory. Bloom adopts terms like 'post-Enlightenment' and 'Romantic Crisis-poem' without question. The crisis-poem takes for granted a unique self, always there, however divided, ready for a crisis, to turn into a strong or weak poet. Though it is a general truth that the meanings of a person in power can be subverted by someone without power, Bloom writes as if his poet–poet confrontation were *sui generis*. But the confrontation is not merely that of the defensive tropings of one set of isolated individuals against another: there are societies/cultures/histories involved. The firm presupposition of a-historical single selves, with their past crystallized around them, makes Bloom's critical practice self-validating in a trivial way, for he thereby keeps out meanings that cannot be directly lodged upon these selves. It is the institution itself which calls for an antithetical reading, including the institution of psychoanalysis, and it is to such a reading that I now finally turn.

PART IV

9

Psychoanalysis and ideology: focus on the unconscious and society

Psychoanalysis as a discourse: sexuality and power

To speak of psychoanalysis as a discourse is to dispose of two contradictory assumptions: that it has sprung up as the fruits of genius at a particular moment in the history of the human sciences, or, as is still asserted, that it emerged in response to the specific needs of neurotic ladies in Vienna at the turn of the century. Both assumptions merely situate psychoanalysis in the domain of cultural history, whereas to call it a discourse is to situate it in a field which questions the very concept of history as traditionally defined.

Michel Foucault, historian of thought, has been writing since the 1960s on the subject of history as a discourse. By that, he means history as a set of linguistic practices which generate social and cultural activity, governed by rules that are unformulated and characteristically unrecognized by the speakers concerned. Thus rules of exclusion operate which keep out unqualified persons in fields such as law and medicine, and define what is to be considered irrelevant and unmentionable. Such activity is largely unconscious, creating what Foucault calls an 'archive', a kind of cultural unconscious to be sharply distinguished from the archetypal kind (Jung), since it is characterized by being subject to constant flux and change, to discontinuity rather than continuity. Certain forces of constraint will shape what is to serve as fact and truth in any particular discourse and what methods can be used to display them.

What keeps knowledge moving is the 'will to power' in the public arena of history. Foucault uncovers strategies of power within a discourse in order to show that power is inescapable because it is inextricably combined with the will to knowledge. Power, therefore, is not to be seen as simply oppressive, for it always has a double effect: it is bad in so far as it constrains both those at the top and those at the bottom in frozen gestures of domination and submission, but because this inevitably leads to counter-strategies of evasion and subversion it cannot help but also be productive:

> For, if it is true that at the heart of power relations and as a permanent condition of their existence there is an insubordination and a certain essential obstinacy on the part of the principles of freedom, then there is no relationship of power without the means of escape or possible flight. Every power relationship implies, at least in potential, a strategy of struggle, in which the two forces are not superimposed, do not lose their specific nature, do not finally become confused. Each constitutes for the other a kind of permanent limit, a point of possible reversal.
>
> (Foucault 1982, p. 225)

Since every will to power cannot but meet with opposition from other wills oppression must perforce open channels for its own subversion.

Psychoanalysis is a discourse of power which Foucault sees as having produced knowledge of both a general and specific nature. In this he provides ammunition for radical critics of psychoanalytic practice, such as Deleuze and Guattari, whose critique of society and textual criticism is to be considered next. As regards the general contribution made by psychoanalysis, he sees it as a master-science, in marked contrast to those who refuse to give it the status of a science at all:

> Psychoanalysis stands as close as possible, in fact, to that critical function which, as we have seen, exists within all human sciences. In setting itself the task of making the discourse of the unconscious speak through consciousness, psychoanalysis is advancing in the direction of that fun-

damental region in which the relations of representation and finitude come into play.

(Foucault 1974, p. 374)

Through challenging the very nature of representation, in revealing the unconscious elements within it, psychoanalysis calls all discourses into question. But this does not mean that it is itself immune to cross-questioning. With regard to its specific contribution, psychoanalysis has revealed the central importance of sexuality at a particular moment in western culture. In *The History of Sexuality* (1981) Foucault sets out to investigate why, since the Renaissance, sexuality has moved towards becoming the sole indicator of selfhood, how it has come to dominate not only discourses but institutions and practices. As an instance he cites the promotion of a 'children's sexuality' at a moment when family power was in decline and needed shoring up by giving the family special rights over the body and soul of its progeny. This then became the cue for the state professions to step in and offer their expert help, and thus began the age of psychiatry and the 'surveillance' of the body. The point Foucault wishes to make is that the resultant power-relations were not simply repressive but led to new knowledge via confession and self-revelation. From this it became obvious that knowing the body leads to a sensualization of power. Watching the forbidden creates pleasure, precisely the kind of prurience which D. H. Lawrence objected to, and which he saw as wholly negative. As will be seen in Deleuze and Guattari's account of Kafka, literature can be made to attest to the *productiveness* of this kind of perverse pleasure, in that power will thereby be disseminated, put into disarray, and not reinforced, as Lawrence would have it.

Foucault's position is counter to all those post-Freudian idealist sexologists, Wilhelm Reich, Herbert Marcuse, Norman O. Brown, who believe in the liberation of the body and the emergence of a true sexuality, away from the unnecessary repression exacted by a capitalist society, which forces its members to make work rather than love. For Foucault 'the good genius of Freud' has located sex as a strategy of power and knowledge at a critical moment in history (Foucault 1981, p. 159). The discourse of psychoanalysis is the modern form of the confessional: sexuality has become the secret which leads to the truth of man's being, a truth not on the side of freedom, but on that of power, the authority installed in the psyche. Deleuze and Guattari will turn from psychoanalysis as a discourse of power to schizoanalysis as a liberation of desire.

Deleuze and Guattari: schizoanalysis and Kafka

Gilles Deleuze, a philosopher, and Félix Guattari, a radical analyst who has been opposing orthodox psychiatry since the 1950s, are considerably less appreciative of Freud and psychoanalysis, although their enterprise is unthinkable outside that framework. They are a godsend to the critic surveying the scene of psychoanalysis and literature, who is engaged in anticipating objections from all sides. In exploding the whole oedipal apparatus they cater for a sizeable group of readers, but at the same time they give new fuel to the psychoanalytic critical enterprise because they are pouring new wine into old bottles. The 'schizoanalysis' of texts, as the example of Kafka will show, actually provides a *method* (even if this is not centrally relevant to their purpose), a textual critical practice which pays close attention to images and motifs, and which, unlike the New Criticism, gives the author a properly delimited place, one functionally related to the system of literary discourse as a whole (see Foucault 1980b, 'What is an author?').

'Schizoanalysis' is a mode of analysis which refuses the idea of an 'oedipalized' unconscious. For Deleuze and Guattari the process of 'free association', whereby a patient undertakes to speak whatever comes to mind, is an example of chaining desire to representations already singled out before desire ever had a chance to get going. The oedipal prohibitions are the very means by which desire is channelled towards the prohibited: 'The law tells us: You will not marry your mother and you will not kill your father. And we docile subjects say to ourselves: so *that's* what I wanted!' (Deleuze and Guattari 1977a, p. 114). They differ from the movement of anti-psychiatry as represented by Laing and his co-workers in not believing that there is a unitary and wholesome self that would emerge if only the narrow family network, together with a society which is seen as no more than an extension of the family, did not deform and distort it.

Anti-Oedipus: Capitalism and Schizophrenia (1977a) is a rebellion against psychoanalysis for presenting desire as rooted in lack. This is seen as a capitalist ploy, because the unconscious is being forced into a position where desire is characterized by insufficiency and hunger. Psychoanalysis has deformed the unconscious. Even though it is not to be held responsible for inventing the Oedipus complex, 'it merely provides the latter a last territoriality, the couch, and a last Law, the analyst as despot and money collector' (p. 269). Schizoanalysis *constructs* an unconscious, sees libido as still fluid, able to be directed into new channels, not already stabilized according to oedipal con-straints. Deleuze and Guattari are not interested in a sexual liberation of any particular group, but in a general liberation of desire. Desire is a 'flow' (of libido) prior to representation and production. What has been 'territorialized' into Nation, Fam-ily, Church, School, Party, can be 'deterritorialized'. They maintain that, instead of there being these unifying totalities outside the body and a unique autonomous self within, 'the unconscious is an orphan' (p. 49). It is not bound to any particular social definition, but is produced in the body as an inescapable part of man within nature, needing the support of other bodies, equally partial.

Deleuze and Guattari postulate a material flow, a *hylé* as they term it (p. 36) – the Greek for a basic world-stuff – which the machines of the body cut into and divide up into partial objects. The unconscious is that part of the flux which escapes the sign-system. Hence their term 'partial objects' to stress that this system need not 'naturally' lead to whole objects. There is a pre-linguistic experience, which they regard as crucial; in this they differ from Lacan for whom the unconscious does not exist before language. For them, as for others discussed in this book (Lawrence, Ehrenzweig, Kristeva), desire is present from the beginning, whereas for Lacan there is a level of physiological need which pre-exists desire. They concede the need of a primal repression, without which an entry into the 'socius' (their term for the community) would be impossible, but turn the full force of their attack upon the secondary repression, the preconscious investment of the libidinal flow that the capitalist world, via the shrunken oedipal family, has imposed upon its children. They praise Melanie Klein 'for the marvellous discovery of partial objects, that world of explosions, rotations, vibrations' (p. 44), but make a vital distinction. What Klein saw as an early oedipal pattern they see as obtaining prior to 'oedipalization': the parts are not fantasies derived from global persons but genuine productions, testifying to 'the absolutely *anoedipal* nature of the production of desire' (p. 45). The Kleinian unconscious is closer to the social nature of desire, whereas the Freudian unconscious is a capitalist construction, an internalized set of power-relations, the result of repression produced for capitalism by the family. Deleuze and Guattari believe that psychoanalysis aids and abets this process. As already mentioned (see p. 83) they comment on the case-history of the psychotic child 'Dick': 'The psychoanalyst no longer says to the patient: "Tell me a little bit about your desiring-machines, won't you?" Instead he screams: "Answer daddy-and-mommy when I speak to you!" Even Melanie Klein' (ibid.).

Bodies are 'desiring-machines, because machines arrange and connect flows, and do not recognize distinctions between a person's organs, material flows, and semiotic flows'. According to Deleuze and Guattari, unconscious desire tends to one or the other of two poles, a schizophrenic one or a paranoiac one. The former is characterized by multiplicity, proliferation, becoming, flowing, a breaking of boundaries, and is constituted by partial objects, fragments of experience, memory and feeling, linked in chance and unexpected ways. The latter is marked by its unifying procedures, its search for order, similarity, wholeness, assuming identity and completeness of objects and selves within conforming constraints and recognized limits. At the schizophrenic pole there is a 'deterritorializing' tendency, shifting boundaries, transforming identities, ignoring the familiarly specified. At the paranoiac pole there is an incessant pressure to 'territorialize', to mark out and maintain the directions of desire. Deleuze and Guattari's 'material psychiatry' becomes a political factor in the active undermining of such territorializing.

There is, however, a problem concerning their project as a whole. Whereas Foucault sees psychoanalysis as a discourse of power which brings in the beneficial side-effects of more knowledge, Deleuze and Guattari see it as entirely harmful. They fully acknowledge the presence of oedipal repression, but they stress that in all cases it is possible and needful to get away from it. They rely upon the concept of the 'schizo' as part of their attack upon the system, for they wish to prove (unlike Laing) that it is not the case that society has driven him 'mad', but instead that he has miraculously escaped the effects of the bourgeois repression-by-signifier and may therefore be held up as representative of a potentially desirable and natural human condition. Instead of Freud's distinction between neurotic/normal and psychotic/mad they distinguish between schizo/normal and paranoiac/mad. Both sets of terms equally belong to a discourse of sanity and madness, precisely what their politics of desire would seem to want to deconstruct. To point to a negative of a hated positive as an escape is still to be bound to the patterns supposedly false (see Rajchman on this issue, 1977, pp. 54–5).

So where does literature come into all this? Literature is like schizophrenia in that it breaks out of the system: 'an author is great because he cannot prevent himself from tracing flows and causing them to circulate, flows that split asunder the catholic and despotic signifier of his work, and that necessarily nourish a revolutionary machine on the horizon' (Deleuze and Guattari 1977a, p. 133). But the author cannot do it without some help. So now yet another type of reader is required, the desire-liberating reader, the schizoanalyst, whose task it is to convert the text into a desiring-machine, or better still, into a revolutionary machine. For Deleuze and Guattari the work of Franz Kafka particularly lends itself to such an enterprise:

> Kafka's machine plugs desire into the premonition of a perverse bureaucratic and technocratic machine, a machine that is already fascist, in which the names of the family lose their consistency in order to open onto the motley Austrian Empire of the machine-castle, onto the condition of Jews without identity, onto Russia, America, China, continents situated well beyond the persons and the names of familialism.
>
> (1977b, p. 123)

Their study is entitled *Kafka: Pour une littérature mineure* (1975; page references are to the German translation, 1976). Deleuze and Guattari are not using the term 'minor literature' in its accepted sense, that of relatively unimportant works. For them it means the literature of a minority which must needs use the language of a majority from which it feels alienated. There are three characteristics: the 'minor' writer will use words of the 'major' language in 'deterritorialized' ways, shifting meanings across customary boundaries. The individual case presented in 'major' literature, in particular the familial triangle, is directly connected to and determined by political events outside; it will become the expression of alternative possibilities, new ways of viewing communal life. Contrast this with 'A dissenting opinion on Kafka' (Edmund Wilson) from the 1950s (just after the defeat of an oppressive regime, that of the Nazis), which places him as minor in a pejorative sense, seeing both him and his characters as nothing but victims:

> The denationalized, discouraged, disaffected, disabled Kafka, though for the moment he may frighten or amuse us, can in the end only let us down. He is quite true to his time and place, but it is surely a time and place in which few of us will want to linger – whether as stunned and hypnotized helots of totalitarian states or as citizens of freer societies, who have relapsed into taking Kafka's stories as evidence that God's law and man's purpose are conceived in terms so different that we may as well give up hope of ever identifying the one with the other.
>
> (Wilson 1962, p. 96; orig. publ. 1950)

Deleuze and Guattari's schizoanalytic project actively opposes such a critical assumption. They reject the whole idea of the domination of a 'subjugated group' via a group-fantasy, myths and propaganda of all kinds. The work of the unconscious endeavours to ensure that the fantasy of subjugation (the ideology that has kept desire under constraint) is transformed into one of revolutionary potential for a 'subject-group' (the power to liberate those so oppressed). For them Kafka's text performs this operation by showing how desire exists simultaneously in two forms of the law, a 'paranoiac transcendental law' (the oedipal system) whose action is to mark out and rigidify into separable and recognizable units, and an 'immanent schizo-law' (the rightful demands of the unconscious), which loosens what has been made rigid, erases the marks, and discovers what has been left undefined. Both forms are co-present in Kafka, but what Deleuze and Guattari are bent on demonstrating is how at every point the schizo-law disassembles the paranoiac law, how writing breaks up the codes of language. They engage in a virtuoso textual and scholarly performance which contrasts oddly with their revolutionary enterprise, but which provides new access to Kafka as a writer, particularly as a comic writer, often acknowledged, but never adequately demonstrated.

The two states of law present in the text correspond to two states of desire. One law channels desire into the production goals of the capitalist system: the Oedipus complex ensures that the law gets inside the subject and sets up a paranoiac structure of competition. This law is 'transcendental' because the interdiction seems to be coming from some ideal source outside the self. But this law is constantly undermined: for every assembling of the fascist machine, the political machine, the bureaucratic machine, a simultaneous disassembling goes on via the operations of an anti-law, which subverts the repressive representations from within the system, hence an 'immanent' law. According to Deleuze and Guattari, Kafka's work is a 'rhizome' (Deleuze and Guattari 1976, p. 7), a favourite image of theirs: a fertile tuber that sprouts a dozen unexpected plants out of concealment. Thus certain elements found together in Kafka's work enact a constant dialectic of repression and expression of desire, but these elements are not in any simple binary opposition because they constantly combine and recombine with others. Typically, there is a kind of submission ritual which finds every possible way to get itself represented. Its favoured representations are the bowed head and the framed photograph. The two together have the effect of neutralizing and blocking desire. The framed forbidden photo that one may not touch, may not love, that can only satisfy desire through the look, and the head kept down by means of roof or ceiling, together function as images of repression. This effect is reversed by a set of counter-images, a general raising of limbs and eyes, of objects raised high (spires and turrets), accompanied by the random sounds of music, all of which function as images of the lifting of repression. Deleuze and Guattari are far from wishing to practise yet another form of image criticism; what they are after is the recapturing of pre-linguistic experience, unconscious investments of the sensory field (sounds and sights), which stimulate resistance to repression, liberating desire (1976, chapter 1, 'Content and expression').

Whereas childhood memory is 'hopelessly oedipal', reterritorializing by constantly saying 'father!' and 'mother!', the deterritorializing is done by what Deleuze and Guattari call 'blocks of childhood', pointing to a field of unbounded sexual and social activity, play with sisters, friends and all kinds of companions. These memories, 'higher intensities' not bound by the oedipal experience, make no distinction between the child and the adult. Deleuze and Guattari cite an incident in *The Castle*, where men are sitting in washtubs, splashing among the suds, while solemn-eyed children look on or, an unpleasant converse, a scene in *The Trial*, where two warders are beaten, an event conceived in a manner and tone (the men react with child-like pain and fear) which suggest that children are being punished. These 'affectations' (*maniérismes*), as Deleuze and Guattari call them, are to be seen as a hallmark of Kafka's style, for with this 'childhood affectation' goes another, a 'politeness affectation', for instance the excessive politeness and worldliness of the two carefully cleansed and exquisitely dressed executioners who collect and prepare Joseph K. for his end. The first affectation reflects an endeavour to return to the free sensuous experience of childhood in the 'flows' of the soapy water. The second affectation is a false representation of an authority which seems intent on the well-being of those in its power while exercising that power in its ultimate form: the executioners, for example, walk Joseph K. up and down to keep him warm, then place a stone under his head for comfort.

> Together they constitute – as two poles of affectation – the schizo-clownishness so typical of Kafka. The schizophrenic is well-acquainted with both, it is his mode of deterritorializing society's given. Kafka has utilized them – or so it seems to us – in a most admirable way, in his life as in his art: the machinic art of the marionette.
>
> (chapter 8, 'Blocks, series, intensities', p. 111)

The clown represents the fearful authority in a comic manner by caricaturing its apparent ceremonious concern for the private wish.

Deleuze and Guattari are intent upon showing that unconscious investment of desire in the social field, the so-called 'higher intensities', have primacy over narrow familial investments of desire, made in the name of Oedipus. All desire is first and foremost social production. Throughout *Anti-Oedipus* they argue that, before sexuality has gone through the process of secondary repression, it is all a flow of unbound libido, 'a body without organs' (they quote Artaud). The 'body without organs' means that the body has not yet been subjected to limiting definitions of its parts; it has not yet been transformed into a single unit within a state-system, accepting its castration. Marxism and psychoanalysis have both made the same discovery of the pattern of production that has emerged in capitalism, but Marxism ignores desire while Freudianism has hampered the class struggle in chaining desire to the family. Kafka's work is revolutionary for Deleuze and Guattari, because their schizoanalysis reveals the unconscious investments of desire as more powerful than those induced by the state-system. That is to say, desire is not tied to a particular representation of power: bodies and objects are constantly on the move, thwarting capitalism in its efforts to maintain its representations. Desire refuses a final embodiment in a particular power-machine; it will always find a way out (*Ausweg* – a key word in Kafka's writings).

Kafka's way out is to write. The letters, stories and novels articulate this theme in three distinct ways. In the famous letter to his father Kafka abjures Oedipus by projecting an absurd father-image into the world at large, for his 'writing-machine' constantly converts the familial triangles into an infinitude of legal, economic, bureaucratic and political triangles, turning the threatening into the comic.

In his stories he stages a transformation process in parallel, a double flight. On the one hand there is the becoming-beetle, -ape, -mouse, anything rather than becoming-bureaucrat, -policeman or -judge. On the other hand there is the reverse effect of the becoming-human of the animal, the ape who wants to find a way out. The simultaneous transformation of human into animal, and animal into human, functions both as an escape from and a reassertion of the oedipal system, because the animals, in their effort to imitate their supposed superiors, also suffer from oedipalization, particularly the dog, 'the Oedipus-animal *par excellence* (chapter 2, 'All too great an Oedipus', p. 23).

In the novels the flight from oedipal authority is achieved through the disassembling of the great power-machines. The single subject (the protagonist Karl or K.) is always at the centre of a vast complex, in contact with a variety of 'machinic' sections (a metaphor for the human beings and objects which constitute the power-structure). The machine, whether tech-nocratic (*America*), or legal (*The Trial*), or bureaucratic (*The Castle*), is governed simultaneously by social and erotic forces: each section of the machine has its own erotic component. As a bank official K. is in touch with one particular woman, as a witness with another, as a defendant with another still. People are assigned to different parts of the machine, where they make love, work or argue. The buildings themselves are part of a vast topography of desire, rooms whose entrances and exits lead from one section to the next in unexpected ways, a continuum of moving barriers. The law machine consists of chambers, books, judges, women, pornographic law. The unexpected irrupts in the office next door or in doorways. Desire dwells within the law: where there is power there is sensual satisfaction to be had. Power produces gains of pleasure through surveillance, an inevitable form of voyeurism (Foucault 1981). Desire itself is deterritorialized and cannot judge, for the judges are full of desire. The verdict gets postponed. Authority is always in a different part of the desiring machine. A series of triangles proliferates in Kafka's text: three bank clerks, three lodgers, three voyeurs, three bureaucrats. No triangle is eternal. The women, too, although assigned to specific sections, 'overflow' the precise position allocated them; they have 'connections' with the total power structure and that is why they can 'help' K. They function at the intersection points of the great machine. The washerwoman makes love to the student in the doorway of the law court, a woman extracts K. from the chamber of the advocate. The women are part-sisters, part-servants, part-whores, occupying positions that are anti-marriage and anti-familial. Like Foucault, Deleuze and Guattari believe that:

As soon as there is a relationship of power, there is a possibility of resistance. We are never trapped by power: it is always possible to modify its hold, in determined conditions and following a precise strategy.

(Foucault 1980a, p. 13)

Deleuze and Guattari's schizoanalytic criticism may be seen as a bold attempt to deterritorialize psychoanalytic criticism. They substitute a provoking textual practice which recovers some of the scandal which psychoanalytic criticism lost in its various stages of naturalization, on its way from id- to ego-psychology. They subvert its representations, playing havoc with so-called typical symbols. They refuse to believe that desire is forbidden from the start. Theirs is an attempt to make reading into a revolutionary political activity, discovering omissions, non-sequiturs, mismatch between style and purpose in texts and patients, more radical than deconstruction in the refusal to reassemble the text, more radical than Lacan in seeing the patient as a 'body without organs' (as essentially uncoded) rather than as a text. The revolutionary writer/reader conducts experiments, trying to find a way out of the given representation. Desire has to begin with a line of flight, a deterritorializing move. Yet the problem of how to escape remains, for the way out of representation inevitably leads through it. Hence there is an ironic success in their schizoanalysis of Kafka's text, because it becomes a new form of traditional literary criticism. Schizoanalysis rebels against psychoanalysis, yet like psychoanalysis it finds itself in literature, finds its own strategies anticipated in it. So it is interesting finally to turn back to *Gradiva* and see what happens to this text when appropriated by a schizoanalytic literary critic.

Gradiva rediviva: towards a way out

For Freud, Jensen's *Gradiva* is a story that neatly illustrates the 'cornerstone' of his theory: the return of the repressed (see pp. 30ff.). He is able to turn the story into an allegory of psychoanalysis: one character, the heroine, is able to perform a successful analysis on another character, the hero, 'curing' him of his 'delusion'. Freud called his piece of psychoanalytic criticism *Delusions and Dreams in Jensen's 'Gradiva'*. In *Anti-Oedipus* Deleuze and Guattari write: 'Never was Freud more adventurous than in *Gradiva*' (1977a, p. 352). How can this be? Surely they cannot approve of the psychoanalytic rehabilitation of the central character. Nor do they. But the very effect that caught that character's attention, a desire caught by the movement of a limb, is the place where schizoanalysis wants to install itself, where it wants to take up the battle with psychoanalysis. In an article called 'The fiction of analysis' (1977), Sylvère Lotringer, a French critic, develops the hint dropped by Deleuze and Guattari. He takes up where Deleuze and Guattari left off, wondering 'whether the revolutionary aspect of *Gradiva* comes from Freud or from Jensen' (Lotringer 1977, p. 173). What is this revolutionary aspect? It is the '"Gradivian" gait', which Freud wants to see as the return of a repressed complex. But there is actually nothing in the text to indicate why the hero, Norbert Hanold, should have a repressed complex about women (pp. 175–6). Fastening on this omission, Lotringer refutes Freud's textual analysis step by step. His central argument is that Norbert's interest in the gait of Gradiva is not a fetishistic fixation on a woman's foot. What captures him is an image of the freedom of walking, a movement of the body, a 'walking-towards':

> Nomadic form, without specific territory, and from no definite epoch: transhistoric. And the archaeologist is moved not by formal beauty nor even by the woman's (indifferent) face, but rather by the vertical position of her right foot. The representation of someone *in motion*. This is moreover the name with which he dubs her: Gradiva, 'she who walks in splendour'. (p. 177)

Norbert's restlessness to get away from his native city and to visit Pompeii is not the response to the return of the repressed in his dream, but the desire to get away from his narrow familial world. The couples in Pompeii that arouse his hatred do so not because of incest-anxiety but because he wishes to get out of the oedipal world into a wider social field. Archaeological excavation need not be a metaphor for the digging up of Norbert's repressed childhood, nor need his love of knowledge be desire for oedipal sexual knowledge: 'the libido does not have to be desexualized or sublimated, ie. repressed in varying degrees, in order to cathect the socio-historical arena' (p. 178).

The revolutionary element is that the 'Gradiva-effect' is one of deterritorialization. The movement of the foot has little to do with its being that of a woman: 'Gradiva is the proper name of a singularity without individuation, a delimitation of the global person . . . a moving region to which sexes, qualities, and races come each in turn to communicate' (p. 178). Where Freud saw the foot as a fetishistic fixation of one unable to move to the genital stage of oedipal development, Lotringer argues for the case being the reverse of a fixation, the foot's movement being the significant feature. Instead of being a delusion, a turning away from reality, it represents Norbert Hanold's attempt to throw off the restrictions of the oedipal family. The motion of the foot is the flow of libido, a movement of desire: 'What then is an *active* fantasy if not libido in full flow storming the walls of representation and overthrowing all the significations that attempt to shackle it' (p. 186). Norbert's own journey re-enacts this search to overthrow. Pompeii is no longer the ground for precisely named objects but a place where naming has to begin anew. Lotringer quotes from Jensen's text:

> Anyone who harboured a desire for such a comprehension had to stand alone, among the remains of the past, the only living person in the hot noonday silence, in order not to see with physical eyes nor hear with corporal ears. *Then something came forth everywhere without movement and a soundless speech began*; then the sun dissolved the tomb-like rigidity of the old stones, a glowing thrill passed through them, the dead awoke, and Pompeii began to live again. (ibid.)

Noon is the hour of the god Pan, the Greek god of *hylé*, the flowing source of all being. Is this just another Lawrentian celebration of a life-force? (Deleuze and Guattari frequently cite Lawrence with approval.) Lotringer sees it rather as a material process, 'a cosmic enunciation free of all subjective appropriation' (p. 187). The becoming impersonal of the person, the 'machinic "it"', is like the awakening of the dead that Jensen describes, a resurrection of what Deleuze and Guattari call 'the body without organs'. Depersonalization is here seen as a redemptive experience because it liberates man/woman from the repression of civilization. Indeed, civilization is redefined and seen as part of desiring production.

Gradiva is thus read through *Anti-Oedipus*. Zoe Bertgang, Norbert's childhood sweetheart, does not become the walking *woman*, but rather *walking* woman, the flow rather than the gender-identification being the key element in the fantasy. Lotringer indeed sees Zoe as an agent of repression in the text, for in 'curing' Norbert, acting as his analyst, she returns him 'to becoming-sensible . . . to becoming-husband' (ibid.). Thus the oedipal unconscious wins over the anti-oedipal 'productive' unconscious; the repression is reinforced. For Freud the delusion was a turning away from reality, but the schizoanalytic critic goes beyond even those psychoanalysts and critics who see illusion and play as a means of mediating the Real. For him 'delusion' need not be a delirium but may be the awakening of a sixth sense.

Both readings, the psychoanalytic and the schizoanalytic, call into question the nature of representation while allowing new forms of it. Freud's reading avoids the challenge coming from the ambiguous wish: the returning repressed must be pacified and returned whence it came. Lotringer's reading, on the other hand, centres on the radical implications of the ambiguous representation, thereby revealing a particular repression to be counter-productive, and pointing to the possibility of a way out of 'the text', both story and system.

10

Conclusion

Psychoanalysis as a clinical practice has been concerned with those bodies whose entry into the social order is fraught with difficulty. In its investigation of these cases it was brought face to face with the very principle of the genesis and construction of selves. Freud discovered that psychoanalysis has to deal with the body caught up in the tropes and figures of language. The relation of psychoanalysis to language and literature is patent, even though its explanatory power is different. To free the patient from his or her symptom, to release the incessant flow of desire from where it has got trapped, the analyst has to rely on the living response of the patient. Nevertheless, both analysands and readers (and all analysts and critics are these in the first instance) are engaged in pursuing undecidable meanings: ambiguity, ambivalence, fantasy, illusion and play are their joint stock-in-trade.

It was inevitable that psychoanalysis should become controversial. The patient with his symptom is an example of inadequacy at the meeting-place of body and society. Where the inadequacy is to be lodged, in the body in question or the society of which it is a member, or both, cannot be simply decided. Troping has been seen as a mechanism of defence, a mechanism of subversion, or even both. The multiple meanings arise precisely because at the interface between body and society the conscious and unconscious hold place together. For Lacan language creates the two in one operation. There is an incessant struggle at work within language, because it is at once cause and effect of the body's desire.

These theoretical implications have gradually led away from the enclosed space of applied psychoanalytic criticism to wider pastures. I do not myself think that applied psychoanalytic criticism is either intrinsically wicked or totally without relevance to literature, even if literature is being 'used' to prove psychoanalytic claims. After all, psychoanalysis is now being 'used' to show how clever literature is. To the familiar Freudian and Jungian criticism, concerning itself with the psychosexual or archetypal fortunes of the author or character or both, can now be added a Winnicottian applied criticism (see Further reading), analysing the figurations of the text in terms of the identity-problems of the characters and their author. These contributions will obviously vary in the rigour of their execution, but at their best, as I hope to have shown with the example of Bonaparte, they might be seen as the 'popular' literature of psychoanalysis, as 'texts' in their own right, often done better by the psychoanalyst than by the critic who tries to emulate her. Properly read, such texts are still the most accessible form of psychoanalytic criticism.

At the other end of the pendulum's swing there is the impressive way in which psychoanalysis and rhetoric have been combined in recent French and Anglo-American criticism, so much so that psychoanalytic theory has been absorbed in the rhetoric of deconstruction, as the outstanding work of Barbara Johnson shows. Focusing as it does on what is repressed in our culture, this kind of criticism is unthinkable, unwritable and, perhaps more to the point, unreadable, without a proper understanding of psychoanalytic rhetoric, as distinct from the bandying about of psychoanalytic terminology. Without such an understanding the new and original ways in which Freudian theory has been assimilated into literary criticism cannot be appreciated and adequately criticized. For, of course, the traffic has not gone one way only: there is a body of work which does not regard Freudian theory as canonical, but instead interrogates literature for possible revisions or additions to that theory, so that it comes to be modified by the literary texts themselves, which are read as proposing other, less repressive ways of

mediating the relations between the unconscious an
order (see Further reading).

The account in this book tries to provide a framewo
which such different types of criticism might be
understood. The psychoanalytic and the aesthetic process overlap because in each case the rhetorical leads to a negotiation in
which reference and representation can be partially achieved,
subject to ever new agreements. To assess the persuasive force
of a text is to discover in what way writer, reader and critic, and
analyst, analysand and society, can enter into transforming
relationships that are integral to structures of desire, relationships all of them have a measure of freedom to create.

Three elements in particular have been shown to characterize
these transformations. First, there is the question of the
mechanisms of language. What Freud detected in dreams, the
tropings of the unconscious in its evasions of the censor, has
been seen to be operative in texts in general. The demonstra-
tions of both id- and ego-psychology as regards the workings of
psychic mechanisms contribute to the understanding of desire
in language. They need not be dismissed just because we
happen to disagree with the conclusions drawn. Whether desire
in language is seen as social or asocial is a matter of interpretation and not a general truth about the unconscious. Second,
there is an overlap in the 'reader theory' of psychoanalysis and
literature. As has been seen, the assumptions of classical criticism, that the text is the patient and the reader the analyst, no
longer hold. The text is not a stable object, immutably fixed for
all time by the 'intentions' of its creator, whether these be seen
as conscious or unconscious. Nor can the situation be simply
reversed, giving all power to the reader. The literary-critical
debate on the 'intentional' and the 'affective' fallacies has been
concerned with similar issues (Wimsatt and Beardsley 1954).
Psychoanalytic theory has shown that an artist/writer is always
an artist/writer-in-transference: the material with which she
works, be it stone or paint or word, is invested with desire before
and as soon as she works with it. The reader-cum-critic's
position is then vastly complicated, for she is subject to the
effects the work produces in her as reader, and at the same time
committed to the analysis of these effects as critic. These
transference phenomena have much to contribute to the old

problem of 'aesthetic distance', for that is also what the analyst and analysand have to achieve in order to bring the analysis to a satisfactory conclusion. Third, there is the force of history as it affects the participants in both the psychoanalytic and the literary situation. As has been seen throughout this book, there is no simple choice between the author or critic as master of the text, and the text as master of the author or critic, because both leave out the field over which interpretative play must range, the field of human action from which history is derived. History is both cause and effect, determining men and women, and being determined by them. It is a field not directly accessible: to negotiate it both psychoanalytic and literary-critical readers need to resort to play, fiction and illusion.

Literature and the arts are generally valued for their 'aesthetic ambiguity'. Psychoanalytic critics, even those with a declared political intent, seem to prefer to work on the culture's store of 'literature'. Radical critics, whose allegiance is to the principle of 'the text', want their criticism to be a political intervention, but at the same time they find themselves drawn into a contradiction, because they are reinforcing the aesthetic value of the 'canon', the classical repertoire. Thus a radical anti-psychoanalytic criticism turns to Kafka (Deleuze and Guattari 1976), a Lacanian feminist criticism to Balzac (Felman 1981), a Marxist/Freudian myth criticism to Racine (Orlando 1978). The 'aesthetic' text seems to have in it more of what is wanted, at least for those who have learnt to 'read' it, than any other text: 'Poetry is incorrigibly conservative yet subversive at the same time' (Orlando 1978, p. 19). In theory, of course, this can also apply to other texts, say legal documents, and clearly being a lawyer involves the study of ambiguity in a peculiar way. While lawyers, presumably, derive pleasure from wrestling with the ambiguities of their text, the majority might not regard this as an aesthetic pursuit. Whereas the legal text has to be made to yield a clear decision, the equivocal justice of Solomon being a 'fiction', the literary text offers what psychoanalysis calls 'compromise formations' to its readers: some desire may be satisfied. This much is promised by aesthetic ambiguity.

Aesthetic ambiguity does not exist of itself: it is an aspect of interaction between persons. The convergence and divergence of desires over what is taken to be the same knot of understanding emerged as the essential feature of the psychoanalytic encounter, and this can be extrapolated to the aesthetic interaction. For the best psychoanalytic model of the aesthetic interaction we need to go to the joke. The joke not only typifies the interchange of conflicting interpretations along with other psychic phenomena such as dreams or symptoms, but, as has been seen, it is also to be distinguished for the peculiarity of its structure and its effects. The joke – and the aesthetic text – offer a site for negotiation, but this negotiation involves not only two participants, but their relation to language and power. Aesthetic response is the joint and agreed release or maintenance of repression. While there is a risk involved (as to who will have the last laugh), neither author, nor text, nor critic can reign supreme. Which way the laughter is to go will depend on the individuals and societies concerned: jokes have the same structure of ambiguity whether they are the conformist's or the rebel's. Tempting as it has been for psychoanalytic critics and theorists to use the structure as a weapon against those they oppose, they cannot claim that the theory of the Joke is theirs because a particular joke serves their turn. This is indeed to mistake practice for theory. The joke of language appears in the Russian tale that serves as my epigraph: the pretence that there is no desire in language, no unconscious, no body. If all desires are parallel, then all vanishes and no one speaks. Since all desires are not parallel, some bodies may be forced to make an untimely exit from society. Under Stalin's regime the teller of the tale, Daniil Kharms, was arrested and put to silence. Equally, where there is no regime, the body in pieces may be all that is left when no one can be heard for the din. Psychoanalytic criticism explores texts for the 'free' associations that tell of the struggle between a body and the society on which it depends.

References

Althusser, Louis (1977) 'Freud and Lacan', in Althusser, Louis, *Lenin and Philosophy and Other Essays*. London: New Left Books (tr. from 'Freud et Lacan', *La nouvelle critique*, 161 (1964), 88–108).

Bachelard, Gaston (1938) *La formation de l'esprit scientifique*. Paris: Vrin.

—— (1968) *The Psychoanalysis of Fire*. Boston: Beacon Press (tr. from *La psychanalyse du feu*, Paris: 1938).

—— (1969) *The Poetics of Space*. Boston: Beacon Press (tr. from *La poétique de l'espace*, Paris: 1958).

—— (1971) *The Poetics of Reverie: Childhood, Language and the Cosmos*. Boston: Beacon Press (tr. from *La poétique de la rêverie*, Paris: 1960).

Bakhtin, Mikhail (1968) *Rabelais and his World*. Cambridge, Massachusetts: Massachusetts Institute of Technology (tr. from *Tvorchestvo Fransua Rable*, Moscow: 1965).

Barthes, Roland (1972) 'To write: an intransitive verb?', in Macksey, Richard and Donato, Eugenio (eds), *The Structuralist Controversy*. Baltimore and London: The Johns Hopkins University Press, pp. 134–45.

—— (1975) *S/Z*. London: Jonathan Cape (tr. from *S/Z*, Paris: 1970).

—— (1976) *The Pleasure of the Text*. London: Jonathan Cape (tr. from *Le plaisir du texte*, Paris: 1975).

—— (1977) 'The death of the author', in Heath, Stephen (ed.), *Image – Music – Text*. London: Fontana/Collins (tr. from 'La mort de l'auteur', *Mantéia*, 5 (1968)), pp. 142–8.

—— (1979) *A Lover's Discourse*. New York: Hill and Wang (tr. from *Fragments d'un discours amoureux*, Paris: 1977).

Beckett, Samuel (1973) *Not I*. London: Faber & Faber.

Bloom, Harold (1975) *The Anxiety of Influence: A Theory of Poetry*. London: Oxford University Press.

—— (1977) *Wallace Stevens: The Poems of our Climate*. Ithaca, New York: Cornell University Press.

—— (1979) 'The breaking of form', in Bloom, Harold, de Man, Paul, Derrida, Jacques, Hartman, Geoffrey and Miller, J. Hillis (eds), *Deconstruction and Criticism*. London: Routledge & Kegan Paul, pp. 1–37.

—— (1980) *A Map of Misreading*. Oxford and New York: Oxford University Press.

—— (1982) *Agon: Towards a Theory of Revisionism*. Oxford and New York: Oxford University Press.

Bodkin, Maud (1934) *Archetypal Patterns in Poetry*. London: Oxford University Press.

Bollas, Christopher (1976) 'Melville's lost self: *Bartleby*', in Tennenhouse, Leonard (ed.), *The Practice of Psychoanalytic Criticism*. Detroit: Wayne State University Press, pp. 226–36.

Bonaparte, Marie (1949) *The Life and Works of Edgar Allan Poe*. London: Imago (tr. from *Edgar Poe: Étude psychanalytique*, Paris: 1933).

Bowie, Malcolm (1979) 'Jacques Lacan', in Sturrock, John (ed.), *Structuralism and Since: From Lévi-Strauss to Derrida*. Oxford: Oxford University Press, pp. 116–53.

Chasseguet-Smirgel, Janine (1981) *Female Sexuality*. London: Virago (tr. from *La sexualité féminine, recherches psychanalytiques nouvelles*, Paris: 1964).

Cixous, Hélène (1976) 'Fiction and its phantoms: a reading of Freud's *Das Unheimliche*', *New Literary History*, 7, 525–48 (tr. from 'La fiction et ses fantômes', *Poétique*, 10 (1972), 199–216).

Crews, Frederick (1966) *The Sins of the Fathers: Hawthorne's Psychological Themes*. New York: Oxford University Press.

—— (1976) *Out of My System: Psychology, Ideology and Critical Method*. New York: Oxford University Press.

—— (1980) 'The American literary critic explains why he has rejected Freud', *London Review of Books*, 4 December, 3–6.

Culler, Jonathan (1983) *On Deconstruction: Theory and Criticism after Structuralism*. London: Routledge & Kegan Paul.

Deleuze, Gilles and Guattari, Félix (1976) *Kafka: Für eine kleine Literatur*. Frankfurt am Main: Suhrkamp Verlag (tr. from *Kafka: Pour une littérature mineure*, Paris: 1975).

—— (1977a) *Anti-Oedipus: Capitalism and Schizophrenia*. New York: The Viking Press (tr. from *L'anti-Oedipe: Vol. I, Capitalisme et schizophrenie*, Paris: 1972).

—— (1977b) 'Balance sheet-program for desiring machines', *Semiotext(e)*, *Anti-Oedipus: From Psychoanalysis to Schizopolitics*, 2, 117–35 (tr. from 'Bilan-programme pour machines désirantes', *Minuit*, 2 (January 1973)).

Derrida, Jacques (1975) 'The purveyor of truth', *Yale French Studies*, 52, 31–113 (tr. from 'Le facteur de la vérité', *Poétique*, 21 (1975)).

—— (1978) 'Freud and the scene of writing', in *Writing and Difference*. Chicago: University of Chicago Press (tr. from *L'écriture et la difference*, Paris: 1967), pp. 196–231.

—— (1982) *Dissemination*. Chicago: University of Chicago Press (tr. from *La dissémination*, Paris: 1972).

Ehrenzweig, Anton (1970) *The Hidden Order of Art: A Study in the Psychology of Artistic Imagination*. London: Paladin (orig. publ. Weidenfeld & Nicolson, 1967).

Empson, William (1930) *Seven Types of Ambiguity*. London: Chatto & Windus.

Farrell, B. A. (1981) *The Standing of Psychoanalysis*. Oxford and New York: Oxford University Press.

Felman, Shoshana (1977) 'Turning the screw of interpretation', *Yale French Studies*, 55/56, 94–207.

—— (1980) 'On reading poetry: reflections on the limits and possibilities of psychoanalytical approaches', in Smith, Joseph H. (ed.), *The Literary Freud*. New Haven and London: Yale University Press, pp. 119–48.

—— (1981) 'Rereading femininity', *Yale French Studies*, 62, 19–44.

Fischer, Jens Malte (ed.) (1980) *Psychoanalytische Literaturinterpretation*. Tübingen: Max Niemeyer Verlag.

Foucault, Michel (1974) *The Order of Things: An Archaeology of the Human Sciences*. London: Tavistock Publications (tr. from *Les mots et les choses*, Paris: 1966).

—— (1980a) 'The history of sexuality: interview', *Oxford Literary Review*, 4, 3–19.

—— (1980b) 'What is an author?', in Harari, Josué V. (ed.), *Textual Strategies: Perspectives in Post-Structuralist Criticism*. London: Methuen, pp. 141–60.

—— (1981) *The History of Sexuality, I*. Harmondsworth: Penguin (tr. from *La volonté de savoir*, Paris: 1976).

—— (1982) 'The subject and power', in Dreyfus, Hubert L. and Rabinow, Paul (eds), *Michel Foucault: Beyond Structuralism and Hermeneutics*. Brighton: Harvester Press, pp. 208–26.

Freud, Anna (1966) *The Ego and the Mechanisms of Defence*. New York: International Universities Press (tr. from *Das Ich und die Abwehrmechanismen*, Vienna: 1936).

Freud, Sigmund (1953) *The Standard Edition of the Complete Psychological Works* (24 vols). London: The Hogarth Press and the Institute of Psychoanalysis (tr. from *Gesammelte Werke*, vols I–XVIII, London and Frankfurt: 1940–68). The *Standard Edition* includes the following works:

—— (1895) 'Project for a scientific psychology', I, pp. 281–397.

—— (1893–5) *Studies in Hysteria* (with Josef Breuer), II.

—— (1900) *The Interpretation of Dreams*, IV and V.

—— (1905) *Three Essays on the Theory of Sexuality*, VII, pp. 123–246.

—— (1905/6) 'Psychopathic characters on the stage', VII, pp. 303–10.

—— (1905) *Jokes and their Relation to the Unconscious*, VIII.

—— (1907) *Delusions and Dreams in Jensen's 'Gradiva'*, IX, pp. 1–97.

—— (1908) 'Creative writers and day-dreaming', IX, pp. 141–54.

—— (1910) '"Wild" psychoanalysis', XI, pp. 219–30.

—— (1910) 'Leonardo da Vinci and a memory of his childhood', XI, pp. 59–138.

—— (1913) 'The claims of psycho-analysis to scientific interest', XIII, pp. 163–90.

—— (1914) 'On narcissism: an introduction', XIV, pp. 163–90.

—— (1914) 'On the history of the psycho-analytic movement', XIV, pp. 1–66.

—— (1915) 'Repression', XIV, pp. 141–53.

—— (1916–17) *Introductory Lectures on Psycho-Analysis*, XV and XVI.

—— (1918) 'From the history of an infantile neurosis', XVII, pp. 1–124.

—— (1919) 'The uncanny', XVII, pp. 217–56.

—— (1920) *Beyond the Pleasure Principle*, XVIII, pp. 1–64.

—— (1923) *The Ego and the Id*, XIX, pp. 1–66.

—— (1924) 'The economic problem of masochism', XIX, pp. 155–72.

—— (1925) 'A note upon the "mystic writing pad"', XIX, pp. 227–34.

—— (1925) 'Negation', XIX, pp. 235–40.

—— (1925) 'Some psychical consequences of the anatomical distinction between the sexes', XIX, pp. 241–60.

—— (1926) *Inhibitions, Symptoms and Anxiety*, XX, pp. 75–176.

—— (1926) 'Psycho-analysis', XX, pp. 259–70.

—— (1928) 'Dostoevsky and parricide', XXI, pp. 173–96.

—— (1930) *Civilization and its Discontents*, XXI, pp. 57–146.

—— (1933) Preface to Marie Bonaparte's *The Life and Works of Edgar Allan Poe: A Psycho-Analytic Interpretation*, XXII, p. 254.

—— (1933) *New Introductory Lectures on Psychoanalysis*, XXII, pp. 1–182.

—— (1937) 'Analysis terminable and interminable', XXIII, pp. 209–54.

—— (1940) 'An outline of psycho-analysis', XXIII, pp. 139–208.

—— (1940) 'Splitting of the ego in the process of defence', XXIII, pp. 271–8.

Frye, Northrop (1957) *Anatomy of Criticism: Four Essays*. Princeton, New Jersey: Princeton University Press.

—— (1978) 'Forming fours', in Denham, Robert D. (ed.), *Culture and Literature*. Chicago: University of Chicago Press, pp. 117–29. Orig. publ. 1954.

—— (1981) *The Critical Path: An Essay on the Social Content of Literary Criticism*. Bloomington and London: Indiana University Press.

Fuller, Peter (1980) *Art and Psychoanalysis*. London: Writers and Readers Publishing Cooperative.

Gallop, Jane (1982) *The Daughter's Seduction: Feminism and Psychoanalysis*. Ithaca, New York: Cornell University Press.

Gargano, James W. (1967) 'The question of Poe's narrators', in Regan, Robert (ed.), *Poe: Twentieth-Century Views*. Englewood Cliffs, New Jersey: Prentice-Hall, pp. 164–71.

Gombrich, Ernst (1977) *Art and Illusion: A Study in the Psychology of Pictorial Representation*. London: Phaidon Press.

—— (1983) 'Freud's aesthetics', in Kurzweil, Edith and Phillips, William (eds), *Literature and Psychoanalysis*. New York: Columbia University Press. Orig. publ. 1966.

Green, André (1978a) 'Potential space in psychoanalysis: the object in the setting', in Grolnick, Simon G. and Barkin, Leonard (eds), *Between Reality and Fantasy: Transitional Objects and Phenomena*. New York and London: Jason Aronson.

—— (1978b) 'The double and the absent', in Roland, Alan (ed.), *Psychoanalysis, Creativity, and Literature: A French–American Inquiry*. New York: Columbia University Press, pp. 271–92.

—— (1979) *The Tragic Effect*. Cambridge: Cambridge University Press (tr. from *Un oeil en trop*, Paris: 1969).

Greenacre, Phyllis (1970) 'The transitional object and the fetish, with special reference to the role of illusion', *International Journal of Psychoanalysis*, 51, 442–56.

Hartmann, Heinz (1964) 'Notes on the theory of sublimation', in Hartmann, Heinz, *Essays in Ego-Psychology*. New York: International Universities Press, pp. 215–40. Orig. publ. 1955.

Hawthorne, Nathaniel (1978) *The Scarlet Letter*. New York and London: W. W. Norton.

Hertz, Neil (1979) 'Freud and the Sandman', in Harari, Josué V. (ed.), *Textual Strategies: Perspectives in Post-Structuralist Criticism*. London: Methuen, pp. 296–321.

Hirsch, E. D. (1976) *The Aims of Interpretation*. Chicago: Chicago University Press.

Hoffmann, E. T. A. (1969) *Selected Writings of E. T. A. Hoffmann*, 2 vols, ed. Knight, Elizabeth C. and Kent, Leonard J. Chicago: Chicago University Press. 'The Sandman', I, pp. 137–67 (tr. from 'Der

Sandmann', 1816); *The Life and Opinions of Kater Murr*, II (tr. from *Lebens-Ansichten des Katers Murr*, 1820/1).

Holland, Norman N. (1968) *The Dynamics of Literary Response*. New York: Oxford University Press.

—— (1975a) *Poems in Persons*. New York: W. W. Norton.

—— (1975b) *Five Readers Reading*. New Haven: Yale University Press.

—— (1980) 'Re-covering "The Purloined Letter"', in Suleiman, Susan R. and Crosman, Inge (eds), *The Reader in the Text*. Princeton, New Jersey: Princeton University Press, pp. 350–70.

—— (1982) 'Why this is transference, nor am I out of it', *Psychoanalysis and Contemporary Thought*, 5, 27–34.

Jacobi, Jolande (1968) *The Psychology of C. G. Jung: An Introduction with Illustrations*. London: Routledge & Kegan Paul.

Jakobson, Roman and Halle, Morris (1956) *Fundamentals of Language*. The Hague: Mouton, pp. 76–82.

Johnson, Barbara (1977) 'The frame of reference: Poe, Lacan, Derrida', *Yale French Studies*, 55/56, 457–505.

—— (1978) 'The critical difference', *Diacritics*, 10, 2–9.

Jones, Richard M. (1978) *The New Psychology of Dreaming*. Harmondsworth: Penguin.

Jung, Carl Gustav (1972a) *Two Essays on Analytical Psychology*. Princeton, New Jersey; Princeton University Press (tr. from *Über die Psychologie des Unbewussten*, Zurich: 1943, and *Die Beziehungen zwischen dem Ich und dem Unbewussten*, Zurich: 1928).

—— (1972b) 'On the relation of analytical psychology to poetry', in *The Spirit in Man, Art and Literature*. Princeton, New Jersey: Princeton University Press (tr. from 'Über die Beziehungen der analytischen Psychologie zum dichterischen Kunstwerk', Zurich: 1931), pp. 65–83.

—— (1976) *Symbols of Transformation*. Princeton, New Jersey: Princeton University Press (tr. from *Symbole der Wandlung*, Zurich: 1952).

—— (ed.) (1978) *Man and His Symbols*. London: Picador. Orig. publ. 1964.

Kaplan, Morton and Kloss, Robert (1973) *The Unspoken Motive: A Guide to Psychoanalytic Literary Criticism*. New York: Free Press.

Kaul, A. N. (ed.) (1966) *Hawthorne: Twentieth-Century Views*. Englewood Cliffs, New Jersey: Prentice-Hall.

Kharms, Daniil (1974) 'Ministories', in *Russia's Lost Literature of the Absurd; Selected Works of Daniil Kharms and Alexander Vvedensky*, tr. and ed. Gibian, George. New York: W. W. Norton.

Kittler, Friedrich (1977) 'Das Phantom unseres Ichs und die Literaturpsychologie', in Kittler, Friedrich and Turk, Horst (eds), *Urszenen*. Frankfurt am Main: Suhrkamp, pp. 139–66.

Klein, Melanie (1977) 'The importance of symbol formation in the development of the ego', in *Love, Guilt and Reparation and Other Works*,

1921–1945. London: The Hogarth Press, pp. 219–32. Orig. publ. 1930.

Kris, Ernst (1964) *Psychoanalytic Explorations in Art*. New York: Schocken Books. Orig. publ. 1952.

Kristeva, Julia (1980) *Desire in Language*. New York: Columbia University Press.

Kuhn, Thomas S. (1970) *The Structure of Scientific Revolutions*. Chicago: Chicago University Press.

Kuhns, Richard (1983) *Psychoanalytic Theory of Art: A Philosophy of Art on Developmental Principles*. New York: Columbia University Press.

Lacan, Jacques (1970) 'Of structure as an inmixing of an Otherness prerequisite to any subject whatever', in Macksey, Richard and Donato, Eugenio (eds), *The Structuralist Controversy*. Baltimore and London: The Johns Hopkins University Press, pp. 186–95.

—— (1972) 'Seminar on "The Purloined Letter"', *Yale French Studies*, 48, 39–72 (orig. publ. in *Écrits*, Paris: 1966).

—— (1975) 'Seminar of 21st January 1975', in Mitchell, Juliet and Rose, Jacqueline (eds), *Feminine Sexuality: Jacques Lacan and the école freudienne*. London: Macmillan, pp. 162–71 (tr. from *Ornicar?*, 3, 104–10).

——(1977a) *Écrits: A Selection*. London: Tavistock Publications.

—— (1977b) *The Four Fundamental Concepts of Psycho-Analysis*. London: The Hogarth Press (tr. from *Le séminaire de Jacques Lacan, Livre XI*, 'Les quatre concepts fondamentaux de la psychanalyse', Paris: 1973).

—— (1978) *Das Seminar von Jacques Lacan, Buch I (1953–54): Freuds technische Schriften*. Olten and Freiburg-im-Breisgua: Walter-Verlag (tr. from *Les écrits techniques de Freud: Le Séminaire I, 1953–54*, Paris: 1975).

—— (1980) *Das Seminar von Jacques Lacan, Buch II (1954–55)*. Olten and Freiburg-im-Breisgau: Walter-Verlag (tr. from *Le moi dans la théorie de Freud et dans la technique de la psychanalyse: Le Séminaire II*, Paris: 1978).

Lacoue-Labarthe, Philipe (1977) 'Theatricum analyticum', *Glyph*, 2, 122–43.

Laing, R. D. (1974) *Knots*. Harmondsworth: Penguin.

Langer, Suzanne (1942) *Philosophy in a New Key*. Cambridge, Massachusetts: Harvard University Press.

Laplanche, Jean (1976) *Life and Death in Psychoanalysis*. Baltimore and London: The Johns Hopkins University Press (tr. from *Vie et mort en psychanalyse*, Paris: 1970).

Laplanche, Jean and Leclaire, Serge (1972) 'The unconscious: a psychoanalytic study', *Yale French Studies*, 48, 118–75 (tr. from de Brouwer, Desclée (ed.), 'L'inconscient' (VIe Colloque de Bonneval), Bonneval: 1966).

Laplanche, Jean and Pontalis, Jean-Baptiste (1973) *The Language of Psycho-Analysis*. London: The Hogarth Press (tr. from *Vocabulaire de la Psychanalyse*, Paris: 1967).

Lauder, Afferbeck (1965) *Let Stalk Strine*. Sydney, Australia: Ure Smith.

Lawrence, D. H. (1961a) *Fantasia of the Unconscious*. London: Heinemann. Orig. publ. 1923.

—— (1961b) *Psychoanalysis of the Unconscious*. London: Heinemann. Orig. publ. 1923.

—— (1962) *The Symbolic Meaning: The Uncollected Versions of Studies in Classic American Literature* ed. Armin, Arnold. Arundel: The Centaur Press.

—— (1977) *Studies in Classical American Literature*. Harmondsworth: Penguin.

Leitch, Vincent B. (1983) *Deconstructive Criticism: An Advanced Introduction*. London: Hutchinson.

Lesser, Simon O. (1957) *Fiction and the Unconscious*. Chicago: University of Chicago Press.

Lichtenstein, Heinz (1961) 'Identity and sexuality', *Journal of the American Psychoanalytic Association*, 9, 179–260.

—— (1965) 'Towards a metapsychological definition of the concept of self', *International Review of Psycho-Analysis*, 46, 117–28.

Lombroso, Cesare (1891) *The Man of Genius*. London: Walter Scott (tr. from *Genio e follia*, Milan: 1864).

Lorenzer, Alfred and Orban, Peter (1978) 'Transitional objects and phenomena: socialization and symbolization', in Grolnick, Simon A. and Barkin, Leonard (eds), *Between Reality and Fantasy: Transitional Objects and Phenomena*. New York: Jason Aronson pp. 472–82.

Lotringer, Sylvère (1977) 'The fiction of analysis', *Semiotext(e)*, 2, 173–89.

Lyotard, Jean-François (1974) 'Au delà de la représentation', preface to Ehrenzweig, Anton, *L'ordre caché de l'art. Essai sur la psychologie de l'imagination esthétique*. Paris: Gallimard.

—— (1983) 'Answering the question: what is post-modernism?', in Hassan, Ihab and Hassan, Sally (eds), *Innovation/Renovation: New Perspectives on the Humanities*. Madison, Wisconsin: University of Wisconsin Press, pp. 329–41.

—— (1984) 'The sublime and the avant-garde', lecture at Cambridge, 12 March.

Mannoni, Maud (1970) *The Retarded Child and the Mother*. London: Tavistock Publications (tr. from *L'enfant arrière et sa mère*, Paris: 1964).

—— (1973) *The Child, his 'Illness' and the Others*. Harmondsworth: Penguin (tr. from *L'enfant, sa 'maladie' et les autres*, Paris: 1967).

Mehlman, Jeffrey (1975) 'How to read Freud on jokes: the critic as *Schadchen*', *Poétique*, 6, 439–61.

Meisel, Perry (ed.) (1981) *Freud: A Collection of Critical Essays*. Englewood Cliffs, New Jersey: Prentice-Hall.

Meltzer, Françoise (1982) 'The uncanny rendered canny: Freud's blind spot in reading Hoffmann's "Sandman"', in Gilman, Sander L. (ed.), *Introducing Psychoanalytic Theory*. New York: Brunner/Mazel, pp. 218–39.

Metz, Christian (1982) *Psychoanalysis and Cinema: The Imaginary Signifier*. London: Macmillan (tr. from *Le signifiant imaginaire. Psychanalyse et cinéma*, Paris: 1977).

Mitchell, Juliet and Rose, Jacqueline (1982) *Feminine Sexuality: Jacques Lacan and the école freudienne*. London: Macmillan.

Muller, John P. (1979) 'The analogy of the gap in Lacan's *Écrits: A Selection*', *The Psychohistory Review*, 8, 38–45.

Nordau, Max (1895) *Degeneration*. London: Heinemann (tr. from *Entartung*, Berlin: 1892/3).

Orlando, Francesco (1978) *Toward a Freudian Theory of Literature*. Baltimore and London: The Johns Hopkins University Press (tr. from *Lettura Freudiana della Phèdre*, Turin: 1971, and *Per una teoria Freudiana della Letteratura*, Turin: 1973).

Prawer, Siegbert S. (1965) 'Hoffmann's uncanny guest; a reading of *Der Sandmann*', *German Life and Letters*, 18, 297–308.

Rajchman, John (1977) 'Analysis in power: a few Foucauldian theses', *Semiotext(e)*, *Anti-Oedipus: From Psychoanalysis to Schizopolitics*, 2, 45–58.

Ricoeur, Paul (1970) *Freud and Philosophy: An Essay on Interpretation*. New Haven and London: Yale University Press (tr. from *De l'interpretation: essai sur Freud*, Paris: 1965).

Rimmon-Kenan, Shlomith (1983) *Narrative Fiction: Contemporary Poetics*. London: Methuen.

Rose, Gilbert J. (1980) *The Power of Form: A Psychoanalytic Approach to Aesthetic Form*. New York: International Universities Press.

Rubin, Bernard (1982) 'Freud and Hoffmann: "The Sandman"', in Gilman, Sander L. (ed.), *Introducing Psychoanalytic Theory*. New York: Brunner/Mazel, pp. 205–17.

Saussure, Ferdinand de (1977) *Course in General Linguistics*, ed. Bally, Charles and Sechehaye, Albert. London: Fontana/Collins. Orig. publ. 1915.

Segal, Hanna (1977) 'A psycho-analytical approach to aesthetics', in Klein, Melanie, Heimann, Paula and Money-Kyrle, Roger (eds), *New Directions in Psycho-Analysis*. London: Maresfield Reprints, pp. 384–405. Orig. publ. 1955.

Stokes, Adrian (1977) 'Form in art', in Klein, Melanie, Heimann, Paula and Money-Kyrle, Roger (eds), *New Directions in Psycho-*

Analysis. London: Maresfield Reprints, pp. 406–20. Orig. publ. 1955.

—— (1978) *The Critical Writings of Adrian Stokes*, 3 vols. London: Thames and Hudson. 'The Quattrocento' (1932) I, pp. 29–80; 'Stones of Rimini' (1934) I, pp. 181–259; 'Three essays on the painting of our time' (1961) III, pp. 143–84; 'Painting and the inner world' (1963) III, pp. 209–59; 'Reflections on the nude' (1967) III, pp. 303–42.

Sulloway, Frank J. (1979) *Freud, Biologist of the Mind: Beyond the Psycho-Analytic Legend*. London: André Deutsch.

Timms, Edward (1983) 'Novelle and case history: Freud in pursuit of the falcon', *London German Studies*, 2, 115–34.

Trilling, Lionel (1964a) 'Art and neurosis', in *The Liberal Imagination*. London: Heinemann, pp. 160–80. Orig. publ. 1945.

—— (1964b) 'Freud and literature', in *The Liberal Imagination*. London: Heinemann, pp. 34–57. Orig. publ. 1947.

Ulmer, Gregory (1980) 'The discourse of the Imaginary', *Diacritics*, 10, 61–75.

Weber, Samuel (1973) 'The sideshow or: Remarks on a canny moment', *Modern Language Notes*, 88, 1102–33.

—— (1977) 'The divaricator: remarks on Freud's *Witz*', *Glyph*, 1, 1–27.

—— (1978) 'It', *Glyph*, 4, 1–31.

—— (1982) *The Legend of Freud*. Minneapolis: University of Minnesota.

White, Allon (1983) 'Exposition and critique of Julia Kristeva', Centre for Contemporary Cultural Studies, University of Birmingham, Series SP, No. 49.

Williams, Judith (1978) *Decoding Advertisements: Ideology and Meaning in Advertising*. London: Marion Boyars.

Wilson, Edmund (1962) 'A dissenting opinion on Kafka' in Gray, Ronald (ed.), *Kafka: A Collection of Critical Essays*. Englewood Cliffs, New Jersey: Prentice-Hall, pp. 91–7. Orig. publ. 1950.

Wimsatt, W. K. (with Beardsley, Monroe) (1954) *The Verbal Icon*. Lexington: University of Kentucky Press.

Winnicott, D. W. (1974) *Playing and Reality*. Harmondsworth: Penguin.

—— (1977) *The Piggle: An Account of the Psychoanalytic Treatment of a Little Girl*. Harmondsworth: Penguin.

Wollheim, Richard (1971) *Freud*. London: Fontana/Collins.

—— (1973) *Art and the Mind*. London: Allen Lane. 'Freud and the understanding of art', pp. 202–19; 'Adrian Stokes', pp. 315–35.

Wright, Elizabeth (1982a) 'Modern psychoanalytic criticism', in Jefferson, Ann and Robey, David (eds), *Modern Literary Theory: A Comparative Introduction*. London: Batsford, pp. 113–33.

—— (1982b) 'The new psychoanalysis and literary criticism: a reading of Hawthorne and Melville', *Poetics Today*, 3, 89–105.

Further reading

The aim of this section is to help the reader in further exploring the issues raised in each part, and the books suggested are therefore grouped accordingly. In pursuit of this aim I am providing both material which introduces principles and particular fields, and that which extends the discussion of them. The lists contain a few works already referred to but are mainly composed of additional texts that may prove useful.

Part I: Classical psychoanalysis

Bettelheim, Bruno (1976) *The Uses of Enchantment: The Meaning and Importance of Fairy Tales*. London: Thames & Hudson. A clear example of classical applied ego-psychological criticism; Grimm, Perrault, Anderson, etc., read as allegories of self-development.

Fischer, Jens Malte (ed.) (1980) *Psychoanalytische Literaturinterpretation*. Tübingen: Max Niemeyer Verlag. Contains the earliest examples of psychoanalytic criticism, produced by Freud's circle (including Otto Rank and Theodor Reik), with an excellent historical introduction by the editor.

Gilman, Sander L. (ed.) (1982) *Introducing Psychoanalytic Theory*. New York: Brunner/Mazel. Basic concepts clearly explained, some from a new ego-psychological point of view (Otto Kernberg on narcissism), others taking a more general approach (see the comprehensive essay on transference). Includes contextualizing papers, e.g. literature, philosophy of science.

Homans, Peter (1979) *Jung in Context*. Chicago: University of Chicago

Press. A considered critical account of Jung in his relation to Freud. Clear on Jung's thought and historically informative.

Laplanche, Jean and Pontalis, Jean-Baptiste (1973) *The Language of Psycho-Analysis*. London: The Hogarth Press. A remarkable work of encyclopaedic scholarship, which examines and collates the principal notions of psychoanalysis, defining and discussing almost 300 basic concepts in all their complexity. An indispensable aid for anyone trying to find their way through Freudian theory.

Phillips, William (ed.) (1957) *Art and Psychoanalysis*. New York: Criterion Books. A compendium of classical-theoretical and -applied criticism. Includes contributions by Simon Lesser, Otto Rank, William Empson, Kenneth Burke, and a long extract from Marie Bonaparte's book on Poe.

Rieff, Philip (1979) *Freud; The Mind of the Moralist*. Chicago and London: University of Chicago Press. Orig. publ. 1959. An erudite and urbane study of the relevance of Freud for our culture. Still one of the best – and most readable – introductions to Freud's general significance.

Spector, Jack J. (1973) *The Aesthetics of Freud*. New York: Praeger Publications. Too prolix to provide a consistent critical viewpoint, but nevertheless very useful for its mass of information and wide-ranging reference.

Wollheim, Richard (1971) *Freud*. London: Fontana/Collins. An admirably clear though perhaps not easy exposition of Freud's theories and their logic.

Part II: Object-relations theory

Dettmering, Peter (1981) *Psychoanalyse als Instrument der Literaturwissenschaft*. Frankfurt am Main: Fachbuchhandlung für Psychologie. A psychoanalyst applies a combination of English, French and American object-relations theory (Winnicott, Green and Kohut), putting the emphasis on imagery. Includes interpretations of works by Rilke, Kafka, Musil, James.

Fuller, Peter (1980) *Art and Psychoanalysis*. London: Writers and Readers Publishing Cooperative. A wholly committed application of object-relations principles to painting and sculpture. Discussed in Part II.

Klein, Melanie (1977) *Love, Guilt and Reparation and Other Works, 1921–1945*. New York: Dell Publishing. See particularly 'The role of the school in the libidinal development of the child' (1923), and 'The importance of symbol-formation in the development of the ego'

(1930), discussed in Part II.

Klein, Melanie, Heimann, Paula and Money-Kyrle, Roger (1977) *New Directions in Psycho-Analysis*. London: Maresfield Reprints. Orig. publ. 1955. Includes contributions by Melanie Klein, Hanna Segal, Adrian Stokes and Wilfred Bion.

Milner, Marion (1968) *The Hands of the Living God*. London: The Hogarth Press. A remarkably detailed account of the analysis of a schizophrenic patient, conducted via drawings, made over many years by an analyst of the object-relations school who has been influential in its aesthetics.

Mitscherlich, Alexander (ed.) (1982) *Psycho-Pathographien des Alltags: Schriftsteller und Psychoanalyse*. Frankfurt: Suhrkamp. Recent attempts at explaining an author's work via his pathology, from a variety of psychoanalytic approaches. Contains a critical essay on methodology by Janine Chasseguet-Smirgel with reference to the film *Last Year in Marienbad*.

New Literary History (1980), *Psychology and Literature: Some Contemporary Directions*, 12, No. 1. See particularly the theoretical contribution of André Green, 'The unbinding process', as well as the account of Kohutian criticism by Ernest Wolf, of Jungian criticism by Marie-Louise von Franz (relevant to Part I), and of Lacan's *Hamlet* interpretation by John Muller (relevant to Part IV).

Skura, Meredith Anne (1981) *The Literary Use of the Psychoanalytic Process*. New Haven and London: Yale University Press. This is an ambitious attempt to make the most general use of psychoanalytic theory for the interpretation of literature by taking a number of major topics in psychoanalysis – case-history, fantasy, dream, transference – and applying them to a variety of texts. The main parallel is between the therapeutic effects of analysis and the organizing power of literature. In the attempt to integrate all theories, essential differences in position are disregarded; however, the interpretations are markedly object-relational.

Tennenhouse, Leonard (1976) *The Practice of Psychoanalytic Criticism*. Detroit: Wayne State University Press. An eclectic volume of mainly applied criticism, including Jungian, Winnicottian and Reichian approaches. See particularly a review essay by Anton Ehrenzweig, in which his ideas are more concisely expressed than in *The Hidden Order of Art* (1970).

Wollheim, Richard (1972) *The Image in Form: Selected Writings of Adrian Stokes*. Harmondsworth: Penguin.

—— (1973) 'Adrian Stokes', in *Art and the Mind*. London: Allen Lane, pp. 315–35. The above selection, together with this essay, provide an authoritative introduction and guide to Stokes's work.

Part III: Structural psychoanalysis

Bowie, Malcolm (1979) 'Jacques Lacan', in Sturrock, John (ed.), *Structuralism and Since: From Lévi-Strauss to Derrida*. Oxford: Oxford University Press. A coherent and comprehensive introductory essay.

Clément, Catherine (1983) *The Lives and Legends of Jacques Lacan*. New York: Columbia University Press (tr. from *Vies et légendes de Jacques Lacan*, Paris: 1981). A successful popularization, evocative in its combination of biography and lively theoretical exposition.

Derrida, Jacques (1981) *Positions*. London: The Athlone Press (tr. from *Positions*, Paris: 1972). Three interviews, in the third of which Derrida explains his position vis-à-vis Lacan; see pp. 81–7 and 107–14.

Forrester, John (1981) 'Psychoanalysis or literature?', *French Studies*, 35, 170–9. A comprehensive review article which critically evaluates the contemporary scene in France and America.

Gallas, Helga (1981) *Das Textbegehren des 'Michael Kohlhaas': Die Sprache des Unbewussten und der Sinn der Literatur*. Reinbek bei Hamburg: Rowohlt. An excellent example of theory in practice.

Hartman, Geoffrey H. (ed.) (1978) *Psychoanalysis and the Question of the Text: Selected Papers from the English Institute, 1976–77*. Baltimore and London: The Johns Hopkins University Press. Explores the relation of psychoanalytic theories to theories of the text via a collection of essays in which the common ground is the attempt to install an intersubjective criticism.

Johnson, Barbara (1980) *The Critical Difference: Essays in the Contemporary Rhetoric of Reading*. Baltimore: The Johns Hopkins University Press. These essays, collected together from various sources, are distinguished examples of an implicitly psychoanalytically orientated deconstructive criticism that is able to show rivalries of power, repression and the return of the repressed, at work in a text at levels hitherto unsuspected; see particularly 'Melville's fist: The execution of *Billy Budd*' and 'The frame of reference: Poe, Lacan, Derrida'.

—— (1982) 'Teaching ignorance: L'Ecole des Femmes', in *Yale French Studies, The Pedagogical Imperative: Teaching as a Literary Genre*, 63, 165–82.

Kurzweil, Edith and Phillips, William (eds) (1983) *Literature and Psychoanalysis*. New York: Columbia University Press. The latest anthology to date; contains a wide range of material from early Freud to Kristeva, placed into somewhat arbitrary sections, headed with editorial comment. The general introduction openly declares its allegiance to ego-psychological criticism and aversion to the modern theoretical orientations.

Laplanche, Jean (1976) *Life and Death in Psychoanalysis*. Baltimore and

London: The Johns Hopkins University Press. A lucid deconstruction of the key concepts in Freud's thought, which has deservedly become something of a manifesto of the French re-reading of Freud. With a useful introduction by the translator Jeffery Mehlman.

Leitch, Vincent B. (1983) *Deconstructive Criticism: An Advanced Introduction*. London: Hutchinson. A well-integrated exposition. For areas of special relevance see discussions of Lacan, Barthes, Foucault, Bloom, Deleuze and Guattari.

Muller, John P. and Richardson, William J. (1982) *Lacan and Language: A Reader's Guide to Écrits*. New York: International Universities press. A closely annotated manual with detailed commentary on every part of the text, preceded by a summary of each chapter. Contains an invaluable index of terms.

Tanner, Tony (1979) *Adultery in the Novel: Contract and Transgression*. Baltimore and London: The Johns Hopkins University Press. A lively and eclectic use of Lacan, with whose help three major novels are analysed and, by way of a virtuoso close textual reading, shown to question their joint presuppositions.

Turkle, Sherry (1979) *Psychoanalytic Politics: Freud's French Revolution*. London: André Deutsch. Orig. publ. 1978. A detailed record of the course of cultural events surrounding the French rediscovery of Freud.

Weber, Samuel M. (1978) *Rückkehr zu Freud: Jacques Lacans Ent-stellung der Psychoanalyse*. Frankfurt am Main, Berlin, Wien: Ullstein. A concise and rigorous account of Lacan's thought in the context of his importation of linguistic theory into psychoanalysis.

Wilden, Anthony (1968) *The Language of the Self: The Function of Language in Psychoanalysis*. New York: Dell Publishing A comprehensive linguistic and philosophical introduction to Lacan's theory, together with a commentary and annotations on a key paper of Lacan's.

Williams, Linda (1981) *Figures of Desire: A Theory and Analysis of Surrealist Film*. Urbana, Illinois and London: University of Illinois Press. An analysis of the implicit theory in the Surrealist practice of the film, influenced by Christian Metz's study of the relevance of Lacan's theory of the subject to the cinema (Metz is discussed in the present text, Part III, chapter 7).

Wordsworth, Ann (1981) 'An art that will not abandon the self to language: Bloom, Tennyson and the blind world of the wish', in Young, Robert (ed.), *Untying the Text: A Post-Structuralist Reader*. London: Routledge & Kegan Paul, pp. 207–22. A brief principled exposition of Bloom's theory and a persuasive application of it in a reading of Tennyson's 'In Memoriam'. The book itself has a section devoted to deconstructive psychoanalytic criticism which combines theoretical exposition and critical practice.

Yale French Studies (1977), Literature and Psychoanalysis. The Question of Reading: Otherwise, 55/56. Now a classic manifesto of the relationship between literature and modern French psychoanalysis (available in a new paperback edition). A clear itinerary precedes the collection, in which the question of the relation of theory to practice is very much to the fore. Contains a number of items already documented, but see particularly Lacan's remarkable and difficult analysis of Hamlet, and Peter Brooks's 'Freud's masterplot: questions of narrative', which deals with a significant area of overlap between psychoanalysis and literature, for which there was no space in this book.

Part IV: Psychoanalysis and ideology

Bersani, Leo (1976) A Future for Astyanax: Character and Desire in Literature. Boston, Massachusetts: Little, Brown & Co. Challenging Freud's theory of sublimation, Bersani reads a variety of texts, traditional and modern, as covertly or openly resisting oedipal structuration by disturbing our unified images of character and identity.

Doubrovski, Serge (1978) '"The Nine of Hearts": fragment of a psychoreading of La Nausée', in Roland, Alan (ed.), Psychoanalysis, Creativity, and Literature: A French–American Inquiry. New York: Columbia University Press, pp. 312–22 (reprinted in Kurzweil and Phillips: see Further reading for Part III). A remarkably close textual reading of a single episode, which reveals the logic of fantasy within a substratum of imagery, thereby showing how the hero's existential crisis, his 'nausea', is figured via a loss of his sexual identity. 'Psychocriticism' (the term comes from Charles Mauron) is a form of psychoanalytic criticism which closely combines the psychoanalytic and the literary. For a recent account and an eclectic use of it see Berg, William J. and Moskos, George (eds) (1981) Saint Oedipus: Psychocritical Approaches to Flaubert's Art. Ithaca, New York: Cornell University Press; but see also Orlando below, who transforms it into a systematic political textual criticism.

Eagleton, Terry (1983) Literary Theory: An Introduction. Oxford: Basil Blackwell. See chapter 5, 'Psychoanalysis', for a clear and accessible introductory account, with the issue of ideology to the fore.

Felman, Shoshana (1975) 'Women and madness: the critical phallacy', Diacritics, 7, 2–10. An article which reviews two books on women and addresses itself, via a reading of a story by Balzac, to the problem of speaking for those oppressed in discourse – in this case, women, from outside the masculine/feminine divide.

Forrester, John (1980) 'Michel Foucault and the history of psychoanalysis', History of Science, 18, 286–302. Discusses how

Foucault writes the history of psychoanalysis in terms of its relation to other sciences and its position with regard to power.

Girard, René (1965) *Deceit, Desire and the Novel: Self and Other in Literary Discourse*. Baltimore and London: The Johns Hopkins University Press. Orig. publ. 1961. Girard reads the novel as containing a structure of rivalry, based on all desire being an imitation of another's desire; he sees an ineradicable threat of violence issuing from the rivalry with that other for the object of desire, eroding the boundaries between the normal and the pathological as the heroes are caught within a triangular structure, from which there is no escape via Oedipus.

Guattari, Félix (1979) 'A liberation of desire', in Stambolian, George, and Marks, Elaine (eds) *Homosexualities and French Literature: Cultural Contexts/Critical Texts*. Ithaca, New York and London: Cornell University Press, pp. 56–69. An interview, outlining Guattari's views on desire in literature within the book's general discussion of the relation between gender and culture.

Jacoby, Russell (1975) *Social Amnesia: A Critique of Conformist Psychology from Adler to Laing*. Hassocks: The Harvester Press. See particularly chapter 4, 'Negative psychoanalysis and Marxism', which discusses the critique launched against psychoanalysis by Herbert Marcuse and the Frankfurt School.

Kittler, Friedrich and Turk, Horst (eds) (1977) *Urszenen: Literaturwissenschaft als Diskurskritik*. Frankfurt am Main: Suhrkamp. Using the theories of Lacan, Derrida and Foucault, this book examines a variety of texts, literary and philosophical, as discourse: who speaks, of what, to whom, and under what historical conditions. Includes essays on Goethe, Kafka, Benjamin, Kant, and Hegel/Marx.

Lohmann, Hans-Martin (ed.) (1983) *Das Unbehagen in der Psychoanalyse: Eine Streitschrift*. Frankfurt am Main/Paris: Qumran. A critique of psychoanalysis from within, dedicated to Alexander Mitcherlich (1908–82), founder and director of the Sigmund Freud Institute in Frankfurt.

Orlando, Francesco (1978) *Toward a Freudian Theory of Literature*. Baltimore and London: Johns Hopkins University Press. Orig. publ. 1971/3. A brilliant, meticulous and difficult study of the relation between poetry and history, conducted at the level of theory and practice. Taking Racine's *Phèdre* as a practical example, and using Freud's theory of negation as a model, Orlando traces both the lifting and returning of the personal and political repressed (Phèdre's perverse desire) via the key signifiers of *monstre* and *cacher*, in a close textual practice which takes from modern linguistic theory and also acknowledges Charles Mauron's method of 'psycho-criticism'.

Appendix to 1987 reprint: Post-feminist criticism: reading/writing (M)otherwise

In her latest critical assessment of the feminist debate, Moi, following Kristeva (1981), marks out three main positions in the feminist struggle: 1 women demanding 'equal access to the symbolic order', a battle for equal rights; 2 women rejecting the 'male symbolic order in the name of difference', an assertion of the uniqueness of their femininity; and 3 women rejecting 'the dichotomy between masculine and feminine as metaphysical', a deconstructed form of feminism, which Kristeva sees as her own position (Moi 1986a, p. 214). Moi would also like to take this position but points out that to adopt it prematurely risks the danger of making the feminist struggle redundant. You might say, if there were no enemies, who needs friends? A fully politicized feminist criticism, such as Moi clearly sets out, is rightly aware that to reject fixed gender definitions in theory is still to be stuck with them in practice, because at some point feminists may be forced, if only as a political strategy, to make the kind of bad choice that any logocentric system dictates. They can either fight patriarchy from within on a day-to-day practical basis (position 1, more usually taken by Anglo-American feminists), or refute patriarchy from without by constructing alternative positions which stress the uniqueness of the feminine and fall into the danger of a new metaphysic (position 2, more often occupied by leading French feminists).

My aim in this appendix is to relate psychoanalytic feminist criticism to my book, which implicitly adopted position 3, in that it regarded (gender) identity as a cultural construct, in theory equally problematic for both sexes. In my critical investigation of psychoanalytic praxis I was more concerned to reveal the uncertain foundation of any idealized system that considers itself based on ontological givens than in taking up any specific cause. Since then I have increasingly come to see that feminist criticism is of specific relevance to that more general project as it offers the clearest and the most visible instance of the difficulties of trying to subvert or re-form any system from within.

Psychoanalysis has its own bleak theory of the construction of gender (see pp. 14–15 and pp. 108–12), and it is this theory, as was first pointed out over a decade ago (Mitchell 1974), which can be used as an ideological weapon for women to fight their own oppression. It is the double-edged nature of this weapon which has preoccupied feminists ever since: on the one hand it enables them to demonstrate that gender is symbolic and not biological; on the other hand it constructs woman around the phallic sign. The mother's (unconscious) choice is not much of one: either she gives way to the Name of the Father and the Law, or she keeps the child with her in the Imaginary at the level of an inadequate body unable to acquire the language of the Other (see Mannoni 1973). Woman in patriarchy is condemned to occupy the place of signifier for the male other, who can give free reign to his fantasies and obsessions, and, what is more, implicate her in them (see Marie Bonaparte on Poe in this book, pp. 40–2).

It is for their theory and practice of the slippage of language caused by unconscious desire that feminists continue to embrace Freud and Lacan, even if somewhat coolly. It is a matter of continuing debate how far they may be said to serve the feminist cause. In the first instance women derived from them the proofs of their own oppression. They publicized by all means at their disposal the extent to which the subjectivity of woman, what our culture calls femininity, has been and is determined by the discourse of patriarchy, in Freud's theory woman emerging as 'little man'-minus, in Lacan's as 'not-all'. In either case she is implicated in the ambivalences of 'The Daughter's Seduction' (Gallop 1982) as a pre-condition for moving from the desire of the mother to that of the father. Gallop's book is the first full-length literary project which sets out to challenge and subvert the psychoanalytic discourse from within its own feminist ranks, trying to create an intercourse between Lacanian psychoanalysis and feminism whereby each challenges the other's essentialism. Gallop is among those feminists who believe that Lacan's doctrine really does go 'beyond the phallus' in that he has provided a theory about human identity-formation having a generality that applies no matter what the power-structure is at a given historical moment.

In her book *Figuring Lacan*, MacCannell (1986, pp. 139–51) draws a useful comparison between Kant and Lacan. What must not be attributed to Lacan is the idea of the Symbolic Order as a categorical imperative. Lacan's Symbolic Order is a formula not for a realm of ideal judgements but for a mapping of mores that always remain adjustable. Like logic, it is the ghost of agreements, yet it must be applied to phenomena the whole time. The Symbolic Order is based on nothing but the principle of a splitting, a binary yes/no which any subject has to accept in order to emerge from the Real. The trouble comes when a binary content is allowed to become rigid, as though these oppositions had always existed. For it is not the structure in itself which is a threat to any freedom, but those who turn its presumed universality into a warrant for their own discourse of power. In that case human identity will be founded on false distinctions, such as those founded on racism or patriarchy. Under such circumstances language is no longer a proper game, with others having places equivalent to one's own, but a manipulation by others, whereby the subject is placed in a field of force within which it is compelled to adopt a false identity. This is what feminists are up against in the case of gender distinctions. There are those who accuse Lacan of merely shifting the cause of woman's oppression from 'men *per se*' to 'the structural organisation of society, language and exchange' (Gross 1984, p. 85; see also the questions raised in Greene and Kahn (eds) 1985), but others argue that it is his theory and praxis which enables feminists to see woman as a mythical construct and which can and must provoke alternative readings (Mitchell and Rose 1982; Gallop 1982; MacCannell 1986; Ragland-Sullivan 1986). That is to say the old myths are to be abandoned and new ones to be invented. However, as Ragland-Sullivan points out, it is not at the Real level of primary castration (the separation from the mother's body) that the struggle for new forms of gender identity should be waged, but at the level of secondary castration, through the meanings attributed to the father's position in the triangle, for it is there that the masquerade begins:

Woman's history will never appreciably change without a theoretical understanding of why there has ever been discrimination against women along gender lines. If Lacan's new epistemology is valid, however, the task placed before feminists is truly monumental, and, in part, impossible. The 'catch-22' lies in the circular nature of the dilemma itself. After Castration a mother's unconscious Desire is communicated to the infant, along with her attitudes toward the Phallus and messages about the infant's place within the symbolic, structural drama. To short-circuit the system, then, one must either change the gender of the primary source of nurture and identification . . . or change the unconscious Desire of mothers who, by accepting their femininity at all, support a system of phallic values.
(Ragland-Sullivan, op. cit., pp. 298–9)

Those feminists who believe that Lacan's thought provides the basis for re-writing woman's and man's history are engaged in a criticism which does more than go to literature to find proof for the oppression of women. Post-feminist criticism is rethinking the struggle of women for power and recognition because it sees the futility of perpetuating fixed binary oppositions. Instead of reading a text because it is written by a woman or considering the representation of woman, these feminist critics, taking up position 3, read texts for their hypothetical and marginal meanings, maintaining that it is these kinds of meaning which constitute a feminine subjectivity. They argue that a more radical kind of feminist criticism would be one which capitalizes on women's marginal position by refusing to make a clear distinction between subject and object (see Gallop 1985). In support of this they have interrogated the writings of Derrida as much as those of Lacan, finding that 'it is *woman* that must be released from her metaphysical bondage and it is writing, as "feminine operation", that can and does subvert the history of that metaphysics' (Jardine, 1986, p. 183). Jardine sees this 'anti-and/or post-feminism' of the French theorists as 'exemplary of modernity', in that their discourse systematically undermines all the categories we take to be natural ones (pp. 21–5). There is an intrinsic undecidability in writing which is not ambiguity and which is beyond any fixed genderization. Yet is to be called 'feminine', and therein lies the danger of a new metaphysics, despite the fact that men are not barred from this position.

The theorist who has done most to examine the marginal from a feminine if not a feminist perspective is Julia Kristeva. In her introduction to Kristeva's work, Moi (1986b) sets out Kristeva's theory of a subject-in-process, based on a view of language as a mobile and provisional system of signification, its categorizations constantly disrupted by the resonating of early bodily drives. Though this pre-oedipal sexuality returns in both sexes, it has led Kristeva and her followers to pay special attention to the mother's body, around which this early pre-self experience takes place, the mother being the primary object of love for the child's early spasmodic and unco-ordinated sexual drives, satisfying its needs and coding its desires. But this focus on the space occupied by mother and child has now begun to shift to the focus on the mother herself as a devalued subject/object (Kristeva 1982), and on the attempt to find a positive sign for her to replace the various myths of the eternal feminine which idealized her out of corporeal existence in the past, yet at the same time helped to sustain her. Woman's continuing vulnerability in the Symbolic Order has raised new questions regarding the value of the maternal:

> The desire to be a mother, considered alienating and even reactionary by the preceding generation of feminists, has obviously not become a standard for the present generation. But we have seen in

the past few years an increasing number of women who do not only consider their maternity compatible with their professional life or their feminist involvement . . . but also find it indispensable to their discovery, not of the plenitude, but of the complexity of the female experience, with all that this complexity comprises in joy and pain.

('Women's Time', in Moi 1986b, p. 205)

The question of the continuing desire for motherhood can no longer be answered solely either in traditional terms or in psychoanalytic terms. So back to the literary text for its uncanny capacity to reveal the unsaid, this time to let the mother and the maternal speak.

A recent collection of essays (Garner, Kahane, and Sprengnether (eds) 1985) addresses itself to the feminist revision of the maternal narrative, centring particularly on the way psychoanalytic theory from Freud to Klein to Winnicott has constructed her. In psychoanalytic terms the mother's absence from her child indicates her presence not just elsewhere, but somehow attending to or being attended by the father. That is to say, she is always seen from the viewpoint of those who lay claim to her, whether it be the father or the child. To see the mother's need in relation to other women or to her work is not a view that psychoanalytic theory helps to promote.

In an illuminating essay included in this collection, Susan Rubin Suleiman argues that traditional psychoanalytic theory, being a theory of childhood, confines the mother to a purely sacrificial role, condemning her to a total selflessness. Suleiman points out that Melanie Klein speaks with great insight about the murderous impulses the child has towards the loved mother, but has nothing to say about the reverse. The notion that the mother may be in conflict regarding her child and her *work*, or the idea that the mother might be the subject of artistic creation rather than its object (see my book for the various child-centred theories of creativity from Freud through to Winnicott) is a relatively new one: '*Mothers don't write, they are written* . . . this is the underlying assumption of most psychoanalytic theories about writing and artistic creation in general' (Suleiman, p. 356). Suleiman calls for more information in the form of diaries, memoirs, essays by writing mothers. In the meantime she asks the question, 'Is there such a thing as the writing mother's fantasy?' and answers it by examining the 'fiction' of a mother. I shall briefly summarize her first example, a short story entitled 'Good Housekeeping' by Rosellen Brown, herself the mother of two young children. A photographer-mother is going round the house with her camera, taking counter-domestic pictures (the title of the story is ironic). As her baby wakes, crying, she sees 'the baby's uvula quivering like an icicle about to drop' (Suleiman, p. 373, quoting Brown). But as she points her camera at the baby, it stops crying and smiles, thus turning from object into subject. After a moment's pause the mother reaches out and pinches the child's thigh dispassionately, 'found the rosy tightness of it . . . kept pinching hard, till she got that angry uvula again' (ibid.), described in a variety of metaphoric terms, far from the language of 'Good Housekeeping', as Suleiman points out. Suleiman writes: 'The power of the story for me, lies in the fantasy that I read in (or perhaps into) it: "With every word I write, with every metaphor, with every act of genuine creation, I hurt my child".' Hence for her the story is not just a story about what it feels like to be a mother, but 'a story about the *representation* of motherhood by a mother . . . a story about the specular relation between mother-as-artist and her child' (ibid., p. 374), a play of gazes in which the mother's aggression wins over her tenderness.

To realize the long road along which feminist criticism has travelled to be able to produce a piece of sophisticated critical writing such as the above joint production by Rosellen and Suleiman, it might be worth looking at a piece of early feminist criticism, a German film entitled *Mädchen in Uniform (Maidens in Uniform)*, which also indirectly implicates motherhood. It was shown on television (8 September 1986) and the programme note ran as follows: 'Leontine Sagan's study of lesbianism in an upper-class boarding school in Prussia before World War One may have lost much of the power to scandalize that it had in the Thirties, but it still appears remarkably fresh and intelligent.' The film was prefaced by a short American documentary, an autobiographical collage of a lesbian's life. It was thus typecast from the start both by this graft and by the announcement. A post-feminist reading of this film would not reduce it to a simple study of lesbianism. The first impression is that it is a film about women's oppression by women within a military patriarchy which forces its women to adopt the position of 'soldiers' wives' and 'soldiers' daughters', the mothers and aunts who deposit their reluctant daughters at the school. The headmistress is represented as a female commandant, herself oppressed by the aristocracy whom she serves. There is a ceaseless hierarchy of curtseys, the higher the rank the nearer the ground. The film shows the attempt of a schoolmistress, loved and revered by her charges, to satisfy her feminine desire and those of her charges without injuring either their future prospects or her own in a society on which she and they depend for survival and whose underlying values she cannot accept. She plays the part of the (good) phallic mother, a combined parent-figure that insists on rules, yet at the same time knows how to subvert them. Her severe, yet tender gaze (which her charges describe as 'uncanny') provokes general rapture, as does the ceremonial good-night kiss accorded to each pupil in her charge. There is a remarkable panning sequence as she moves from one austere bed to another, with each girl waiting in a kneeling position at the foot of the bed, wearing an ecstatic look. What any criticism which merely places this film within a homosexual context misses is the conscious attempt on the part of the mistress (she finally leaves the school in a gesture of refusal after a near-tragedy following the victimization of one of her pupils) to re-inscribe another discourse than that of Prussian militarism from within, even though this also coincides with what counts within patriarchy as illicit enjoyment (the film certainly images feminine *jouissance*). This enjoyment, however, is not purely in the Imaginary, since at the same time she acts as a Symbolic third term by insisting on rules and a certain distance. In a post-feminist reading it is not easy to separate the narcissistic components of this film (the emphasis on forbidden emotion) from its critical elements, that of writing another discourse for mothers, which need have nothing to do with their biological function, a way of writing (M)otherwise in that particular system. This also raises the question of the extent to which the motherly function is necessarily bound up with procreation, and, hence, the project of writing (M)otherwise is perhaps more disturbing, then as now, than simply that of writing woman.

ELIZABETH WRIGHT
December, 1986

References (titles previously listed are not included)

Gallop, Jane (1985) *Reading Lacan*. Ithaca and London: Cornell University Press.

Garner, Shirley Nelson, Kahane, Clare and Sprengnether, Madelon (eds) (1985) *The M(other) Tongue: Essays in Feminist Psychoanalytic Interpretation*. Ithaca and London: Cornell University Press.

Greene, Gayle and Kahn, Coppélia (eds) (1985) *Making a Difference: Feminist Literary Criticism*. London and New York: Methuen.

Gross, Elizabeth (1984) 'Love Letters in the Sand: Reflections on *Feminine Sexuality: Jacques Lacan and the École Freudienne*, ed. by Juliet Mitchell and Jacqueline Rose', *Critical Philosophy*, 1,2 (1984), 69–87.

Jardine, Alice A. (1985) *Gynesis: Configurations of Woman and Modernity*. Ithaca and London: Cornell University Press.

Kristeva, Julia (1982) *Powers of Horror*. New York: Columbia University Press (tr. from *Pouvoirs de l'horreur*, Paris: 1980).

—— (1986) 'Woman's Time', in Moi (1986) pp. 187–213 (tr. from 'Les temps des femmes', *Cahiers de recherche de sciences des textes et documents*, 33/44 (1979)).

MacCannell, Juliet Flower (1986) *Figuring Lacan: Criticism and the Cultural Unconscious*. London and Sidney: Croom Helm.

Mitchell, Juliet (1974) *Psychoanalysis and Feminism*. Harmondsworth: Penguin Books.

Moi, Toril (1985) *Sexual/Textual Politics: Feminist Literary Theory*. London and New York: Methuen.

—— (1986a) 'Feminist Literary Criticism', in *Modern Literary Theory: A Comparative Introduction*, second edn. London: Batsford, pp. 204–21.

—— (1986b) (ed.) *The Kristeva Reader*. Oxford: Blackwell.

Ragland-Sullivan, Ellie (1986) *Jacques Lacan and the Philosophy of Psychoanalysis*. London and Canberra: Croom Helm.

Sagan, Leontine (1931) *Mädchen in Uniform* (film).

Suleiman, Susan Rubin (1985) 'Writing and Motherhood', in Garner, Kahane and Sprengnether (eds), pp. 352–77.

My thanks go to Gillian Beer and Diane Chisholm for their pertinent comments on this section.

Index